George Whitefield Mead, Charles Lemuel Thompson

Modern methods in church work

The gospel renaissance

George Whitefield Mead, Charles Lemuel Thompson

Modern methods in church work
The gospel renaissance

ISBN/EAN: 9783337284367

Printed in Europe, USA, Canada, Australia, Japan

Cover: Foto ©Lupo / pixelio.de

More available books at **www.hansebooks.com**

MODERN METHODS

IN CHURCH WORK

MODERN METHODS
IN CHURCH WORK

The Gospel Renaissance

BY

REV. GEORGE WHITEFIELD MEAD

WITH AN INTRODUCTION

BY

REV. CHARLES L. THOMPSON, D.D.
PRESIDENT OF THE OPEN AND INSTITUTIONAL CHURCH LEAGUE
UNITED STATES OF AMERICA

"The contribution that this age is to make to Christian thought is that practical Christianity is Christianity"

NEW YORK
DODD, MEAD AND COMPANY
1897

IN CARISSIMAM MEMORIAM

OF

My Father and Mother,

WHOSE LIVES OF PRAYER, LOVE OF GOD, AND SERVICE TO MAN,
HAVE BEEN LIFE'S RICHEST LEGACY AND AN ABIDING
INSPIRATION IN THE WORK OF
THE KINGDOM.

PREFACE.

IN the preparation of this work my thought has not been to magnify WORKS above GRACE, but my theme has been limited largely to that which bears upon the former subject. Yet even in the review of this part of the work of the Church, in the light of the new movement, it must appear, I am sure, that the spiritual mission of the Church instead of being minimized is magnified, made supreme, and extended even to the influence of all things through the dispensation of the Holy Spirit.

I wish to express my obligation to those ministers and Y. M. C. A. Secretaries and other Christian workers who have aided me with addresses and information relative to churches and denominations and to the many ministers who have favored me with documents and information relative to their Free Pew System, men's clubs, and other departments of church work, the review of whose work, though not mentioned for want of space, has been an inspiration in the presentation of this work. To the pastors of churches whose names appear,

PREFACE.

I am indebted for the information which has made possible the helpful mention of their church work. I only regret that it has been necessary so often to condense the reference to their work and methods employed. To the Rev. Walter Laidlaw, Ph.D., and the Rev. Winthrop Hageman, Ph.D., who kindly placed before me the manuscript copy of the report of the Sociological Canvass of the Fifteenth Assembly District, New York, I have to offer my special thanks. I would also make grateful acknowledgment of the helpful assistance of Mrs. Laura C. Dunlap, in matters of tabulation and the arrangement of certain material. It is with regret that I find myself unable to make such mention as I should like to make of the painstaking favors which I have received from Christian workers, and I can only make this general acknowledgment, and express my deep obligation.

G. W. M.

NEW YORK,
    December, 1896.

CONTENTS.

CHAPTER	PAGE
INTRODUCTION	xvii

I. CARDINAL PRINCIPLES   1

1. New era in church and Christian work. 2. Influence of Christianity. 3. Distinguishing marks of the new era in church life and methods. 4. The Free, the Open, and the Institutional Churches illustrative of the new movement. 5. The principles: (1) Evangelism, (2) Consecration, (3) Ministration, (4) Adaptability, (5) Extension, (6) Organization. 6. The recovery of gospel teaching.

II. THE FREE, THE OPEN, AND THE INSTITUTIONAL CHURCH   15

1. Discussion of the name Free. *a.* Does not give comprehensive view of the work. *b.* Misleading in conveying the idea of free pews only. *c.* Misleading as suggesting no financial obligation. 2. Discussion of the name Institutional. *a.* Cumbersome. *b.* Suggests undue emphasis on organization. *c.* Eliminates the personal idea. *d.* Awakens prejudice and necessitates explanation. *e.* Stands for the opposite of what it suggests. 3. Discussion of the name Open. *a.* Lays stress on the spirit of the church. *b.* Expresses figuratively the true idea. *c.* Calls attention to the importance of daily church opening. *d.* Some characteristics of the Open Church. 4. Summary,— no one name entirely satisfactory. This not a misfortune.

III. THE CHURCH-MEMBERS,— WHERE ARE THEY?— WHAT ARE THEY?   22

1. The church should be concerted in work. 2. Knowledge of members necessary. 3. Church rolls and records. 4. Card catalogue explained. 5. Communion cards. 6. Annual roll-call. 7. Visiting staff, different plans in several churches. 8. Teachers' reports.

CONTENTS.

CHAPTER	PAGE
IV. REACHING PEOPLE OUTSIDE THE CHURCH	29

1. Need of knowledge of people about the church. 2. Means of getting such knowledge. I. House-to-house canvass. *a.* Facts to be secured. *b.* How inaugurated. *c.* Records and directions. *d.* Disposition of the results of the canvass. *e.* Remarks. II. House-to-house visitation. *a.* Some methods of. *b.* Results of, in different places. *c.* Means of engaging the personal interest of church-members. 3. Sociological canvass in the City of New York. 4. Value of such canvass.

V. PERSONAL WORK	40

1. Need for. 2. List of non-church-members. 3. Statistics of growth of churches. *a.* Average cost of converts in leading denominations in the United States. *b.* Average number of converts to a church. *c.* Average number of church-members to a convert. *d.* The number of churches reporting no converts after a whole year's work. 4. Workers' training-class. 5. Win One Circles. 6. Workers' Handbook. 7. Enlistment card. 8. Silent evangelism. 9. Evangelistic Sunday-school work.

VI. REACHING STRANGERS AT THE SERVICES	58

1. Number of strangers. 2. Need of welcome. 3. Pastor's welcome. 4. Officers' welcome. 5. Pew cards. 6. Letters and calls to follow signatures to pew cards. 7. Pulpit reception. 8. Reception in rear of church. 9. Reception committee. 10. Vestibule committee.

VII. USHERS' ASSOCIATION	68

1. Importance of the usher. 2. Importance of ushers' associations. 3. Plan of the Ushers' Association of Grace Baptist Church and of the Hollond Memorial Church, Philadelphia. 4. Testimony as to value.

VIII. THE CHOIR	71

1. Different kinds of church music. 2. Some choirs in different churches. 3. Character of church musicians. 4. Prayer for the choir.

CONTENTS.

CHAPTER	PAGE

IX. THE MEN'S SUNDAY-EVENING CLUB 76
   1. The problem of using and interesting the men of the church. 2. The Men's Sunday-Evening Club solves that problem. 3. Model constitution. 4. Elements of strength in the Club. *a.* Stands for a definite object. *b.* Equalization of labor and responsibility. *c.* Develops the feeling of fraternity. *d.* Emphasizes the social side. 5. Work in the Sunday-evening services. 6. Organization of. 7. Results of. 8. Extracts from testimonials.

X. THE SUNDAY-EVENING SERVICE 91
   1. Failure of. 2. Some variations in. *a.* Musical service. *b.* Liturgical service. *c.* Brookfield service. *d.* Special night service. *e.* Special series of sermons. *f.* Illustrated service. (*a*) Object. (*b*) Pictures. (*c*) Stereopticon views. *g.* Special features. (*a*) The Sunday-evening service in Rochester, N. Y. (*b*) The Prelude. (*c*) Sunday-evening service in Dr. Chapman's Church, Philadelphia.

XI. THE AFTER MEETING 104
   1. Value of. 2. Successful features. *a.* Held in adjoining room. *b.* Invitation to. *c.* Music. 3. Different kinds of, and hints for conducting. *a.* General participation. *b.* Spiritual quickening of Christians. *c.* Appeal to the unconverted. *d.* Formal people. *e.* Character of leader. *f.* Close on time. 4. Intermitting the after meeting.

XII. THE PLEASANT SUNDAY AFTERNOON . . . 111
   1. Leisure hour of working-men. 2. How conducted in England. *a.* Programmes. *b.* Music. *c.* Leader. *d.* Committees. *e.* Prizes. 3. Salient features of. 4. Principles of. 5. Movement in this country.

XIII. YOUNG PEOPLE'S SOCIETIES 118
   1. Importance of. 2. Future work of. 3. The three principal Young People's Societies. 4. Committees of the Young People's Society of Christian Endeavor. 5. Departments of the Epworth League and the Baptist Young People's Union. 6. Reading-Circles of the

CONTENTS.

CHAPTER   PAGE

Epworth League. 7. Christian-culture courses in the Baptist Young People's Union. 8. Work of the Young People's Society of Christian Endeavor. 9. Dr. Clark's "Ways and Means."

XIV. THE PRAYER MEETING 122

1. A much-discussed subject. 2. Welcome for new ideas. 3. Plans of different pastors to secure attendance and participation. 4. The family idea of. 5. Special points. *a.* Music. *b.* Topics. *c.* Missionary concerts. *d.* Shall women take part? *e* Leader. 6. Social gathering at the close. 7. Concluding remarks. *a.* Commencing on time. *b.* Preparation of the leader. *c.* Plainness of dress.

XV. THE COTTAGE PRAYER MEETING 130

1. Reasons for holding such meetings. 2. A cottage prayer meeting in New York. Results of. 3. How carried on. 4. The plan of the churches of Oberlin, O. 5. A return to the ways of the early Church.

XVI. OPEN-AIR PREACHING 133

1. Early examples of. 2. Work in England. 3. Work in this country. 4. Tent meetings. 5. Gospel wagons. 6. Gospel push-carts. 7. Work of this kind by the country church.

XVII. CHAPELS AND MISSIONS 138

1. Need for. 2. Religious services of. *a.* Speakers. *b.* Methods of conducting. *c.* Enrolment cards. 3. Expenses of. *a.* Lay speakers. *b.* Officers of the home church. *c.* Societies. 4. The Buffalo plan. 5. Must make use of lay workers.

XVIII. COUNTRY EVANGELIZATION 147

1. Value of the institutions of the country. 2. Need of Christian work in the country. 3. "Stations." *a.* Outline of work. *b.* How organized. 4. Home department of the Sunday-school. 5. How begin the work of country evangelization. *a.* Revival meetings. *b.* Organization of stations. *c.* House-to-house canvass. 6. The missionary spirit a condition of spiritual blessing

CONTENTS.

CHAPTER	PAGE

XIX. MEN'S CLUBS 154

I. Comprehensive society. 1. Need of. 2. Westminster Club of Buffalo, N. Y. *a.* Plan of. *b.* Results. 3. Men's Society of the Church of the Covenant, Washington, D. C. II. Laboring-men's clubs. 1. Need for. 2. Examples of, and features of. 3. The Christian Industrial League.

XX. REACHING AND HOLDING YOUNG MEN . . . 162

1. Increasing interest of young men in church work. 2. Means of reaching them. I. Brotherhood of St. Andrew. *a.* Organization. *b.* Work. II. Brotherhood of Andrew and Philip. *a.* Committees. *b.* Work. III. Alling Class. *a.* Duties of officers. *b.* Work of class. *c.* Mr. Wanamaker's record plan. *d.* Other like classes. IV. Young men's clubs. *a.* Need of. *b.* How to conduct. V. Annual Suppers.

XXI. ATHLETICS 177

1. Interest in. 2. Value of. 3. Purifying effects of Christianity on athletics. 4. Need for physical improvement. 5. Gymnastics. 6. Athletics as an amusement. 7. Bicycle-riding a source of Sabbath-breaking. 8. The opportunity of the Church.

XXII. CHURCH LIBRARIES, READING-ROOMS, LITERARY SOCIETIES, AND ENTERTAINMENT COURSES 184

XXIII. TEACHING BY MEANS OF CLASSES . . . 194

1. Need of. 2. Way to be undertaken by the church. 3. How carried on. *a.* Educational classes. *b.* Night schools. *c.* Colleges under the charge of the church. 4. Winter-night college. *a.* How inaugurated. *b.* How conducted. 5. The church in relation to culture.

XXIV. WOMEN'S WORK 200

1. Value of. 2. Branches of. 3. Some examples of comprehensive women's societies. 4. Missionary societies. 5. Aid societies. 6. A model Women's Society. 7. The Helping Hand. 8. Work in country churches. Mrs. Frost's work in Berea, Ky. 9. Self-denial the basis of women's work.

xi

CONTENTS.

CHAPTER	PAGE
XXV. WORK WITH GIRLS AND YOUNG WOMEN	207

1. Work of Rev. F. B. Meyer, B. A., London, with young women. 2. Young Women's Aid Society. 3. Young Women's Missionary Societies. 4. Fresh-air work by young women. 5. Some societies of young women. *a.* Young Women's Temperance Union. *b.* Daughters of the King. *c.* King's Daughters and Sons. (*a*) The work of the different circles.

XXVI. THE SOCIAL PROBLEM OF THE CHURCH . 216

1. Mary and Martha League. *a.* Necessity for such a society. *b.* Constitution of. *c.* Work of its committees. *d.* Monthly meeting. *e.* Special features of. *f.* The president of. 2. Church socials. *a.* How to make attractive. *b.* Some special forms of. 3. The "Shawmut Church Evenings at Home," plan of. 4. The real value of social life.

XXVII. THE CHILDREN OF THE CHURCH. . . . 226

1. Great importance of education of the youth. 2. Agencies for working with children. *a.* The Sunday-school special days. *b.* Sermons to children, outlines of sermons. *c.* Children's societies, children's service of song. *d.* Missionary work for children, stamp albums, temperance cards.

XXVIII. THE SUNDAY-SCHOOL 235

1. Dr. A. F. Schauffler's "Ways of Working." 2. Rev. Carlos Tracy Chester's "Sunday-school Ways of Working." 3. Ways of securing attendance employed by different churches. 4. Reports of Sunday-schools. *a.* Used to indicate the spiritual condition of the classes. *b.* Used to find facts about the children's families. 5. Home department of the Sunday-school. 6. Teachers' meeting. 7. Normal classes. 8. Suggestions of Rev. E. P. Armstrong.

XXIX. LECTURES TO BOYS ONLY 242

1. Need of, not realized. 2. Lectures to men only, come too late in life. 3. Objections to, answered. 4. Reasons for. *a.* To counteract evil influences. *b.* To keep them from being entrapped. *c.* To restrain them through the

| CHAPTER | PAGE |

knowledge of the consequences of transgression. 5. The White Cross Society and the Silver Cross Society. *a.* Pledges of.

XXX. THE BOYS' CLUB 249
  1. Anecdote of twin brothers. 2. Need of work for boys. 3. The Boys' Club. 4. Plan of conducting. 5. Outings. 6. Membership ticket. 7. Results of. 8. Other kinds of clubs. *a.* Military. *b.* Temperance. *c.* Harry Wadsworth, or Lend-a-hand clubs.

XXXI. THE BOYS' BRIGADE 255
  1. When organized. 2. Meetings of. 3. Special points. *a.* Headquarters. *b.* Officers. *c.* Uniforms. 4. Benefit to the boy. *a.* Mental and Moral. *b.* Physical. 5. Objections to, answered. 6. The boys for Christ.

XXXII. INDUSTRIAL CLASSES 261
  1. Importance of industrial training as an educator. 2. Some things that may be undertaken by the church. I. Carpentering-classes. *a.* Leader. *b.* Use of simple materials. *c.* Sloyd system. II. Kitchen-garden. *a.* Outline of plan. *b.* What is taught. *c.* Value of. *d.* How carried on. III. Cooking-classes. *a.* Bad cooking a promoter of intemperance, of waste, of extravagance. *b.* Remedy found in cooking-classes for women, for children. *c.* Expenses of. *d.* How carried on. IV. Sewing-classes. *a.* Value to all classes of a knowledge of sewing. *b.* Requisites for a sewing-class. *c.* Outline of work. *d.* Benefit of sewing-classes.

XXXIII. DAY NURSERIES AND KINDERGARTENS . 273
  1. Day nurseries. *a.* Necessity for. *b.* Working plan. *c.* Sunday nurseries. 2. Kindergartens. *a.* Value of. *b.* Some points concerning. *c.* Applied to Sunday-school teaching.

XXXIV. TEMPERANCE WORK 278
  1. Knotty problem of. 2. Three kinds of temperance work. I. Educational. *a.* Temperance Society of the Brick Church of Rochester, N. Y. *b.* Work in other churches. *c.* Scientific instruction, cooking-classes, etc.

CONTENTS.

Chapter   **Page**

II. Prevention. (1) Substitute for the saloon. *a.* Social amusements. *b.* Temperance refreshments, coffee-houses, drinking-houses, etc. (2) Temperance legislation. III. Rescue. *a.* Need for. *b.* Work in St. Bartholomew's Mission, New York. *c.* How to organize and carry on rescue work. *d.* Co-operative Rescue Mission. 3. Influence of temperance upon the church.

XXXV. HEALING 286

1. Duty of the church to care for the sick. 2. Medical missionaries. 3. Free dispensaries. 4. Church hospitals. 5. Sick committees. 6. Order of deaconesses and private deaconesses. 7. Diet kitchens. 8. Unofficial care of the sick by the church.

XXXVI. RELIEF WORK 292

1. This work binding on the church. 2. Need for discrimination. 3. Church laundries, wood-yards, and tailor-shops. 4. Employment bureaus. 5. Boarding-houses. 6. Coal Club. 7. Legal and medical advice.

XXXVII. BENEFICIARY AND LOAN ASSOCIATIONS, AND THE PENNY PROVIDENT FUND . 296

a. Shall the church undertake? 1. Beneficiary Association. *a.* Churches in Philadelphia, testimonials of pastors as to value. 2. Loan Association of the Church of St. Bartholomew, New York, and the Provident Loan Society, New York. 3. The Penny Provident Fund. *a.* Working of. *b.* Value of.

XXXVIII. THE PLURAL PASTORATE 303

1. Need for, the Scriptural idea. 2. Co-pastorates unsuccessful. 3. Different plans for plural pastorates. 4. The relationship of the pastors. 5. Lay assistant. 6. Strength in numbers.

XXXIX. THE FREE-PEW AND VOLUNTARY-OFFERING SYSTEM 307

1. Advantages of the pew-rental system. 2. Meaning of the free-pew plan. 3. The pew-rental system not the supplanted system, but the supplanter. 4. Advantages

CONTENTS.

CHAPTER   **PAGE**

of the free-pew system. (1) Claims all the advantages without any of the disadvantages of the pew-rental system. (2) Claims advantages over the pew-rental system. *a.* More in accord with Scriptural ideal. *b.* Increases revenue of the church. *c.* Avoids social distinctions. 5. Results of. 6. Growth of. 7. Voluntary offering. *a.* How conducted. *b.* Vestibule record card. 6. How to substitute the free-pew plan for the pew-rental system.

XL. CHURCH PROGRAMMES, YEAR-BOOKS, BULLETINS, VESTIBULE CARDS, PAPERS, LETTERS, AND ADVERTISING 317

XLI. CHURCH ARCHITECTURE 326
1. New Methods of. 2. The Plymouth Congregational Church of Cleveland, O. 3. Arrangement of other churches. 4. Parish-houses. 5. Roof-gardens. 6. Attention to details. 7. Need of the best that art can give.

XLII. MOBILIZING THE WORK 330
I. The individual church. 1. Danger in the multiplication of societies in. 2. Pastor's council or cabinet. *a.* How carried on. *b.* Value of. 3. Reference to women's work. II. Mobilizing the work of the churches in the community. *a.* Need of. *b.* The plan of the Evangelical Alliance. *c.* Importance of.

XLIII. RESULTS OF THE NEW METHODS 336
1. Success of the new methods. 2. Different conditions demand different methods. 3. Testimonials as to success. 4. Comparative statistics. *a.* A church compared with itself, under the old and the new methods. *b.* Several Congregational churches compared with the whole Congregational Church in the United States. 5. The results commend the methods.

XLIV. THE INSPIRATION OF THE NEW MOVEMENT AND THE REALIZATION OF THE KINGDOM 345

INTRODUCTION.

By CHARLES L. THOMPSON, D.D.

This book is timely. It speaks to an opportunity. An intelligent discussion of the best methods of church work is one of the strongest needs of the times. It is often said that what the Church needs, to secure her purity and progress, is to get back to Christ. There is a truth in this, although it is sometimes over-stated. We have some inheritance of mistakes in the theology of the fathers, and it would doubtless advance the simplicity of theological statement and conduce to the unity and harmony of the Church, if we would be content to express truth in the divine simplicity which marked his words. But we have departed from the simplicity of the early Church quite as much in the principles and methods of church work as in the forms of theological statement. The simple ways of apostolic times have very much been lost sight of in the modern administration of church affairs. Both in the principles of Christian life and in our ways of expressing them, we have gone a long way from the early Church, and without any sharp sense of our departure.

Christ himself organized no church. From him we get the foundations of religious belief, for he was a religious teacher. But we cannot get from his words or example an illustration of the divine order of Chris-

INTRODUCTION.

tian service as developed in an organization. To be sure, the germs of Christian life are all to be found in what he said and did. But we must look to the lives of the apostles and of Christ for an exemplification of the principles they received from the Master. Their hands had touched the hand of Jesus Christ, and in considering the life and ways of the early Church, we are as near to Christ in organic church life as it is possible to get. Christ promised to his disciples the guidance of the Holy Spirit in organizing the Church. They sought that guidance and yielded themselves to the promised direction and control.

The Acts of the Apostles is, therefore, a hand-book of Christian life and work, to which we must look as expressing the mind of Christ himself. At the same time we must not forget that it was also a development. Its essential principles were immutable; but its methods easily took form and color from their surroundings. In general, we may say the Apostolic Church consisted less in definite forms of thought or systems of administration than in a certain great spirit which enabled its members to mould it to the necessities of the times and to give themselves without stint to its service, and die without hesitation for its extension. In the second chapter of that book, four great characteristics of the Apostolic Church are given to us in the familiar words, "They continued steadfastly in the apostles' doctrine and fellowship, and in the breaking of bread, and in prayer." Here are four great truths on which as on four pillars the early Church rested: love of truth, love of one another, frequent remembrance of Christ, and constant prayer. These are the changeless factors of the church life. Now when we think how the primitive Church lived on these truths with joy and gladness, and died for them

INTRODUCTION.

in triumph, and when by contrast we consider how formal and spiritless a thing modern church life frequently is, we cannot but be impressed that there has been a departure from the divine ideal, and that it will be only by a struggle that the Church will get back to the power of those truths as they inspired those lowly disciples. The power of the truth is measured by its effects. So measured, these truths are seen to be almighty. It was a time when all God's people were God's priests, when there was no proxy service of one for another, when all men, women, and children held themselves, as under personal obligations, to give themselves for Jesus Christ. The spirit of sacrifice was not the privilege of the few, but was for a time the common heritage of all the people of the Lord.

It is the purpose of this book to hold these cardinal principles in strong light and to show how the Church of to-day has peculiar opportunity for translating them into a service somewhat akin to the noble service of the Apostolic Church. Thus, for example, this book lays stress on church co-operation or the unity of the Church, in that it carries our thought back to the unity of the early Church, one of whose first articles was this, "the people were together." That should be as true to-day as it was eighteen centuries ago. The distinguishing mark of the Church of Christ is found in the simple fact that her members are believers in the person and teaching of Jesus Christ. The Church, therefore, is not a company of people organized on congenial social lines; it is not a school compacted on theological lines; it is not a club banded together to do benevolent work. The bond that binds them is the bond of Christian faith; it is communion of faith, and it is as strong as the power of Him on whom that faith rests. Recent studies in church history have disclosed the fact that the unity of the churches of the first century consisted not in the identity of the organization, but in a common faith and love. The germs of the different organizations of to-day may all be found in apostolic or sub-apostolic times. Varying forms of government did not then prevent unity of life and service. They should not do so now.

Another characteristic of the early Church was, that they had all things in common. That does not mean communism. It only means that believers held all possessions as the stewards of Christ, ever ready to distribute according to the necessities of his people and his kingdom. In harmony with this idea it is one purpose of this book to declare that the commercial spirit should not rule in the house of God, and that distinctions between rich and poor are not in harmony with the mind of the Master or the practice of the early disciples. The right use of money is one of the living questions in the administration of church affairs. In these days, when tremendous wealth is in the hands of God's people, what results might be anticipated if the spirit of the consecration of property ruled them as it ruled the early Church!

The chapters of this book which insist that the property of the church should be in daily and common use for church work illustrates that article of the Apostolic Church which says that they "continued daily with one accord in the temple." The temple then was a far more sacred building than any of our modern churches are, but at the descent of the Holy Ghost the temple doors were flung open. Henceforth it was not to be a place of occasional resort, but an every-day home, its doors open every day, and every day thronged by those who gathered there to meet each other and meet the Lord. That does not mean that there should be public services constantly; but it means that Christianity should be so active that its central gathering-place should manifest that activity, as closed doors and darkened windows cannot do. If the Church is a lighthouse, its light should be burning every day; if a rescue station, its boats should be manned every day; if a school, its classes should be open every day; if a temple, its altar should be accessible every day.

The church building should be the centre, but it should not be the circumference, of Christian activity. The diffusion of Christian activity throughout the community is expressed in that article of the early Church which says, the disciples "were breaking bread from house to house." Their life was an evidence of Christ's words of commission to his people, "I send you forth." If the Church has healing power, let her go to the sick; if comforting power, let her be as an angel to the sorrowing; if lifting power, let her find those who have fallen. The Church must not stand and beckon; she must "go." Her ministry should be as penetrating as human misery and as comprehensive as the pity of God; and her members should be swift to seek and to save that which is lost, — lost anywhere and in any sense. The church which would be true to the principles which Christ announced and the example he set must ferret out human sin, sorrow, and ignorance and bring them to the light of the truth which she possesses.

Considering now the divine model of what the Church should be, it must be evident that in some things we have departed a long way from that noble example. We have gone away from the simplicity, from the personal devotion, from the self-sacrifice of the Apostolic Church. The Church is rich and powerful and has the eye of the nations; but we have lost something to secure which we could well afford to give

INTRODUCTION.

up some of the visible signs of our greatness and power. And whatever we may think of particular forms and methods of church work, the conviction is getting hold on the conscience of Christendom, that if we would be equal to the tremendous obligations of these times, some of that simple faith and that cheerful consecration of the primitive Church must come back to us. We talk of the dangers of scepticism, and that Christianity to be secure must meet it; and so it must, but the cogency of the argument which Christianity presents depends at last upon the vigor of Christian life that is back of the argument. We speak of the social trials that surround the community, the alienation of class from class, and the conflicts these conditions render inevitable. We must meet these trials and engage in these conflicts, not in a lifeless round of merely respectable and nominal Christianity, but in a certain intensity of Christian truth and sentiment, in the union of believers panoplied in the old doctrine, locking arms across the dividing lines, in the old fellowship of the apostles, living every day and everywhere the great truths that we profess.

All great ages of church history have been adventurous, from the days when Joshua claimed Canaan to the day when the Wesleys left the Church that they might dwell among and uplift the people. We are coming upon the most adventurous times now, — a crusade not for the dead Christ's tomb, but for the living Christ's cross. To be a Christian is to be a crossbearer, to enter into the sacrificial spirit of the Master, like Paul to be the slave of Jesus Christ; and all this that the Kingdom of Heaven may take its place on the earth, that all life may be divine, and that the blessings of society, education, and government may be inbreathed with the spirit of the living God. To secure this result

INTRODUCTION.

there need be nothing new, but the old Gospel in the full measure of its power applied to individuals and to the whole structure of society.

There must be the preaching of the Gospel: "As ye go, preach." Every great work has begun there, — Paul at Ephesus, Augustine at Rome, Savonarola in Florence, Luther at Erfurth, Wesley and Whitfield among the colliers and peasants in England.

There must be continuous evangelistic work, by which is not meant continuous revival service, but such personal work as will bring people at all times to personal commitment to Christ.

There must be a purpose to apply the whole Gospel to the whole man, to meet the people at every point of need, physical, intellectual, moral, and spiritual.

Surrounding all church work there must be a spiritual atmosphere, secured by the character of the workers, by religious exercises connected with all the departments of the work, and by keeping always supreme the principle that we do it all in His Name and for the supreme end of saving souls. There will then be no danger in any kind of institutional work. Above all and sanctifying all, we must get nearer to Christ. We must recall the words of the Master to his disciples when they were striving for pre-eminence, " I, your lord and master, am among you as he that serveth." Then we shall see the divine dignity and glory of the service committed to us.

This book deals chiefly with methods of church work; but it suggests methods and pleads for activity on no ground lower than the top of Calvary. Christ sacrificed for us necessitates a sacrificial church, whose ways of working are flexible to every new occasion, but whose spirit is as changeless as the spirit of Christ.

MODERN METHODS IN CHURCH WORK.

CHAPTER I.

CARDINAL PRINCIPLES.

It would be strange indeed if the closing years of this century, which stand so signally for progress, for invention, for unparalleled industrial and commercial achievement, for material and political development and attainment, when philosophers are writing of the "Evolution of Evolution" and a decade marks greater results than a century was wont to do, — it would be strange if these closing years recorded that all other departments of life had moved forward with accelerated energy and power, but that the Church alone in its great mission had stood still. And the Church, we are wont to say, has before it infinite possibilities!

Whatever may be suggested by a superficial glance at the religious world, a careful study of the facts shows that the Christian Church has entered upon a new era, — an era of fast spreading the Kingdom. The prophecy "Greater works than these shall he do; because I go unto my Father,"[1] is being fulfilled. More souls are being reached daily in this dawn of the twentieth century than ever before in the history of the

---
[1] John xiv. 12.

Church. New methods have been adopted. Work is aggressive. There is a "sound of a going in the tops of the mulberry trees." True, this era has not fully come, but it has come as day has come when

"doth the morning starre appeare
Out of the East, with flaming locks bedight."[1]

The growth of Christianity is shown "in that in 1800 there was one Evangelical communicant in every 14.50 inhabitants in the whole country. In 1850 there was one in every 6.57 inhabitants. In 1870 there was one in every 5.78 inhabitants. In 1880 there was one in every 5 inhabitants. In 1890 there was one in every 4.53 inhabitants. These figures indicate a very large relative gain upon the population, — three communicants in the same number of inhabitants where there was one in 1800. . . . Where the population since 1800 has increased twelve fold the communicants of these churches increased thirty-eight fold, or over three times as fast relatively."[2]

The wide and increasing influence of Christianity on the thought and life of the world is shown in many ways: a few years ago any consideration of the Gospel principles in the study of sociology was regarded as unscientific; now the commandment LOVE ONE ANOTHER AS I HAVE LOVED YOU is the basis of our sociology. The influence of Christianity is further seen in its raising the tone of citizenship; creating a regard for the rights of others; imposing obligations upon the wealthy to share their abundance with those less fortunate; inculcating the principles of justice; emphasizing the duty of humanity to children, to the poor, to prisoners, and to all suffering classes; inciting to con-

[1] Spenser's Faerie Queene, canto viii.
[2] Problem of Religious Progress, by Rev. Daniel Dorchester, D.D., pp. 594, 595.

stant endeavor in the interests of peace and the arbitration of grievances between men and nations.

Along with this increasing influence and extended power of Christianity, a great change has been coming over our churches. The indications of a return to the Christianity of Christ lie open to our sight on every side. A new and more strenuous spirit of helpfulness characterizes the inner and outer life of the churches; they are becoming more humanitarian. And in the larger and more vital appreciation of the gospel of service, of love, and of human brotherhood, they are becoming more practical,— going into the fuller life of human relationships, in which the capabilities of fellowship, love, and sympathetic helpfulness are liberated, expanded, and enriched,— and are seeking that the spirit of Christ may be realized in the life of the family, the community, the church, and the nation, and become wholly the informing life of the world. In other words, that which marks the new era in church life and methods is the recovery of the full teaching of the early Church, — that the office of the church is to heal and to teach as well as to preach. If we call such work "new," it is only because we have lost sight of it for several hundred years; for the work is as old as the Apostles, and bases its claim upon the teachings of the Son of Man.

Those unfamiliar with the nature of the new movement which stands for the realization of this Gospel idea of healing, teaching, and preaching, erroneously suppose that it finds expression only in churches working with what is called the "mission element," and therefore not adapted to the wealthier churches, and of such colossal undertaking as to be impracticable for the poorer, country and village parishes. This popular impression has its rise, no doubt, in the attention which the signal success of the Institutional church has attracted to itself, especially in the mission districts. But the forward Christian movement of our day is in the avenues of our city and in the suburban and country churches no less than in the mission "downtown" districts. Considering the environment of each church, the number of people within its reach, the results of the new methods in the avenue, village, and country churches have been as large proportionately as have those of the mission churches.

For churches *illustrative* of the forward Christian movement, I would mention the Open, the Free, and the Institutional church.[1] Though different in name, they are one in spirit and aim, the detail work of the church being worked out according to the environment of each church. It is in the principles which underlie their work, therefore, that we are to find the idea for which the movement stands. A study of the movement reveals six cardinal principles: —

1. EVANGELISM is the first principle to be mentioned. By this is meant especially the saving of souls and the training and nurturing of Christian character; the same emphasis being placed on the sacraments and preaching as has been done heretofore. The only reason for speaking of this is to present all the underlying principles of the new movement. This seems necessary, since there has been some confusion of thought, on the part of those who know the work only at a distance, as to just what the new movement means and represents. Those persons are wide of the truth who think the sensationalist its representative, or who attribute to it any new doctrines.

That this is the spirit of the movement is evidenced

---

[1] For convenience the term "Open church" will be used throughout this chapter as a comprehensive term for the new movement.

by the following quotations from two of its leaders and well-known men in the church. The Rev. Charles L. Thompson, D.D., President of the Open and Institutional Church League, in speaking of the Open church says: "It believes there is no other name but the name of Christ whereby men must be saved. It believes it will profit us nothing to gain the world and lose our soul, or life. It holds firmly to the supremacy of eternal life. Its ultimate is to bring men to the knowledge, faith, and service of the Redeemer. It would count church work a failure that did not result in lives renewed by the power of the Holy Ghost. More than this, it is willing to have its work tested and judged by its fealty to and success in the supreme work of bringing men to Christ."[1]

Unmistakable, too, are the words of the Rev. Russell H. Conwell, D.D., pastor of the Baptist Temple, Philadelphia, one of the largest and most successful Institutional churches in the country. Dr. Conwell says: "The mission of the Church is to save the souls of men. That is its true mission. It is the only mission of the Church. That should be its only thought. The moment any church admits a singer who does not sing to save souls; the moment a church calls a pastor who does not preach to save souls; the moment a church elects a deacon who does not work to save souls; the moment a church gives a supper or an entertainment of any kind not for the purpose of saving souls, — it ceases in so much to be a church, and to fulfil the magnificent mission God gave to it. Every concert, every choir service, every preaching service, every Lord's Supper, every agency used in the church must have the great mission plainly before its eyes. We are here to save the souls of dying sinners; we are here for

---

[1] The Sacredness of the Secular, p. 5.

no other purpose; and, the mission of the Church being so clear, that is the only test of a real church."

But it will be helpful not only to have the statement of leaders in this work, but also the judgment of men outside the movement who have investigated the work.

Said the *Congregationalist*, in an editorial a short time ago: "To the query so often put, Is the Institutional church secularizing religion? this much at least can be said: It certainly has not had that effect upon the pastors and their fellow-laborers. It would be hard to find a set of men more ardent in their devotion to Christ than the men who are identified with Institutional work. Moreover, as respects the body of the membership, if the prayer-meeting be taken as the thermometer of spiritual life, or if a visitor comes in contact with the rank and file, he gains the impression that a strong and constant desire to save men permeates the entire church."

2. CONSECRATION is the second cardinal principle; and a consecration too that is electric in its very thought. Not the consecration merely of one day in the seven, or of a part of a man, or a part of his income, but the consecration of all of the man, all of his income, and all of the three hundred and sixty-five days of the year. The spirit of the new movement is all-inclusive in its claims, claiming not only that all of the man — body, soul, and spirit — and all that he has — time, talents, and possessions — are God's, but also claiming that all society — its business, labor, commerce, laws, institutions, everything — is His also. The Open church, therefore, believes in " sanctifying all days and all means to the end of saving the WORLD for Christ." And this emphasis on the sacredness of all things and of all the man is one of the principles which differentiates the new movement from the work of the past. Dr.

Josiah Strong recognized this when he said: "This broader conception of the mission of the Church, while it has been held by individuals, has never been grasped by the Church herself. She has deemed the world a hopeless wreck, and herself commissioned to save out of it as many as possible, whom she is to land on the heavenly shore. It has not yet dawned on her that she is to save the wreck itself. She has sought to fit men to do God's perfect will in heaven instead of consciously aiming to hasten the answer to her Lord's prayer, 'Thy will be done *in earth* as it is in heaven.' She does not seem to have perceived that God had the *world* in his heart and plan. 'God so loved the *world*' that he gave his Son for its redemption. Christ came into the world, not to condemn it, ' but that the *world* through him might be saved.'"[1]

3. MINISTRATION is the third cardinal principle of the Open church. It aims, as Christ's body, to furnish the material environment through which his spirit can be practically expressed to the age in which it exists.[2] It seeks to reach all sides of a man, — not only the spiritual side, but also the physical, intellectual, and social nature of man. It therefore "seeks to become the centre and source of all beneficent and philanthropic effort, and to take part in every movement which has for its end the alleviation of all human suffering, the elevation of man, and the betterment of the world."[2] This is simply following the example of Him who came not to be ministered unto but to minister; who went about doing good, healing the sick, comforting the afflicted, feeding the hungry, and sitting with the sinner that he might show him the way of Life. The

---

[1] The New Era, p. 236.
[2] *Platform* of the Open and Institutional Church League, United States of America.

welcome of Jesus Christ was a gracious welcome, his ministry was for *all*, and the common people heard him gladly. "The men who are active in the new religious movement are not foolish enough to suppose that they can literally imitate Christ under the conditions of modern life and have any good grow out of it; but they endeavor in all ways to put his spirit into the life of to-day, so that the churches may be to the men of the present time what he was to the men of his time."[1] Therefore the Open church seeks to minister unto others so freely and nobly that the plainest people will gladly come; and ministers, with the church open seven days in the week, with provision for helpful amusements and recreation removed from temptation, with libraries and reading-rooms and means for social intercourse, and ever ready and helping hands in time of misfortune, loss, sorrow, disaster, and affliction. This ministering unto the whole man means too, where needed, kindergartens for children, club-rooms for men, training-classes for young men and young women, the Helping Hand for mothers, and nurseries where mothers who are compelled to work out for the day may leave their children knowing that their care and education will be provided for.

It is in this work, at least in a part of this work, that the new movement has been criticised; it being urged that such beneficent and philanthropic efforts should be left to charitable societies instituted for that purpose. It may be answered that if the Church delegates such work to outside societies it loses a great blessing. The good of doing is reactive upon the doer, is not alone felt by the recipient. The curse of men has been their content to do for others by proxy. Let

---

[1] The Institutional Church, by George Willis Cooke, "The New England Magazine," August, 1896, p. 647.

CARDINAL PRINCIPLES.

the Church go and do as the very hands and feet of God, and it will soon find that loving deeds are as potent as ever, that hard hearts are melted by the Christ spirit of love. God committed the poor to the care of the Church. It is the doing of beneficent and philanthropic work — precisely this kind of work — which Jesus declared is the test that is to determine eternal destiny.[1]

The Duke of Argyle, speaking of Dr. Chalmers, says: "He obeyed the call of the Psalmist in considering the poor. And the result of his consideration was that the relief of and care for unavoidable poverty is the special duty and function of the Christian Church in its fullest and highest organization of combined laity and clergy. . . . He was not content with holding this view in theory. He undertook to show how it could be worked out in practice in one of the parishes of the great city of Glasgow with a population of more than one hundred thousand. He undertook to show that the free-will offering of his own parochial congregation could be made adequate to the discharge of this great duty. He desired to show that the Christian Church, if it only knew how to drill and marshal its spiritual forces in facing and dealing with the causes of secular suffering and distress, could be and would be the greatest and best of all agencies in the world. And he did show it."[2]

Those who attack the new movement must do it along different lines from that of ministration, for here it is too close to the Christ principle, — not to be ministered unto, but to minister.

It is at once apparent that the nature and extent of

---

[1] Matthew xxv. 31–46.
[2] Christian Socialism, "Eclectic Magazine," 1895, p. 20. Reprint from the "Nineteenth Century."

ministration must vary as the need varies. This leads to the mention of the fourth cardinal principle underlying the new movement, which is —

4. ADAPTABILITY. He who fails to grasp the significance of this principle will never understand the Open church. It is an institutional organism varying its features according to local needs. If upon the wealthy avenue, or in a village of homes, the church must adopt means suited to its environment for bringing the people to Christ and keeping them there. Methods essential in the tenement district might prove ruinous in a community of homes. Because new methods succeed in one locality is not always reason for inaugurating them in another. We must not make our appeal to the poor alone, any more than to the rich alone.

This principle of adaptability has not always been remembered in Christian work. It was said by the Rev. A. F. Schauffler, D.D., in 1888, that during the twenty years preceding, nearly two hundred thousand people had moved in below Fourteenth Street, New York, and seventeen Protestant churches had moved out.[1] This "uptown" movement has been going on in all our larger cities; and why? Because the Church could not, or would not, adjust its methods to meet the conditions of its new environment.

But it is not the "uptown" movement that best shows the want of adaptation to local need. In fact, this moving may be proof of adaptability to changed conditions. We owe a duty to the well-to-do and to the rich as well as to the artisan and the poor, and the Church must keep her hold on the people on whose gifts the support of missions depends; but the loss of

---

[1] The New Era, by Dr. Josiah Strong, p. 200.

flexibility and adaptation has been apparent in the Church in its want of large persuasive appeal to the people of all classes.

The principle of adaptability, therefore, is seen to be a most important one, and the pastor who fails to recognize its claims is sure to fail of truest success. Methods suitable to-day may require large modification to-morrow. We cannot, therefore, hold to cold, mechanical methods. Eternal verities will stand, but the application of gospel principles must vary with the ever-varying, ever-changing conditions of human life and the changing circumstances of society.

5. EXTENSION is the fifth cardinal principle. The Church has always, I believe, recognized that its purpose is to multiply itself, to reproduce itself in new churches. Like young birds that mature in strength and then fly away from the mother home to build nests of their own, — nests which in turn send out other young to build other nests, — so the Church should multiply itself, reproduce itself, till the world over there shall be churches of the living God. The extension idea of the new movement, however, includes not only giving to missions and the established boards of the Church, and sustaining some little adjunct church or mission, and building new churches, but also emphasizes that the Church is to multiply itself through *all* its individual members, — that wherever there is a human heart there is the temple of God and opportunity for service, and also emphasizes the importance of regular systematic and *personal* effort for extending the Kingdom throughout the community.

6. ORGANIZATION is the sixth principle. The principles already mentioned give rise to certain forms of organization, to certain definite, distinct lines of

activity, — such organization as shall give to the "builders every one his sword," and shall put into battle line every one within the pale of the church.

We are in an age of organization. It is a necessary condition of success in any enterprise whatsoever. Dr. Lyman Abbott once said, "Neither a mob of brave men nor an organized body of cowards ever made an army." Yet thousands of our churches are literally falling to pieces because of loose, haphazard, unbusinesslike ways; falling to pieces, too, when there is infinite power in a willing people. We need to utilize that power, as the power of Niagara is being utilized. For centuries the water-fall of Niagara had gone on into its great plunge only to break into maddening fury where its waves are tossed in grandeur and lashed into spray at the whirlpool two miles below. Then men thought to make use of that power. Now it supplies the force which generates the electricity for lighting the Empire State and for running the machinery of its great manufactories.

"To organize is not to create opportunities," but to use those which already exist, to utilize the powers already flowing through the Church. It is but bringing the people together in right relations to one another and in right relations to God; and the result is that they are as lights upon a thousand hills, and a moving power in the great work of the Kingdom. General Von Moltke was asked what was the pivotal hour between Prussia and France and the consummation of the German Empire. He replied, "The hour when I completed the maps of Alsace-Lorraine, and put the armies face to face on paper." Most Christians long to do something to advance God's Kingdom, but many of them do not know how or what to do. There is no more stupendous blunder than the assumption that they are not willing, or that they know just how and where to begin. Some are too timid to express their willingness. Others check and freeze the fountain of aspiration by minimizing their powers. But people are put to doing, work for the church is practically accomplished, when some capable mind maps out the work to be done, — completed, as was Prussia's victory with Moltke's maps of Alsace-Lorraine. The organized church not only shows to every man his work, but maps it out for him when necessary, so that a wayfaring man cannot err therein. And a value of having different societies is to appeal by "all means" to all people. If one society will not appeal to a member, perhaps another will.

There are so many counter-attractions to the church at the present time, that a successful minister must not only be a good preacher and a faithful pastor but also a good organizer.

Such are the cardinal principles which underlie the Forward Christian movement of this closing century. We see that these principles are not new, but, now applied in their simplicity and business-like directness, they bear the breath of omnipotence and are as exhilarating as on the morn when first proclaimed on the Galilean hills.

Rev. James Roscoe Day, D.D., Chancellor of Syracuse University, and former pastor of Calvary Methodist Episcopal Church, New York, in speaking of this new movement, said: "The whole matter resolves itself into this, — an attempt to get the Christian Church back to Christ, and to have it stand for Christ among men. . . . I think the day has passed and will never be recovered when that old-time church will have any power over the men and women of this world. They want something to enter into their lives, to help them and to bless them; and they want it done in a natural kind of way too."[1]

One remark must be made before closing this chapter. The churches representing the new movement do not claim to be perfect, nor to have made no mistakes. If one plan fails, they believe in trying another. "He is not the best Christian nor the best general who makes the fewest false steps," said the Rev. F. W. Robertson, "but he is the best who makes the most splendid victories by the retrieval of false steps. Forget mistakes; organize victory out of mistakes." Certainly no greater mistake could be made than has long been made by the Church of the past, — not to try new methods when the old methods have failed to advance the Kingdom of God among men, and have left the roadway stained with the blood of the impenitent, and this sad world ringing with the cries of the hopeless dying.

[1] Address before the Open or Institutional Church League, New York, 1894.

CHAPTER II.

THE FREE, THE OPEN, AND THE INSTITUTIONAL CHURCH.

Churches standing for the principles enumerated in the preceding chapter — namely, evangelism, consecration, ministration, adaptability, extension, and organization — have experienced great difficulty in finding a name "broad and distinctive enough to cover the idea." The names, "Free," "Open," and "Institutional" have been used most commonly, and sometimes interchangeably. But not one of these terms fully meets the need, and the first and last names mentioned are open to the serious objection of being positively misleading.

The term "Free church" has sometimes been applied to churches that have undertaken a broad Christian work. But the popular impression of a free church is one with free pews; therefore the term "Free," instead of being an expression and setting forth of great underlying principles, suggests that free sittings are the *terminus ad quem*. In fact, the term was originally applied to churches only that had abolished pew rentals. It is true that a large number of churches that have engaged in aggressive work have deemed it best to have free pews, but there are notable exceptions to the rule. And where the free-pew idea is concurred in, it is but a single phenomenon of a great underlying principle; otherwise free pews in a church may mean very little. It is possible to conduct the system on as low a mercantile basis as any other system. Again, it is painfully evident that a church which has free pews yet is closed six days out of seven is farther from the Apostolic idea than is the church which sells its sittings and holds them for the owners at certain services, but has other services which are free to the public and doors that are open all the time during the week. This latter modification of the free-pew system is justified even by so strong an advocate as the Hon. Silas McBee, when the church is so popular that, unless protected, the members on whom the church is dependent for support would only now and then find opportunity to worship at its services.

But the term "Free church" is otherwise misleading. It is suggestive of a church which places little or no emphasis on financial support. But, as a matter of fact, all free churches do emphasize financial obligation, though they may emphasize it under the gentler term of "voluntary offering." A church cannot be conducted without expense, and church boards must be supported. The only free thing about giving in the Free church is the freedom of giving as each man is able or as each man will.

It is not strange that there is an increasing tendency to drop the term "Free" and to use the term "Open," or only the old denominational name.

The term "Institutional," as applied to the church, is also open to serious objection. It is a cumbersome and ill-suited word. "An institution," as one has happily put it, "is an organization for the realization of an idea." The true church does stand for organization, that is to say, for "a due construction of parts;" but organization is but one of the underlying cardinal principles. Therefore, to call the church "Institutional" is to magnify organization unduly, and to suggest the doing of Christian work by machinery, handling the masses by cold mechanical methods, — which is the very opposite of what is meant. In the true church societies and departments are but open doors by which we may enter in and win the people personally, and organization is but the orderly arrangement of affairs and the preparation for personal work. This is far different from delegating that personal work to something that is impersonal. We have had quite enough of that! Dr. Josiah Strong has well said: "The average Christian to-day is hiring his Christian work done by proxy, — by societies, institutions, the minister, the city missionary. He is so very busy that he would rather give his money than his time. His interest in his fellow-men, therefore, is expressed through various organizations which make a business of philanthropy. Thus our Christian work has become largely *institutional* instead of *personal*, and therefore largely mechanical instead of vital!"[1]

It is not surprising that the term "Institutional," as applied to the church, meets with cordial prejudice. The term savors of the secular and the mechanical, and is void of inspiration or aught that suggests Christian kindness, personal interest, and self-sacrificing love. The term will necessitate continuous explanation, or else it must continue to awaken prejudice and opposition, and bring the new movement under suspicion and into disfavor. In either event it defeats the very purpose for which it was chosen, and militates against the coming of the Kingdom. I would prefer to speak of a church carrying on Institutional work rather than call it an Institutional church.

It must be said, however, that the term "Insti-

[1] The New Era, p. 218.

tutional" has not been satisfactory, for the most part, even to the leaders of the work which has borne that name. Let us forget, then, the unfortunate christening, and hope for a better name or none at all.

What shall we say of the term "Open"? This term, too, has come about naturally. It was used in the first place to distinguish those churches with doors open every day in the week from the churches which stand locked and bolted from Sunday to Sunday. The word "Open" is far less objectionable than the terms "Free" and "Institutional." No one principle is emphasized so much as a great spirit back of the open house is suggested. Figuratively, the term "Open" is beautiful in its thought, implying open pews, open hearts, open opportunities, and is a suggestive symbol of the open arms of Everlasting Love. The term arouses no prejudice, but rather awakens interest and sympathy, and excites investigation.

The word "Open" is otherwise of service. It calls attention to the importance of having church doors open day and evening, and seven days in the week. The *Chicago Mail* has estimated the net capital value represented by the churches of Chicago at $22,500,000. After reference to the estimate, and the proposition of some of the Chicago papers that the returns on the part of the churches were inadequate, Mr. W. T. Stead says: —

"Considering that London is more than twice the size of Chicago, and that the churches are far more costly structures than those built on the shores of Lake Michigan, it would not be out of the way to put the money locked up in church buildings and sites at nearer $100,000,000 than $75,000,000. Every penny of that immense sum is trust-money for God Almighty. Is it well invested?

THE OPEN CHURCH.

"The first principle of investing money is that it should bear interest all the time it is invested. Rain or shine, week in, week out, all the days of the week, the man of the world expects his money to bear interest. At present the rate of interest is low. He counts himself lucky if he can get a safe three per cent per annum. But what business man would lock up his capital in any undertaking that only yielded a return one day in seven? If he invests it in a public house, Boniface earns his dividend seven days a week; if he puts it in any other business, the investment bears harvest six days a week. But if the saints invest it for God Almighty, it bears fruit only one day in seven. This is not very good business for the children of light, who in this respect have much to learn from children of the world."[1]

But there are other reasons for the churches being open all the time. The Psalmist said that his desire was to dwell in the house of the Lord and to inquire in his temple.[2] Can we inquire in his temple only when the choir and the preacher are present? Can we come to him only through the priest? True, the streets are open, so are the saloons; but the church is quiet and restful and precious through association. Here our thoughts, like the Psalmist's, must be of His loving kindness. What a help, what an object lesson, what a beautiful privilege, "to *daily* inquire in His temple"! Such a church would also be a blessing to strangers. Thousands of people are every day passing idle hours in the cities and towns, waiting some errand, and would gladly accept the hospitality of the open church. Thus living streams of blessing would flow out from all our churches and from community to community as the very rivers of our God.

[1] The Independent, April 11, 1895, p. 5. [2] Psalms xxvii. 4.

The Episcopal churches have largely taken the lead in keeping some part of the church open daily, with an inscription on the outside of the church inviting strangers and others to come in at any time " for meditation and prayer." I can but feel that a church which will not do so much as that is in a lamentable condition.

It remains to be said, however, that few people, comparatively, would avail themselves of the open temple. Therefore it is not enough that we merely open the church doors. We must meet the varied needs of the community, stand as in the place of Jesus Christ, the friend of man, — body, soul and spirit, — and minister in His name. I recognize, however, that there are a *few* church constituencies which have little need of a church outside its spiritual ministry. But for the most part the needs of every community are many, and these needs cannot be met by one large, barren, empty room. For instance, if a church is to meet the social and educational needs of the community, there must be rooms where the people can read, study, or pass a leisure hour in pleasant social intercourse, or find diversion amid ennobling surroundings. The children and young people too need to be provided for by play-rooms and halls where they can have entertainments and social gatherings. There is dire need for such arrangements in almost every community. What a shame, then, for the church to stand bolted and barred as though its sacred courts would be desecrated by helpful ministries to suffering humanity! If the church is to reach society on all its sides, come into touch with all classes of people, — touch them where their needs are real and help them in ways which they must appreciate and so gain a lasting influence upon them, — it must recognize that man has more than one side to his being; and when the church recognizes this fact, we can expect her courts to be open always with provision for meeting the varied needs of the community and freely giving her loving ministries to all.

Such is the idea of the Open church. It is evident that even this word is not adequately descriptive. Yet it is by far the best of any that has been suggested. It may not altogether be regarded as a misfortune, however, that no one name fully meets the need. Denominational preferences promise to exist, and churches are already known by their individual names. Let us hope that the time may come when every church will stand for the salvation of, and ministration to, the whole man and for the redemption of the whole world, and stand with as large a welcome as the welcome of the Father, " Whosoever will may come;" and go, as did Jesus, " TEACHING . . . and PREACHING the gospel of the kingdom, and HEALING all manner of sickness and all manner of disease among the people."[1]

[1] Matthew iv. 23.

CHAPTER III.

THE CHURCH-MEMBERS, — WHERE ARE THEY? — WHAT ARE THEY?

THE logical starting-point of church work is with the church itself. Xerxes, when at the Hellespont with his army of a million and a half of men, cried pathetically, "I would I had as many soldiers as men!" That army is little prepared for war which goes with scattered, broken, or wavering lines. As a matter of fact, many church-members are not in battle line, some are never there. But the fault is not altogether that of the people. Some are waiting to be drafted; others do not know how to enlist.

One of the first steps for marshalling people, making concerted action possible, is personal knowledge of the church-members, — knowing who they are, and where they are, whether in line or out of it. For this purpose it is necessary to keep a church roll. But a church roll is more than the old-time notion, "a history of important dates." It is not our purpose to speak of church records and roll-books, which are as numerous as they are varied in their nature. There have been some new record books in this line, providing for a record of dates, of reception into church-membership, marriage, dismissal, or death. But these record books are sometimes cumbersome, and cannot be kept in alphabetical order with such convenience as a card catalogue of the members; nor have the books the advantage of blanks to be filled in with a cross, indicating the several societies to which the member may belong. The following card is used by the Madison Avenue Presbyterian Church of New York City: —

M	SS	LBA	BM	MS	FMS	HMS	YLAS	WS	A&P	CEW	GW	MC	E	*Street*, Madison Ave. No. 506.
2,4,'95	×									×	×	×		Smith, Mr. H. L.
2,4,'95		×	×	×	×							×		" Mrs. H. L.
2,4,'95	×	Dismissed to Central Ch. Rochester, 4,4,'96.				×	×					×		" Charles W.
	×					×			×	×		×		" Bertha Louise.
														" Gertrude.
														(See Miller, Mrs. R. B.)

The letters at the head of the card stand for the several societies of the church. The crosses opposite the name indicate the societies of which the person is a member. The figures, 2, 4, '95, indicate that on the second day of the fourth month of 1895 the person was received into active membership of the church. It should also be noticed that the letters indicating the various societies which are to the right of this card represent the societies of the men, and the letters to the left, those of the women. This gives space, in the event of marriage, dismissal, or death, for making such record. The name Miller, in parenthesis at the bottom of the card, refers us to the M cards, and indicates that there is some close relationship between the families represented by the two cards. Sometimes this relationship is indicated by a brief note upon the back of the card. If members of the church be given access to the card catalogue, then the notes must be colorless.

The above card is valuable, not only because it shows at a glance just what the member of the church is doing or is not doing, but also because it is a family card. It contains the names of the members of the family. It will be an unusual church where the record does not show a goodly number of non-church-goers in the families represented by membership in the church. It is for such non-church-goers that the individual church is especially and directly responsible.

Another system of cataloguing the church-membership is by different colored cards. It practically incorporates the ideas of the above card, but uses one colored card for the church-members, and a card of different color for the attendants of the church.

Some churches have a system by which the roll of the communicants is checked at each communion Sunday so as to ascertain the absentees. Absence from communion is a very great evil. This system is suggestive to the pastor of those members who are becoming lax in the discharge of their church duties, and who possibly may be losing interest in the great work of the Kingdom. If followed more closely, we doubt if some churches would suffer annually so many "lost sheep." The following simple card is used by the Ruggles Street Baptist Church of Boston: —

COMMUNION CARD.

RUGGLES STREET BAPTIST CHURCH.

Name,..
Residence,..
Remarks,..

....

Each Communicant is requested to write his name and address legibly, that the attendance may be accurately kept. Strangers will kindly record the church of which they are members. Any information of cases of sickness or need will be gladly received by the Deacons.

THE CHURCH-MEMBERS.

The Bethany Presbyterian Church, Philadelphia, uses the communicants' card system. The following is a copy of the communication and card coupons which are mailed to every member at the commencement of the year: —

Bethany Communion Card No...
Name,............................ Residence,............................
JANUARY COMMUNION

Bethany Communion Card No...
Name,............................ Residence,............................
MARCH COMMUNION

Bethany Communion Card No...
Name,............................ Residence,............................
MAY COMMUNION

Bethany Communion Card No...
Name,............................ Residence,............................
JULY COMMUNION

Bethany Communion Card No...
Name,............................ Residence,............................
SEPTEMBER COMMUNION

Bethany Communion Card No...
Name,............................ Residence,............................
NOVEMBER COMMUNION

BETHANY PRESBYTERIAN CHURCH.

Communicant's Card No...............
Name,..................................
Address,...............................

The membership of this Church is large, and without some system of record, members may be absent for months without their absence being noted, or its cause known. The object of this card is to correct the register of the names and residences of members, and to enable Pastors and Elders to give needed sympathy and counsel in sickness, trouble, or prolonged absence from Church services. The coupon is to be detached and dropped into the basket at the Communion service. The number on the card and on the coupons corresponds to the number of your name on the Church Roll. Please write your name and residence in full on the coupon. Requests for visitation made on the back of the coupons, or otherwise, will receive attention; but the Pastors and Elders cannot be expected to know of cases where they might be helpful unless notified. Neglect to use cards will cause members to be treated as absentees; due diligence should be, therefore, exercised to deposit the coupons.

The names and addresses of Pastors and Elders are as follows:—

REV. J. WILBUR CHAPMAN, D.D., PASTOR,
2211 St. James Place.

REV. GEORGE VAN DEURS, ASSISTANT PASTOR,
3932 Sansom Street.

REV. JAMES M. FARR, JR., ASSISTANT PASTOR,
26 South Thirty-Fourth Street.

It of course takes considerable time to enter the returns of these cards, but it is one way of proving a faithful shepherd and bishop of souls.

Another system of keeping in close touch with the members and of obtaining information as to change in the family address, and a plan which also magnifies their relation to the church, is that of an annual roll-call of the members of the church. Such annual roll-call is an established thing with some denominations, and is growing in favor with others.

But good as these plans are, they are not enough to keep the pastor informed as to the needs of his people. The sick and other sufferers, absentees and back-sliders, would not, without systematic assistance, always be known to the minister, at least until the time of truest assistance is past. The wise pastor, therefore, surrounds himself by a good visiting-staff, which is of value in many ways; not only to acquaint the minister with the needs of the parish, but also to help him meet them; to bring the people through acquaintance into closer sympathy, and promote that fellowship which should be a distinguishing feature of every community of worshipping Christians.

Several different plans are being pursued in parish visitation. The Rev. John L. Scudder, D.D., pastor of the Tabernacle, Jersey City, N. J., has a band of sixty helpers for visiting, whom he calls "sub-pastors." The staff is made up of both men and women; each has a list of names of persons belonging to the Tabernacle Constituency who are kept track of, and of whom reports are made at the time of the meeting of the committee with the pastor at the hour preceding the preparatory lecture. In this way the needs of the people are known; in case of absence they realize that they have been remembered, and are led to feel that, in some measure at least, they are a part of, and are important to, the work.

Another system of parish visitation may be called the "block" or "district" plan. The membership of the congregation is divided geographically into a convenient number of districts, and the districts into sections; over each district is placed an officer of the church, or a deaconess, who is supposed to interest himself or herself in the spiritual or material welfare of the people, as the need may be. That the most available person may be obtained, the leaders of these districts are sometimes appointed from the membership of the church at large. Such leaders are usually appointed by the pastor, who also suggests the names of a committee to work with them. In other churches the district leaders choose their own committee. Reports are made by the members of the visiting staff to the leader, who in turn reports to the pastor; urgent cases being reported at once.

The parish of the Presbyterian Church of Austin, Ill., is divided into four districts, with three deaconesses over each, and with two deacons to assist in a general way as they may be able. I take the following from a leaflet by the pastor, Rev. John Clark Hill, D.D., bearing suggestions on the work of the deaconesses: —

"The committee designated will call to their aid any of the ladies (and men too) to the work that demands attention, and to distribute the 'calling lists' as furnished by the pastor for the general benefit of all. . . . The work should be done in the most quiet and unobtrusive manner. We should say nothing about it in a public way; the less its organized character appears on the surface, the more influential it will be in its working."

MODERN METHODS IN CHURCH WORK.

Teachers' reports in the Sunday-school are also valuable for keeping the pastor acquainted with the needs of his people. Names and addresses of scholars absent for two or more successive Sundays are reported not only to the superintendent, but also to the minister.

The people of a parish are a precious charge, and every effort should be made to shepherd them closely.

CHAPTER IV.

REACHING PEOPLE OUTSIDE THE CHURCH.

"The parish priest of austerity climbed into the high church steeple,
   That he might be near to God, to hand His word down to the people;
Every day in sermon script, he wrote what he thought came from
      heaven,
   And threw it down on the people's heads two times one day in seven.
In his age God called him down to die, and he cried from out the steeple,
   'Where art thou, Lord?' and the Lord replied, 'Down here, among
      my people.'"

It is not enough that the pastor know the people of his church; he should also know the people about his church. One thing absolutely essential to thorough work on the part of the church is a personal knowledge of the country and people whose business it is to conquer.

Previous to the Japo-Chinese war, the Japanese knew thoroughly every harbor, river, and hill of their enemy's territories. The Japanese had sounded the waters, and surveyed the lands of the Chinese. When the time for fighting came, the Mikado's people knew how advantageously to face their enemy. The Japanese, too, did not wait for the enemy to come to them, but went out to the enemy.

The true church does not wait for the people to come to it; it goes to the people, following the commandment of Jesus Christ: "Go out into the highways and hedges, and compel them to come in."[1] Can it be

---
[1] Luke xiv. 23.

gainsaid that the Church has not, comparatively speaking, followed this method in working for souls? Pastors have been content to preach from the pulpit. In the face of a well-nigh empty church, a decreasing membership, and a depleted treasury, some of them have asserted by practice — if not by word — that two services on the Sabbath and one in mid-week are sufficient to evangelize the world. When we awaken to the fact that he who preaches only from the pulpit preaches only in part, we shall have taken one step toward the Christ ideal, — going after the people, and working for them by such painstaking persistency as will make applicable the golden metaphor, "fishers of men;" doing anything and everything that will bring the gospel to bear upon the hearts of the people.

I. A successful and systematic method in reaching people outside the church is a house-to-house canvass. The purpose of such a canvass is to learn who and where the people are; what have been, if any, their church affiliations; and what are their church preferences, — in a word, what is the religious and social status of the community. Much may be said in favor of such a canvass. "If it is useful to the Federal Government to accumulate, every decade, facts concerning the population living beneath the Stars and Stripes, it cannot but be useful to the associated Christianity of our country to accumulate facts to direct its policy. . . . Shall the Church of Christ be willing to allow the State to surpass her in care and culture of the individual?"[1]

In the city a number of churches usually co-operate in making such canvass. In the country or smaller city the canvass may include all the churches of the

---

[1] Manuscript Report of the Sociological Canvass of the Fifteenth Assembly District, New York, 1896.

community. These churches come together through their pastors or delegates, and apportion sections of the district to be canvassed to each church for the purpose of learning the church status of each person within the district. Each church utilizes such working force as the pastor or person in charge may determine. Some churches have two or three paid canvassers for taking the census. Other churches work on the principle that the visiting-staff should consist largely of the lay-members of the church, believing that it is a work which the Christian has no right to delegate to another.

A careful record is kept of every visit by the canvasser in a blank form provided for that purpose. The following form is that which was used by some of the churches of Philadelphia: —

Visitor, ...					Territory, ...		
Address, ...							
Street.	No. of House.	Name of Family (or Individual).	Language.	No. of Children not in Sabbath-school.	Church attended.	Church Preference (if non-attendants).	Remarks.
....	....	....	......	.....	....	....	....
....	....	....	......	.....	....	....	....
....	....	....	......	.....	....	....	....
....	....	....	......	.....	....	....	....
....	....	....	......	.....	....	....	....

The following are a part of the directions which were given to the canvassers: —

TO VISITORS.

Be careful to see that *each blank* contains your name and address, and the territory assigned you, as called for at the top of the form.

Get information as complete as possible from every house, not neglecting boarders and servants.

Indicate by the abbreviation " Indl." after the name, when it is that of an individual not the head of the family.

Entries are to be made in the column headed "Language" only when divine service conducted in a foreign tongue is preferred. Indicate in this column, also, by the abbreviation "Col." the names of people of color.

In the column of "Remarks" state in a word any circumstance worthy of special notice; for example, "sick," "destitute," "intemperate," "call immediately."

As the blanks are filled, tear them out at the line of perforation, and send them promptly to your District Chairman. When your work is finished, note the fact on the last blank.

Please write legibly.

State your errand plainly and briefly at each house, and be particular to let the parties know that the visitation is general. Avoid, as far as possible, the appearance of formal questioning, and taking notes in the presence of the parties visited.

Remember that the persons visited are under no *obligation* to answer your inquiries. Ask the information courteously and as a favor.

Ascertain, if possible, the name of the family residing in the house, before calling.

Prepare yourself by meditation and prayer for your work, and, with God's help, make it as *spiritual* as you can.

The several churches making the canvass have weekly or bi-weekly meetings, as may seem advisable, presided over by the chairman elected at the first meeting. Reports from each church are given at this time. The names of those persons who have expressed a preference for the Episcopal church are handed over to the Episcopalians, those who have expressed a preference for the Methodist church are handed over to the Methodists, the Congregationalist to the Congregationalists, the Presbyterian to the Presbyterians, and so on through the list. This is the end of the canvassing. Its purpose is simply to locate non-church-goers, and acquaint the churches so far as possible with the conditions of the people about them.

It is to be remembered in this canvass that people will frequently claim church relations and will theoretically have them, when practically they sustain no definite church relationship. Because they were married in, or many years ago the grandmother was a member of, a certain church, they have come to regard that church, in an indefinite way, as theirs. Or it may be that the children recurrently with holiday times attend the Sunday-school, and so the parents will make claim to a church home. Dr. Paden, of the Hollond Memorial Presbyterian Church, Philadelphia, said that in a house-to-house canvass of a considerable district about his church, hardly ten per cent of the people visited were, from their own accounts, without a church home, while practically he believed that a much larger per cent were of the non-church-going classes.

II. The canvass is followed up by everything within the church's power for winning the people to Christ and to his service. One of the most successful means, and one that prepares for other influences, is the house-to-house visitation. This method has been attended with blessed results. It is the way the disciples worked, — "breaking bread from house to house." The people are called upon by one of the pastors, again by some members of the visiting-staff, and again by other members of the church. Acquaintance is commenced, a cordial invitation to the church services and an assurance of welcome to all the church privileges is given. Visits are repeated, letters are written, church notices are mailed, and little attentions are shown in every way. By and by the door of the heart stands ajar. These little things, by the interpreting power of a Christ-like personality, have accomplished the end: the people are won to Jesus Christ and to his service.

In a community of about twenty-four thousand population, the nineteenth monthly report of such visitation "started into the beginnings of church life thirty-eight families."[1] This ought to teach us the lesson of patience and perseverance. It takes time for thoughts to mature and for new purposes to form.

Other results of this canvassing and systematic visitation may be mentioned. In the city of Rochester, N. Y., recently about forty families were anchored within the fellowship of the church, as a result of a house-to-house canvass by two churches of that city. This is the more significant when we remember what a church-going community Rochester is, and that the canvass was made by the Brick Church, which has a membership of 1,935, and by the Central Church, which has a membership of 1,712. It is stirring to see pastors of such large churches with feelings of responsibility even for "sheep not of their fold." In Buffalo, N. Y., 387 families were started into the beginnings of church life in one month's time, — not into active membership, but into definite church connections; children in the Sunday-school, and older people in some department of the church. In the town of Montclair, N. J., at the first monthly report, the churches gave a classified

[1] Rev. Frank Russell, D.D., Report of the Christian Conference, Chickering Hall, New York, 1888, p. 172.

list of an aggregate of 614 names and addresses of young men and young women who were not connected with any evangelical church. One of the pastors present said, "My brethren, would you have guessed a hundred such persons in our little community of less than five thousand population? The fact that we have them is worth twenty times as much as all these conferences that led the way to such lists and classifications have cost us."[1] When Rev. G. R. Pike assumed the pastorate of the Greenstone Presbyterian Church at Pullman, Ill., in 1894, he at once made a study of his new field. A canvass of the town was organized, and the name, residence, and church relationship of every person (at that time some eight thousand) was ascertained. Mr. Pike says: "The striking discovery was made that there was a body of from twelve to fifteen hundred unmarried men scattered about in private families and lodging-houses; obviously, here was a class needing special attention." Dr. Thomas Chalmers had his whole parish in Glasgow divided into districts, containing about twenty-five families in each. He assigned two visitors to each of these little fields, and kept himself informed as to the work by monthly reports. His canvass showed eight hundred families who were without church connections, but through the efforts of the church six hundred families were developed into regular attendants of the church. The Hanson Street Baptist Church of Brooklyn, N. Y., conducted a house-to-house canvass in the immediate vicinity of the church. Although this church is located at the heart of the church-going population of Brooklyn, out of the forty thousand people canvassed eight thousand were found to be without a church home.

[1] Rev. Frank Russell, D.D., Report of the Christian Conference, Chickering Hall, New York, 1888, p. 171.

But it is not necessary to multiply these illustrations. Out of the many who wrote me of their work in this line, only one reported discouragements. A pastor in New York City, while acknowledging that his church through the house-to-house canvass came into possession of the addresses of a goodly number of non-church-going people, said that he did not know of "one person who had come into the church as a result of the canvass." Is not this a humiliating confession? A list of non-church-goers is of no value unless it is used. When Elijah raised the dead boy to life, it was necessary to do more than find the corpse, he had to spread himself upon it. We must keep in close touch with the non-church-going community, follow them up constantly, cling to them, never let go.

There is no larger field for the personal activity of the members of the church than that offered by house-to-house visitation, and it is a comparatively easy thing to go with at least a personal invitation to the church service, when the *entrée* has been given by the house-to-house canvass. Let there be a heart interest born of Christ love, and there will be blessed results. Bishop Andrews has well said: "It will be a new reformation, the proper enlargement and completion of the Lutheran Reformation, when somehow or other it shall come to be understood that all the Lord's people are prophets. When, not out of a mere sense of duty, not because they feel that they must do it, but out of a great sense of the good which Christ offers and the natural desire of loving hearts to give that good to others, all the young men and the young women of the world, and the older men and women, all these shall use this wondrous gift of speech to persuade others to be reconciled to the Lord Jesus Christ. The fault of the churches is this, that we are doing but very little personal labor for the Kingdom of Christ."[1]

Much is accomplished in this personal work, though the people visited are not brought within church affiliations. The various visits in the community are as fountains of water upon an arid desert. Every family visited is another stream of gospel blessing. Thus religious sentiments and ideas percolate the community, and inevitably its whole moral and religious tone is raised and society is uplifted. We should keep in mind, therefore, that the object of our personal work and visitation is for society as well as the individual.

A canvass with a view of ascertaining more than the religious status of the community was undertaken during the past winter by the Federation of the Churches and Christian Workers of New York City. They made a sociological canvass of the Fifteenth Assembly District, and gave their visitors the following instructions: "To ascertain rents from the janitor; to preserve only the surname of each family; to register nationality according to mothers; to enter the age of each child; to ascertain for the Y. M. C. A. the number of male boarders between sixteen and twenty years of age; to specify the church attended by the family and the Sunday-school attended by the children; and on the line 'Water on Floor' to register every family possessing a private bathtub and sanitary conveniences. Visitors were also instructed to make notes concerning cleanliness and thrift, and to inquire, whenever feasible, in what way the church can be most useful to the families visited."[2]

[1] Report of the Christian Convention, Chickering Hall, New York, 1888, p. 181.

[2] Manuscript Report of the Sociological Canvass.

MODERN METHODS IN CHURCH WORK.

What a field for thought, what an opening for activity, such a canvass affords! The Church by this means comes into intimate relationship with the inner life of the community. She finds where the dangers that environ the people lie, where oppression touches them, where sanitation is neglected, where law is violated. She gathers facts that point to the remedy for existing evils. She comes into personal touch with the life of the working man and woman, learns their amusements and their need of amusement, their social as well as their spiritual needs, and, looking at society from this standpoint, understands many things that will prove invaluable in her great work for the regeneration of society.

The Sociological Canvass referred to revealed the fact that within the district covered by it 1,579 families have only seventeen bathtubs, and 1,079 of these families in the poorest part of this district have but five bathtubs. Also that there were one hundred and thirty-one places where liquor is sold to only eight churches, and that these churches had within their territory 5,807 non-church-members and 8,397 non-attendants. The fact is, these non-church-members and non-church-attendants are closely allied to the non-bathtubs, non-playgrounds, and non-healthy conditions, and lastly and chiefly to the non-realization among Christians that we are to work for the salvation of society as well as the salvation of the individual, and that "to put the Lord Jesus Christ into an individual, we must put the Lord Jesus Christ into society."[1] It is of little avail to bring families into church two hours in the week and send them to "Hell's Kitchen" to live one hundred and sixty-six hours in the week, where

[1] Rev. Lyman Abbott, D.D., Second Convention of Christian Workers, New York, 1887, p. 121.

REACHING PEOPLE OUTSIDE THE CHURCH.

vice, vulgarity, profanity, filth, and crime poison and debase, and where every influence breeds moral leprosy and "the spirits of the air" drag to perdition. We must have *society* Christian from centre to circumference, must seek not only to fortify against temptation but also to remove temptation; instead of now and then reclaiming our boys, saving a drunkard, or rescuing a fallen woman, we must make efforts to kill the saloon, shut up the gambling-dens, and wipe out the brothel. True, we must continue to work for the individual; but society is the aggregate of the individuals, and whatever therefore affects their organic relations demands our time and thought. Professor Richard T. Ely well says: "It is as truly a religious work to pass good laws as it is to preach sermons; as holy a work to lead a crusade against filth, vice, and disease in slums of cities, and to seek the abolition of the disgraceful tenement-houses of American cities, as it is to send missionaries to the heathen."[1]

Only as the Church comes into *personal* touch with the people, will it know what is best to do for them and how best to do it. The great mistake of the past, I believe, has been the divorcing of work for society from work for the individual. This has given rise to what is popularly known, on the one hand, as the "religion of humanity" and on the other, what has been too narrowly called "Christianity." Neither position alone is right. Both are fractional. The truth is only in the union of the two. Only as we seek the salvation of men and the redemption of the WORLD are we worthy the name of followers of the Lord Jesus Christ.

[1] Social Aspects of Christianity, p. 73.

CHAPTER V.

PERSONAL WORK.

To win men, one by one, to personal allegiance to Christ is finally the whole problem of the kingdom of God on earth; and to learn to do this is the precise aim of training-class work. A mechanical learning of methods is here, therefore, utterly beside the mark; since a man's relation to Christ must be vital and personal, and there can be no mechanical production of life. In general we may not hope to bring another into any closer relation to Christ than we ourselves hold; for the sake of others, therefore, as well as for ourselves, we need first and most of all to come under the direct impression and influence of Christ; to ripen that acquaintance with God in Christ which is eternal life.

HENRY CHURCHILL KING.

IF all the people who inwardly say, as King Agrippa said to Paul, "Almost thou persuadest me to be a Christian," should stand up, they would, I believe, be like the stars for number!

There are various ways of dealing with these "almosts" and with the non-Christian community.

Systematic personal effort for winning souls is the practice of many churches, and there is an increasing disposition to return to this Apostolic way of working. How often Jesus preached to an audience of one! It was the Rev. Dr. Cumming, of Glasgow, who said, "If I take the last few years of my ministry, I can trace far more decided fruit from personal dealing with individual souls than from all my preaching besides. You cannot tell how it is with a man's heart about religious difficulties, about his understanding of how and what to do when he comes to Christ, till you get side by side with him and get him to tell you what the difficulty is."

PERSONAL WORK.

It is "only a step" between many a soul and Jesus; and it is not always indifference that restrains from taking that step. There are oftentimes real difficulties, and it is not always known that difficulties and doubts can be put down at the Saviour's feet. As Mr. Moody has said, the devil places a straw in the way and magnifies it into a mountain. The real hindrance might not be met by sermons in years. There is a simple and systematic plan of getting at the basis of the trouble. In the chapter on "Church-Members, Who are They and What are They?" the card system suggested gives the religious status of those even distantly connected with the church. From these cards a list may be made, bearing the names and addresses of all who are not Christians, and another list of all who are Christians but not church-members. The list is added to, as new names are obtained. The people should be encouraged to report their interest in the spiritual welfare of others. To this end the Ruggles Street Baptist Church, Boston, uses the following card: —

Dear Pastor, — I am personally and prayerfully interested in the conversion of the following persons:

NAME.	ADDRESS.
....	....
....	....
....	....

Yours very truly, ...
Address, ...

The lists of names are before the pastor constantly, and he either calls personally on these people or assigns some one to call, that the question of their relation to Jesus Christ and to the church may be brought to them, face to face. Such calls, when prompted by sincere interest, are almost always welcome! But if not welcome, why be discouraged? A minister in an Eastern city called on a man of his congregation with view to his soul's interest. The man listened attentively, though he appeared somewhat displeased. The pastor knelt in prayer, but the man kept his seat. The next prayer-meeting night, however, this man came to the meeting, and at its close, when opportunity was given for confessing Jesus Christ, he was the first one to his feet, — much to the joy and comfort of his pastor and family. Another interesting case is that of a young woman who rudely repelled the personal interest of a friend. The two separated and did not meet for a number of years. The young woman with shining face then told her story. "You annoyed me," she said, "but your words were as good seed. I had no rest from the hour you spoke to me till I gave myself to Christ, but I have been happy in his service ever since." Three things are to be remembered in this personal work: prayer, patience, and persistence. *Never let go* of any one. *Never show impatience.* An earnest church-worker told me of writing to a lady friend, asking the privilege of talking with her of her relation to Jesus Christ. The women were of the same social standing; but the letter was never answered, although the woman addressed would not, under other circumstances, have suffered herself to appear discourteous. The friend who wrote the letter was not so foolish, however, as to be offended, but, meeting the woman in public a few days later, took especial pains to shake hands cordially, to show a bright face and friendly interest. Thus she won her friend's heart and prepared the way for winning her to Christ. One church has come before me where pastor and people have worked and prayed for certain families and individuals for a number of years before results were realized.

That two-thirds of the earth's people have not even heard of the name of Jesus is due to the fact, I believe, that Christian people have done little *personal* work, though they may have liberally supported the *general* church work. Can it be gainsaid that the Christian Church has not been reaching the people as she should? Let us consider this question from four different standpoints: the average cost of a convert, the average number of converts to a church, the average number of church-members to a convert, and the number of churches that report no converts after a whole year's work. First, as to the cost of a convert. While it is true that no money value can be placed upon a soul, yet financial matters are hard facts and must be considered whether we want to or not, and in the spirit of honest inquiry we may ask if the money expended annually by the churches is represented by such results as reasonably might be expected. This reasoning does not overlook the varied activities of the church, and the fact that much energy, time, and money must be spent for those gracious ministries whose immediate end is other than reaching the unconverted; does not overlook, because the resultant of all ministry — hearts comforted, sufferings alleviated, persons helped, benevolences given, and all Christian activities — should be the training and placing of Christian soldiers, *soul-winners*, in our Church militant, that the number "added to the Church daily" may increase.

The following tables show the average number of additions by letter and confession (or confirmation), and the average number by confession only, to each church, together with the amount of money expended for parochial purposes, in the United States during the past five years in four different denominations. The amount of money that each convert cost (that is, each church addition by confession or confirmation) is computed from these figures.

1891.							
	No. Churches.	Total No. Additions.	Average No. Additions to each Church.	Total Additions on Confession.	Average No. Additions by Confession or Confirmation.	Congregational Expenses.	Average Cost each Convert.
Episcopal	5,398	41,261	7.6	41,261	7.6	$11,210,095	$271
Presbyterian, N.	6,819	95,909	14	58,102	8.5	9,556,501	164
Congregational	4,985	52,086	10.4	30,614	6.1	6,791,607	222
Baptist	35,860	280,150	7.8	172,261	4.7	7,740,091	44
1892.							
Episcopal	5,546	43,575	7.8	43,575	7.8	$11,210,095	$257
Presbyterian, N.	6,946	93,714	13.4	55,310	7.9	11,032,126	181
Congregational	5,140	54,576	11.2	31,582	6.1	7,140,092	226
Baptist	36,793	288,891	7.8	177,676	5.9	9,999,859	58
1893.							
Episcopal	5,570	42,466	7.6	42,466	7.6	$10,544,737	$248
Presbyterian, N.	7,038	96,483	13.7	57,506	8.1	10,502,208	182
Congregational	5,236	57,561	10.9	34,444	6.5	7,005,338	226
Baptist	38,122	303,344	7.1	189,734	4.9	7,986,668	42

PERSONAL WORK.

	No. Churches.	Total No. Additions.	Average No. Additions to each Church.	Total Additions on Confession.	Average No. Additions by Confession or Confirmation.	Congregational Expenses.	Average Cost each Convert.
1894.							
Episcopal	5,803	42,971	7.4	42,970	7.4	$10,544,737	$245
Presbyterian, N.	7,112	114,353	16	72,967	10.2	10,285,083	140
Congregational	5,342	62,946	11.7	38,853	7.2	7,035,307	185
Baptist	37,910	338,865	89	220,340	5.8	8,046,668	36
1895.							
Episcopal	5,885	45,261	7.6	45,261	7.6	$10,544,737	$232
Presbyterian, N.	7,202	104,146	14.4	65,639	9.1	9,899,691	150
Congregational	5,347	57,932	10.8	35,327	6.6	6,707,613	189
Baptist	40,064	299,109	7.4	188,728	2.1	8,202,985	43[1]

To look at the matter from another standpoint, what has been the harvest of souls resulting from the personal, or the combined personal and general, efforts of church-members? The following table shows the average number of church-members to a convert for each of the past five years in four leading denominations in the United States. No account is made in this reckoning of the ministers; and yet who has

[1] α. The amount of money expended by the Episcopal Church is estimated from the triennial reports of the conventions of that church. β. No estimate of accessions to the Episcopal Church by letter could be obtained. γ. The figures for the Baptist Church include all different branches of that church in the United States. δ. No estimate could be given of other leading denominations in the United States because of the want of accurate figures of those denominations as to their increase on confession. ε. The figures for the Presbyterian Church are for the Presbyterian Church, North.

45

done most in bringing about these conversions, — the ministers or the people? If the former, then the table would make a far more humiliating showing than it does.

Churches.	Ministers.	Members.	Converts.	Average No. Church-members to a Convert.
1891.				
Congregational .	4,886	595,397	30,614	19.44
Presbyterian, N.	5,991	790,827	58,112	13.60
Episcopal . . .	4,088	526,276	41,261	12.75
Baptist	23,800	3,269,806	172,262	18.98
1892.				
Congregational .	5,003	615,757	31,582	19.49
Presbyterian, N.	6,061	813,327	55,310	14.70
Episcopal . . .	4,261	543,275	43,575	12.46
Baptist	24,798	3,383,160	177,676	19.04
1893.				
Congregational .	5,138	637,008	34,444	18.49
Presbyterian, N.	6,236	837,984	57,506	14.57
Episcopal . . .	4,348	561,957	42,466	13.23
Baptist	25,354	3,496,988	189,734	18.43
1894.				
Congregational .	5,287	660,339	38,853	16.99
Presbyterian, N.	6,348	877,896	72,967	12.03
Episcopal . . .	4,384	591,317	42,971	13.76
Baptist	27,091	3,637,421	220,340	16.50

PERSONAL WORK.

Churches.	Ministers.	Members.	Converts.	Average No. Church-members to a Convert.
		1895.		
Congregational	5,347	680,518	35,327	19.26
Presbyterian, N.	6,506	903,648	65,639	13.76
Episcopal	4,487	616,843	45,261	13.62
Baptist	27,774	3,720,235	188,778	19.76

According to these figures, in 1895 for example, it took 19.26 church-members to *one* convert in the Congregational Church, to say nothing of the work of the 5,347 ministers of that denomination; in the Presbyterian Church it took 13.76 members to one convert, in addition to her 6,506 ministers; in the Episcopal Church 13.62 members to every one received by confirmation, not mentioning her 4,487 clergymen; and in the Baptist Church it took 19.76 members to every addition by confession, in addition to the 27,774 ministers of that denomination. As seen by the above table, also, the average cost of every addition by confession (or confirmation) during *each* of the past five years, — averaging the cost to the Congregational, Presbyterian, Baptist, and Episcopal Churches, — is $167.04; and it has taken on an average 16.04 church-members to one convert during each of the past five years, again averaging the same denominations, to say nothing of the work of their thousands of ministers, while the average number of annual additions on confession (or confirmation) to each church of these denominations has been but 6.89 members.

There are yet other facts appalling in their revelation. In the United States there are 7,469 Presbyterian churches, and of this number about one-fifth, or 1,509 churches, according to the minutes of the General Assembly for 1896, reported that they had received no members on confession of their faith during all the months of the preceding year. In the North Central States, out of a total of 2,971 churches, 661 churches, or one church out of every four and one-half churches, reported that they had not one convert after twelve months of work. In California one church out of every three reported no converts. Even in New York State, where the Presbyterian Church is so strongly organized and has the prestige of years, one church out of every eight reported that they had not one convert to show for the work of the entire year.

Turning now to another leading denomination, we find that out of the 5,482 Congregational churches in the United States, according to the Year Book for 1896, 1,438 churches, or, in other words, less than one-fourth of all the churches, reported that they had not so much as *one* convert to show for the year's work.

In the New England States 470 churches out of the 1,582 reported no additions on confession of their faith, and 580 of the 2,188 churches in the North Central States, or one church out of every four, reported no converts after twelve months of toil. In the Rocky Mountain and the Pacific States the record is raised by a fraction, one church out of about every four and one-half reporting no additions by confession.[1] It is to be acknowledged that many of these churches are the smaller churches, but this is by no means true with all.

[1] In preparing these statistics for the Presbyterian and Congregational denominations, I have, when the report of a church was largely incomplete, given the church the benefit of the doubt. These statistics therefore are conservative.

PERSONAL WORK.

Many have close to one hundred members, some over two hundred members, still others over three hundred members. Yet, with all their working forces, — preachers, teachers, officers, Sunday-schools, and organized societies, — there is not *one* convert to show for all the year's work. What a record! While statistics of this kind are not so accessible for other denominations, there is reason for believing that the Presbyterian and Congregational churches are not exceptions in the record of church work.

Dr. Josiah Strong has shown that, taking 80,000 churches together in the United States, their annual additions on confession of faith are only five per cent of their membership, and significantly adds that at this rate it would take these churches twenty years — even though they suffered no losses by death — to make an increase of *one* per cent, to say nothing of an increase of thirty or sixty or a hundred fold of which our Master talked! [1]

If Christians had been faithful in personal work, *could* the results have been so small? At this rate, how long will it take to win the world for Christ? When may we hope that his Kingdom will come? But that so little personal work is done is not always the fault of the church-members. The sins of their neglect will be upon many a minister; or must we go a step farther back, to their training in our theological seminaries, to find the real source of this neglect? The people must be told how to work personally! The pastor, who makes the business of the Kingdom his one business, ought to be fruitful of suggestions to his people for ways of working. To unfold the Word of God and to find ways for its practical application, have been his one study. To this end he labors and

[1] The New Era, p. 357.

toils and plans, only to find himself perplexed oftentimes as to what is wisest to do. If the best way of working, then, is not always patent to the pastor, much less must it be to the people! The minister must come to their aid, — make suggestions out of his larger experience and more thoughtful study. Should not more time be given to the study of ways of winning souls? There are many Christians who would be glad to do the work and hunger for it, but they do not know how, and when they try make a sad failure of it. This need is being met by many pastors in having a Workers' Training-Class. The object of the class is to give practical suggestions as to how to deal with inquirers and the unsaved. Professor Henry C. King, of Oberlin, Ohio, who teaches such a class, takes up six typical cases which practically cover the various conditions of mind and heart with which one is likely to meet. They are as follows: " The willing but ignorant, those lacking conviction, the wilfully indifferent, the doubter, the young Christian, and those turning back." In instructing his class how to deal with these cases, Professor King gives the following plain directions: "State the *condition* of the person to yourself in different forms. Get it clearly and individually before you, — the precise point to be met, the man's attitude and need. Ask, in dealing with just such a person, what *dangers* must be guarded against. Now ask what exactly is involved in the position of this person, — naturally, necessarily involved. And this necessary implication means that some truth is set aside, overlooked, left out of account. What exactly is that *needed truth?* Now search for the passages (maybe whole books or trend of Scripture) enforcing and emphasizing the points brought out in the truth needed."

PERSONAL WORK.

These classes, as conducted by various churches, are composed of both sexes and of all ages. Some of the classes are called "Win-One Circles." The requirement of membership in these circles is that at least one soul shall be selected, prayed for, worked for, and, if possible, by the blessing of God, won. The pastor meets the society as a whole or in divisions at such times as the needs and local conditions render practicable. Instruction is then given and reports heard of work done. The Rev. Arthur Leonard Wadsworth, pastor of the First Baptist Church, Rockland, Mass., in speaking of his "Win-One Circle," says: "Furthermore, my aim is to have a body of Christian workers who shall do whatever is asked of them in time of special services, be able to lead prayer-meetings in cottages and school-houses and to point inquirers to the Lamb of God."

This is, I believe, one of the first circles with which a pastor should be surrounded. What a feeling of strength it would give! What a spiritual force in the church and community it would be! A company of people banded together to study God's Word, — to pray and to plan for the salvation of souls! The "win-one" idea, however, need not be confined to the members of that circle. Why should not the plan of assigning individuals to individuals be carried out in every society and with every church-member? This would mean the ingathering of many who are without the church fold. But those who do this work should realize that it must be done quietly and wisely as well as prayerfully.

For those members of the church who are not able to attend the "Win-One Circle" or the training-class, if not for all, many of the precepts and principles in these workers' classes should be put into definite directions for aiding in the general work of the church.

To this end Rev. Russell H. Conwell, D.D., pastor of the Baptist Temple, Philadelphia, has a printed pamphlet for the members of the church which is called the "Workers' Handbook," containing specific directions to members of all the different societies in the church and other church workers as to how they may best advance the interests of their society or otherwise help in church work.

The following directions to the Business Men's Union is an example of the painstaking care with which these duties are outlined: —

THE BUSINESS MEN'S UNION.

Each member can personally invite each business man who joins the Church to unite with the Society.

He can make it his special duty to welcome to the Church, to the Society, or to the prayer-meetings, each business man he can find present by active searching.

He can look after travelling business men at hotels, and bring them to the Temple.

He can cultivate a fraternal spirit among the business men of the Church.

He can bring in new ideas, and suggest new plans of Christian work.

He can discuss business measures with reference to fraternity and religion.

He can use his influence to put honest and successful business methods into all branches of church work.

He can push enterprises for the payment of church debts, and for the strengthening of the financial, moral, and religious work.

He can interest the Society and his friends in hospital, mission, rescue, temperance, evangelistic, benevolent, and fraternal efforts.

He can cheerfully work with the majority on any useful plans.

He can be punctual and persistent in his attendance on the religious and business meetings of the Union.

He can use his business experience and common-sense on public and private occasions to keep the business of the Church in a prosperous condition.

He can win sincere, influential, enjoyable Christian friends, to whom his own manly Christian character will be a continual blessing.

PERSONAL WORK.

Every person received into the membership of the Baptist Temple receives a "Workers' Handbook" at the time of his reception. Is this not suggestive of what could helpfully be done always when persons are received into the membership of a church? It is a memorable day in the life of those who plight their faith to that body which is the bride of Christ, and we should show in every way possible that we recognize the solemnity and import of the step taken. In appreciation of this, some churches give certificates of membership (not transferable) at the time persons are received into the membership of the church.

Another help in securing the personal interest and of gaining a permanent hold upon the endeavors of the members of the church in Christian work is the enlistment card system. The following is an example of such an enlistment card:—

"LORD, WHAT WILT THOU HAVE ME TO DO?"

I wish to work in some definite way for Christ and the Church, and would like to have my name proposed as a worker in the following.

Check those you wish to work in.

1. Church Prayer Meeting.
2. Young People's Society of Christian Endeavor.
3. Home Sunday School.
4. Whatsoever Society.
5. Ladies' Home Missionary Society.
6. Ladies' Foreign Missionary Society.
7. Ladies' Helping Hand.
8. Ladies' Prayer Meeting.
9. Young Ladies' Society.
10. King's Daughters.
11. Visiting among the Sick and Needy.
12. Calling on Strangers.
13. Temperance work.
14. District Visitation.
15. Distributing Christian Literature.
16. Cottage Prayer Meeting.
17. Men's Club.
18. Brotherhood of Andrew and Philip.
19. Sustaining after Meeting.
20. Work at the Mission.

Name, ...

Address, ...

MODERN METHODS IN CHURCH WORK.

The Jefferson Park Presbyterian Church, Chicago, Ill., has a similar system, but with the following significant addition: —

IF SICK OR AGED, PLEASE MARK THE FOLLOWING.

Praying for each service at the hour when it is held.
Praying daily for the church, its pastor, and its work.
Praying for others who are sick or aged.
Writing letters to such when requested by the pastor.

Remarks: ....
....
....
....

Every member of the church should do something personally to proclaim the gospel of salvation. This is further made possible, even to the most timid, through the system of *Silent Evangelism.* Silent Evangelism is the use of a series of cards, neatly printed in colors and different tints, for the purpose of personal work; the bringing to another's mind in a delicate and direct way the truth of God, and the question of one's relation to Jesus Christ. The system is highly endorsed and commended by the leading clergy, bishops, Christian workers, and college presidents throughout the country.

Time and circumstances do not always give opportunity for conversation as to another's spiritual welfare; again one may be too timid, or may be in doubt as to what is best to say. But it is an easy thing to hand to another a card like the following: —

PERSONAL WORK.

> 𝕸𝖞 𝖋𝖗𝖎𝖊𝖓𝖉, *I was just wondering if you have found the secret of the blessed life. It's a queer and quiet way to ask a question, is n't it, but have you pondered earnestly the Saviour's words,*
>
> "𝖂𝖎𝖙𝖍𝖔𝖚𝖙 𝖒𝖊 𝖞𝖊 𝖈𝖆𝖓 𝖉𝖔 𝖓𝖔𝖙𝖍𝖎𝖓𝖌"?
>
> *and Paul's triumphant saying,*
>
> "𝕴 𝖈𝖆𝖓 𝖉𝖔 𝖆𝖑𝖑 𝖙𝖍𝖎𝖓𝖌𝖘 𝖙𝖍𝖗𝖔𝖚𝖌𝖍 𝕮𝖍𝖗𝖎𝖘𝖙, 𝖜𝖍𝖎𝖈𝖍 𝖘𝖙𝖗𝖊𝖓𝖌𝖙𝖍𝖊𝖓𝖊𝖙𝖍 𝖒𝖊"?
>
> *Oh, this companionship with Jesus! What joys it brings! How it lightens care and helps one toil and win!*
>
> May "the peace of God, which passeth understanding, keep your heart and mind through Christ Jesus."

The card is given. A silent prayer goes with it, and the results are left with God, who has promised that "his word shall not return unto him void."

The following instance is told which shows the splendid results with which the plan has been blessed: "A young man approached a stranger in the streets of Boston, and gave him a Silent Evangelism card. The stranger happened to be a resident of Philadelphia and a Christian. He took the card home, and gave it to a person for whom it bore an appropriate message. As a direct result, union and peace came to a broken family, and eleven persons were brought into relation with the Church of Christ."

The beautifully printed cards of Silent Evangelism bear different messages of sympathy and personal interest, and so are adapted to different people, that is to say, to different ages and conditions. The cost is very little: the use of one card a day will make an average cost of but three and one half cents a week, and the use of one card a week, a cost of but twenty-six cents a year.[1]

Another real service, and one that leads to and encourages personal work, is to place a number of tracts or leaflets in the hands of Christians, and urge them to enclose a suitable one in their various letters. Such a message is often blessed to great good; and as great a blessing and inspiration, I believe, comes to the sender.

But there is yet another way of working to the end of spiritual conviction in our churches. It is the suggestion of the Rev. J. Wilbur Chapman, D.D., Evangelist and pastor of Bethany Presbyterian Church, Philadelphia, that the teaching of the lesson and usual exercises of the Sunday-school occasionally give way to an evangelistic service. The general plan suggested is about as follows: A preliminary conference and prayer-meeting of officers and teachers on the Sabbath, for one-half hour before the opening of the School. The school is opened with the singing of appropriate and familiar hymns and with prayers. The Pastor and Superintendent then make short evangelistic addresses. After this the teachers take their classes in general conference, and heart to heart talk with scholars as to their personal relation to Jesus Christ. The teacher then hands the following card to the several members of the class: —

I have an honest desire henceforth to live a Christian life.
I am willing to follow any light God may give me.
I ask the people of God to pray for me.

Name, ... *Residence*, ...
Name of Teacher, ...

---

[1] Address: The Silent Evangelism Association, 30 Lafayette Place, New York City.

PERSONAL WORK.

Wonderful results have been obtained in this way. A school in Newark, N. J., out of a membership of fifteen hundred had three hundred cards signed, and almost the entire number were received into the church-membership. A school in Burlington, Iowa, out of a membership of two hundred and fifty had fifty cards signed, and forty were received into the church. A small school in New York City out of a membership of one hundred and sixty-four received seventeen cards, another school of two hundred and seventy received sixty cards, and many other schools have obtained like proportionate results. It is worth while to "*suffer the little children* to come!" There is a growing conviction that in work for children lies the hope of the Church. By far the majority of Christians are those who became such before reaching the age of twenty-one.

A little girl came to her mother with the query, "Am I old enough to become a Christian?" "Are you old enough to love mamma?" was the reply. "Yes," said the child; "but am I old enough to become a Christian?" The mother then asked, "Are you old enough to trust mamma?" As the little girl gave assent, a third question was asked, "Are you old enough to obey mamma?" Light came to the little face as the fond mother said, "If you are old enough to love, trust, and obey mamma, you are old enough to love, trust, and obey Jesus; and that is what it is to be a Christian." Here is a lesson for Christian workers!

"They that be wise shall shine as the brightness of the firmament; and they that turn many to righteousness as the stars for ever and ever." [1]

[1] Daniel xii. 3.

CHAPTER VI.

REACHING STRANGERS AT THE SERVICES.

At every church service of every church there are usually present a number of strangers. Some of them are new-comers in the neighborhood, others are those who are "never at home" or whose butler would not admit the church canvasser. Many of these strangers once sustained creditable relationships with a church in some other place, but since moving they have neglected to assume any church responsibilities. They attend one church once, and then in a few weeks attend another, thus becoming church tramps. This class of people is not inconsiderable. Take New York, for instance. The greater part of its English population has come from the country, where the majority of them were a church-going people. If the nominal Christians in that city, those who once happily testified to their faith in some church, would now assume definite church connection and come fully into the Master's service, Manhattan Island would witness a revival of religion that would shake the continent. What is true of New York is true of every large city, and in some degree is true of the smaller city.

Occasionally these sometime-Christians drift into the church services, as do also the occasional church-goers. Now the question arises, How shall we reach these strangers? There is a very simple and satisfactory answer.

REACHING STRANGERS AT THE SERVICES.

The thing to do is to learn who these people are, and where they live, that they may be followed up and persuaded, if possible, to assume Christian responsibilities. The church, therefore, seeks to obtain the names and addresses of strangers when they come into the sanctuary.

Several simple methods are employed. The first method may be called the "Pastor's Welcome." Before the service begins, the pastor or one of the pastors (where there is a plural pastorate) takes his position at the audience room door where the greatest number of strangers enter, and at the place where they wait for ushers to seat them. For these few minutes preceding the service, the pastor really acts in the capacity of head usher. No one is seated on this aisle until he hands the people over to the ushers. Let us see how it works. Several strangers enter: they come in groups of twos and threes and fives; some are alone. The time is brief; it will not do to keep them waiting. The pastor is the first to speak. "Will you have seats?" he asks. "The usher will be here in a moment. I am the pastor; we are glad to welcome you." In introducing himself the minister usually gives his name, and in reply, in most instances, strangers give theirs; if not, he says, "May I ask your name?" Here the name is given, and the pastor writes it down, saying, as he does so, "I should be glad to mail you one of our weekly calendars, if you will give me your address." Or, "I shall be glad to send you notices sometimes of our special meetings; what address will reach you?" The people are found ready and willing to give their names under such circumstances; but unless some excuse, such as the sending of the church calendar or the notices of some meeting, be given *before* their address is asked, the questioner is almost certain to give offence. Ministers who have not tried this simple plan will be surprised to find how many persons they can thus welcome in a very short time. One of the pastors of the Marble Collegiate Church, New York, told me that he had obtained as many as seventy-five names and addresses in one morning. Such a kindly greeting is always well received. Human nature is the same the world over. A sincere welcome and courteous treatment are appreciated. This welcome by the pastor not only secures the stranger's name and address, but it also gives the latter a home feeling *in that* CHURCH, and makes him receptive of the gospel message.

But most churches have more than one entrance, and sometimes lay members, usually officers of the church, stand at such entrance-ways and welcome strangers in the same manner as that described above. It is easy for a man to introduce himself as an officer of the church. Where the congregation is large, it is important that such officer know the people, that he may not make the mistake which a new pastor made in asking an elderly man if he was a stranger. "No, not exactly," said the patriarch; "I have been a member of this church well-nigh forty years." The officer who welcomes strangers should also be able to read them. Some persons will not receive pleasantly even the asking of their names, but all appreciate the reception at the door and provision for being seated without embarrassment.

Notwithstanding such earnest efforts to obtain the names of strangers as they enter the church, many addresses cannot be obtained in this way. The people may have come in too rapidly, or some may have come in late. Other methods must be employed. In the pews or in the hymn-books, — some place where it

REACHING STRANGERS AT THE SERVICES.

cannot escape the eye, — pew cards are placed. Many pew cards have been before me. The following is fairly illustrative of them all: —

THE CONGREGATIONAL CHURCH OF OSWEGO, N. Y.

Cordially invites you to make it your Church home and to join in its work and worship.

Sign your name and address below, and deposit this card when the plate is passed; it will be understood that you wish to be called upon by the pastor as a regular parishioner, and to be assigned a permanent sitting.

Seats are free on application, the expenses of the Church being met exclusively by voluntary weekly offerings, and all privileges of the Church will be open to you whether your offerings be large or small or wholly wanting. It is presumed, however, that all will wish to give something. Kindly indicate by an X before the figure on the back of this card whatever amount you are willing to pledge as your weekly contribution.

M...

No...*St., Oswego, N. Y.*

[Reverse.]

Mark an X in front of the amount you will give, and drop this card on the plate. The treasurer will understand that until further notification you will give this amount weekly, and will keep you informed of the state of your accounts.

The contribution should of course be enclosed in an envelope signed with your name, else it cannot be credited.

.01	.06	.15	.30	.75
.02	.08	.18	.35	1.00
.03	.10	.20	.40	2.00
.05	.12	.25	.50	5.00

An X here ( ) will indicate that you wish to see a copy of the chart of pews, with the vacant sittings marked. Any *unoccupied* seat is at your disposal.

It appears to have been a common experience that strangers have not in great numbers signed these cards. Pastors have acknowledged to me that they believe the failure partly due to an attempt to put too much on one card. In this work we ought to bear in mind that we can lead the people only one step at a time. The object of the stranger's pew card should be one; namely, to obtain his name and address. If the church is faithful, other things will follow. Again, these pew cards, as shown above, are too much in the form of a pledge, in that they appear to commit the signer to the expression of a church preference. The result is that few strangers sign the cards, as their thoughts and desires for a church home have not matured.

A card which is entirely free from the objections given above, and one which has proven very successful, is the following: —

THE MADISON AVENUE PRESBYTERIAN CHURCH

Will be glad to send you special notices, from time to time, of special meetings, if you will write your name and address below.

Name,............................. Address,........................

A cordial welcome always to all.
Seats free.
Please leave this Card in the Pew or hand to one of the Ushers.

This card has several advantages. It is brief. The first visit of a stranger is not the time to acquaint him with the whole system of the workings of the church, or to say that possibly it is his duty to go as a foreign missionary. This card, too, does not commit the signer to any obligation. On the other hand, it will likely be to his pleasure to sign it. Many feel that this is just what they want. They do not care to go to church all the time, but if there is anything *special* going on, they are glad to go. So the card is signed, — its purpose is accomplished: the name and address is obtained.

The ensuing week the pastor writes a letter somewhat as follows: —

MY DEAR MR. SMITH, — We were glad to receive the card signed by you last Sunday in our church. It will give us pleasure to send you notices of our special meetings, and we believe that you will find them interesting and enjoyable.

We cordially welcome you to any and all of our meetings; and we shall be pleased to meet you personally, and hope to have the privilege of calling on you soon.

Trusting that you will always feel at home with us when able to attend our services,

Believe me, sincerely,

....

A call is made as soon as possible. This is followed, from time to time, by notices of special religious and social meetings. Invitations to church socials, to the ladies' receptions, the young men's club, or men's league, the debating society, or young people's society, as the case may be, are sent.

When a person comes, he is cordially received, and is shown every attention. His heart is won by that people and church, and it will be strange, indeed, if it is not soon won to Jesus Christ.

Some churches instead of using cards in the pews have the ushers hand them to strangers, as the following card illustrates: —

> *You are cordially welcomed.*
> *It would afford me pleasure to meet you at the close of the service, and introduce you to our pastor and other members.*
> .... *Usher.*
>
> [Reverse.]
> *Please fill the lines below and drop this card in the collection basket, if you desire the pastor to call on you.*
> *Name,* ....
> *Address,* ....

There is a personal touch about the signature of the usher that commends this card to the stranger and gives the feeling of an individual welcome to the church.

There will be other strangers in the church, doubtless, whose names are not obtained as they enter, and who will not place their addresses on any kind of a card. The method used to reach such persons is also one which pleasantly emphasizes the welcome and hospitality to all. This method is called the "Pastor's Pulpit Reception." At the conclusion of the church notices, or before the offertory, where notices are not read, the pastor says: "It is a pleasure to meet strangers worshipping with us. I shall be in front of the pulpit for this purpose immediately after the service, and will appreciate meeting those of you who will honor me by coming forward." The invitation is given in different forms. The form matters little when coming from the heart. To such invitations the people respond; and there are churches which have obtained large numbers of names and addresses in this way.

REACHING STRANGERS AT THE SERVICES.

Some pastors, instead of having the pulpit reception, go to the rear of the room at the close of the services, and meet the people as they come out. Announcement of the pastor's presence at the door is given from the pulpit. Such ministers are careful to explain, as they extend the invitation to strangers to meet them, that the meeting and the giving of their names entails no obligation, but simply means mutual acquaintance. The value of such explanation from the pulpit is twofold: it prepares the way for an easy approach to the stranger, and emphasizes the hospitality of the church. It also is a delicate suggestion to the church-members that the pastor is at the door at the conclusion of the service especially to express *their* welcome to the new-comers. In the Central Congregational Church of Jamaica Plain, Boston, the following notice appears in the calendar for the evening service, which is conducted by the Young Men's Club:—

NOTE. — During the Gloria Patri, the Pastor and Invitation Committee will pass to the vestibule, where they will be glad to greet as many as possible.

The Gloria Patri is sung immediately after the benediction, and is followed by the usual postlude.

But it is impossible for the pastor to meet all the strangers at the door, and with the pulpit reception it is found that some people are too timid or have no special desire to come forward to meet the ministers. Therefore still other means may be employed for obtaining the names and addresses of strangers present. Some ministers have the church mapped out in sections, a certain number of sittings being apportioned to individuals whose business it is to look out for strangers and to invite them forward to meet the

MODERN METHODS IN CHURCH WORK.

pastor. This work is usually in charge of some one of the church societies.

Whatever society it is under, each individual in charge of a section sends in a written report every week of the previous Sabbath's work. The following is a copy of a blank used for that purpose: —

REPORT ON WELCOMING STRANGERS.

.... *Church.*

Number of strangers in my section,................................
Of these................ *were men,* .... *were women.*
Number to whom greeting was given,........................
Names and Addresses,..

....
....
....

Date,................................ A. M. *or* P. M.
Signed,..

A written report should always be required. It immediately places within the pastor's hand any new names that may have been received, and it keeps the committee "up to time" in their work of welcoming strangers. Other churches also have a Vestibule Committee, which works to the same end of meeting strangers.

For some of the Sabbath services at Grace Church, New York, there is always a committee of young men upon the sidewalk, in waiting to give passers-by an invitation into the services. This is done by printed card of invitation (which is important) and personal word.

In addition to these definite plans for welcoming and reaching strangers at the church services, every

REACHING STRANGERS AT THE SERVICES.

member of the church should be made to feel that to look out for strangers, which is looking out for souls, is a part of true worship.

Many persons hesitate to speak to others of their soul's welfare, but surely the most timid can say to the stranger, "I hope you are going to accept the pastor's invitation to meet him, — will you not let me introduce you to him?" When there is an earnest longing for souls, and the people are filled with the Holy Spirit, how can they refrain from extending a welcome, and giving a stranger to feel that he is in his Father's house and with the Israel of his God! This is the spirit which ought to prevail throughout the Church. When it does, we may expect Pentacostal blessings.

CHAPTER VII.

USHERS' ASSOCIATION.

The ushers at one end of the room are as important as the minister at the other end of the church. The first impression which strangers receive on coming into a church is usually from the ushers. The courteous welcome and ready attention and the prompt seating of visitors, as well as the regular attendants, when necessary, is no small factor in the success of winning the people.

Upon entering the better and larger retail stores in our cities, and even in the smaller villages, the door is not only opened for us, but some one stands ready to check our umbrella, to take our coat, and some one else is prompt in attention to direct us to any part of the building. Is it true that even here the children of this world are wiser than the children of light?

If there is any body of men who need to be prayed for, who ought to pray for themselves, that they may at once realize the importance, delicacy, and dignity of their office, it is the ushers of a church.

I am led to believe that the ushering is most successfully done in those churches which have an Ushers' Association, — where members are stimulated by coming together in an organized society. It is then that there is developed a spirit of *esprit de corps*, that they are inspired with the importance of their work, and fall to their places with military precision.

USHERS' ASSOCIATION.

Grace Temple, Philadelphia, has an Ushers' Association. I take the following significant paragraphs from the resolutions which govern this Society: —

RESOLUTION 4. *Resolved:* That every usher being absent from duty shall pay the Secretary the sum of twenty-five cents, and for being late, the sum of ten cents. These fines may be remitted for sickness, or when said delinquent shall have given the Head Usher two days' notice.

RESOLUTION 6. *Resolved:* That when any usher shall be absent from his post of duty four Sundays in succession without cause, the position shall be declared vacant, and filled by the Head Usher.

The ushers of Grace Temple are also charged twenty-five cents each month to pay for such expenses as may arise from time to time. Those who know of Grace Temple know that it has one of the most efficient bodies of ushers of any church in this country. The business-like way in which they take hold of things is positively refreshing. What pastor has not been exasperated by sleepy officers, nominally in charge of this important work, stumbling into their pews, the latest attendants in the congregation!

The Ushers' Association of the Hollond Memorial Church, Philadelphia, is also deserving of mention. This Society has published in neat attractive form its Constitution and by-laws, together with the names of officers and members of the Association. The suggestions to ushers contained in this little book are so capital that a copy of them should be in the hands of every usher in the country whether he belong to an Ushers' Association or not: —

1. Be at your post thirty minutes before time for service.
2. Be careful to reserve seats when requested to do so.
3. *Fill your front seats first.*
4. Know how many each pew will seat, and see that it is filled when the house is crowded.

MODERN METHODS IN CHURCH WORK.

5. Make an effort to seat friends together.

6. Give strangers the best seats, and see that they have a hymn-book or programme. (Read Hebrews xiii. 2.)

7. The head usher should make it his business to direct the ushering. He should see that the house is evenly seated, and that collectors do their work properly.

8. *Never seat any one during prayer or the rendering of special music.*

9. Be prompt in starting the collection, but *go slow* when taking it, and be careful that you slight no one.

10. Keep the air good. If it becomes close, open windows during the singing.

11. *Be quiet in all your work.*

12. Do not permit groups to assemble in the back part of the church and talk before and during service.

Once a year this Society gives a supper and entertainment to the men of the church. The work of the Association is then briefly reviewed, other short addresses are made, and a general good time is realized. In speaking of this Association, Rev. J. R. Miller, D.D., one of the pastors of the Hollond Church, says: "It has worked admirably. It is a good thing for the young men themselves, and we have no more pleasant and happy Association about the church. It has trained them to thoughtfulness and helpfulness in many ways. They have learned to greet people cordially and take an interest in strangers, the old people, and poor people. Besides, it has been of great advantage to the church, assuring system and order in the seating of people, taking up collections, etc."

There are but few of these Ushers' Associations in the country at present; but a movement so happily conceived is sure to grow, and in time to come it will be a source of wonder to us that for so long we failed to appreciate the magnitude of the office of the "door-keeper in the house of our God."

CHAPTER VIII.

THE CHOIR.

> The power of music over the human heart is something before which we pause in mute admiration, — so clearly does it show God's wondrous plan in keeping for himself one tender spot in the soul on which his voice may fall without rejection.
>
> Mrs. Laura C. Dunlap.

There are various things to be said in favor of different kinds of music: chorus, quartette, vested choir, or congregational singing. One would have the music of the great congregation led simply by a precentor; another, the quartette to lead the congregation and render selections, as duets, trios, and quartettes; but let not any one think that a change of *personnel* without a change of spirit will give new life to the music of the church. Rev. Dr. Rainsford well states this truth when he says: "A man writes that his church has failed as a pew church and with a quartette choir; do I think it will succeed as a free church and with a boy choir? . . . One man can put life-blood into one set of methods, and another into another, but what we want is blood."[1]

There are various plans for conducting church music.

Between the extremes of poor congregational singing and the professional or paid quartette only, lies the middle ground, which is outlined by the Rev.

---

[1] Christianity Practically Applied, p. 179.

MODERN METHODS IN CHURCH WORK.

Charles A. Dickinson, D.D., pastor of Berkeley Temple, Boston, in the introduction to his admirable book, "The Temple Service." He says: "In order to draw upon all the treasures of sacred music, and to make the service of song in the house of God most effective, three things are necessary, — a quartette which is not only competent, but disposed to sing the simplest hymn as well as the most elaborate anthem, a well-trained chorus, and a singing congregation. With this combination it is possible to meet the varied tastes of the people and to secure the most delicate as well as the grandest effects in church service."

Grace Baptist Temple of Philadelphia has the largest permanent choir in the United States, numbering two hundred and eighty singers. They are trained to sing without the baton. Attendance at church and at rehearsals is maintained by the advantages of the musical drill, secured by membership in the choir, and by a fine of twenty-five cents for absence, while absence from a concert subjects the delinquent to a fine of one dollar. There are also associate members who pay five dollars annually, and are entitled to three tickets for each of the concerts of the season. The money that is collected is used in paying for music and other expenses. The choir is assisted by piano, organ, and an orchestra composed mainly of young people from the Sunday-school. This church has excellent facilities for training musicians, as there is a department of music in connection with Temple College, which is under the direction of the church. In the Temple chorus there are several minor musical organizations, such as quartettes of men and women whose services are in demand in the city. All the money these singers make they devote to some branch of the Temple work. One year they contributed $1,200.

In the Clarendon Street Church, Boston, of which the late Rev. A. J. Gordon, D.D., was pastor, there is a large volunteer choir, which consists entirely of church-members. Nothing is paid for music except to the organist. This choir believes that "it is more blessed to give than to receive," and at one time gave $400 to a missionary in Mexico.

The First Congregational Church, Jersey City, has tried the experiment of dispensing with its paid quartette, and devoting the money to paying a chorus. Special singers are engaged for occasional services, but the talent of the chorus is equal to nearly every demand. This plan is working well, and is resulting in binding a large number of families to the church in a very special way.

The Madison Avenue Presbyterian Church, New York, has a large chorus choir which is doing excellent work. The director of the choir, who is also the organist, is a salaried man. The nominal salary of about $100 each is paid the quartette. This latter expense, and the cost of the music, are met by a winter concert given by the choir. No salary is paid to members of the chorus, but they are amply compensated by private singing-lessons given them by the director, for which they agree to sing regularly in the choir. The arrangement is as strictly a business one as that which engages the director of the music. This plan has also met with gratifying success in other churches.

A somewhat different choir is that of St. George's Church, New York. This is a choir of ninety voices. It includes men, women, and boys. The boys are trained for this work by singing in a surpliced choir in the Sunday-school. The Sunday-school choir serve as choristers at the Sunday evening and Wednesday night services, and are promoted to the regular choir on showing proficiency.

Quite different is the method in Grace Episcopal Church, in the same city. This choir consists of men and boys. There is a day school held in the church building for the choir boys. They are thus available at all times for special services, weddings, and funerals. The boys receive private music lessons during the intervals of their classes. The school is an excellent one, having two women instructors and military drill, and boys are counted fortunate who are enrolled on its lists.

In the Congregational Church of Sparta, Wis., they are engaged in what may be called choir-building. The Men's Club of the church has engaged a salaried music-teacher to instruct the young people in music, giving them twenty lessons in twenty weeks. These young people, twenty to forty in number, come into the evening choir as needed, in a body, or in fewer numbers. The pastor, Rev. William Crawford, says, "This is providing good church music for the future as well as for the present."

Whatever the nature of the choir, one thing is needful: let those who lead our worshipping congregations in song be those who can sing with spirit and with a conscious appreciation of their sacred position! True, we want good music, the best possible; none can be too good for such great and sacred themes, nor too good for the humblest people. If the congregation is largely made up of those who are not able to cultivate or gratify their desire for artistic song, so much more the reason for the best that art can give at our church services. But singing which is purely artistic will not do. We have no more right "to put an unconsecrated singer into the choir than we have to put an unconsecrated preacher into the pulpit." [1] Let us be careful how we touch the ark of God!

Dangers beset that church in which the æsthetic taste is paramount. It is not a question of money. The Church cannot afford to be sparing of her funds if she will attain the desired result. But here lies the danger, that by engaging musicians of ability the demand may be created in the congregation for a finished musical skill, which may not at all times be obtainable combined with the spiritual requisites, which far outweigh the merely artistic ones. A sentiment should be developed in the choir and the congregation that the singers are the ministers of God, no less than he who addresses the people from the pulpit; and to this end let the preacher pray for the choir frequently, and in public, as he has prayed for all those who share the services with him. Would we breathe a consecration prayer, let us include that beautiful verse-petition of Frances Ridley Havergal: —

> "Take my voice, and let me sing
> Always, only, for my King.
> . . . . .
> Take my lips, and let them be
> Filled with messages from Thee."

[1] Rev. Dr. A. P. Pierson, Report of Second Convention of Christian Workers, New York, 1887, p. 60.

CHAPTER IX.

THE MEN'S SUNDAY EVENING CLUB.

"The joy of life for strong natures lies in a noble activity: a work adequate to the aspirations of the soul; a work that brings calm by its magnitude, and by its very demands evokes the best and greatest in us."

Not until recently has the executive and business ability represented by the men of the Church been turned to large account. Outside of the few officers and prayer-meeting pillars men have done little or nothing in church work. Here for the most part has been a Niagara of unused power.

The problem of how to use and interest the men in the Church, and how to reach men outside of the Church, is one of the greatest that ever faced a pastor. The minister who first started a men's Sunday Evening Club is deserving the gratitude of his fellow-laborers in the field of church work, for he cut the Gordian knot. One of the greatest movements of modern times, a movement that must stand prominent in the history of the Church, is that of the Sunday Evening Club. The work of these clubs has already passed the experimental stage, and is one of the recognized forces in evangelistic work. The great object of the organization is to increase in every appropriate and legitimate way the attractiveness and effectiveness of the Sunday evening service, and to interest the non-church-going men in church work, that they may become useful members of the Church and faithful followers of Jesus Christ. The organization and the plan of the Men's Club are best indicated by the following constitution, which is practically that of all the clubs doing this work. The constitution, and nine of the committees indicated, are taken from the Club of the Presbyterian Church of Austin, Ill. The first, second, ninth, tenth, and eleventh committees are copied from the Club of the First Congregational Church, Appleton, Wis.

ARTICLE I. NAME. — The name of this Association shall be "The Men's Club of the —— —— Church."

ARTICLE II. OBJECT. — The object of this Club shall be to interest in the . . . Church the men of the community who are not connected with any other congregation, especially by increasing the attractiveness of the evening services.

ARTICLE III. OFFICERS. — The officers of this Club shall be a President, Vice-President, Secretary, and Treasurer, who shall be elected by ballot, by a majority, and hold their office for . . . months, or until their successors are elected.

ARTICLE IV. MEMBERSHIP. — Men who are interested in the purpose of the Club, and willing to co-operate in carrying out its plans, are eligible to membership, and shall become members when accepted by the Membership Committee. It is understood that all who join the Club will, when called upon, serve on committees.

ARTICLE V. COMMITTEES. — The Officers, together with the Pastor, shall appoint the following Committees, who shall serve for three months, namely, —

A Committee on Worship, who, with the Pastor, shall furnish the general plan for each evening service by way of sermon, responsive service, and hymns.

Second: A Committee on Music, who, with the Organist, shall see that the evening service is provided with appropriate vocal and instrumental music.

Third: A Committee on Printing and Advertising, the

duty of which shall be to see that the church and its work is sufficiently advertised.

Fourth: A Committee on Ushers, which shall see that the church services are provided with these officers.

Fifth: A Committee on Invitation, the duty of which shall be to invite strangers and non-attendants of any church, and which shall act also as a hand-shaking or general welcome committee.

Sixth: A Social and Entertainment Committee, the business of which shall be to plan for the social interests of the Club, and provide such entertainments, of a popular character, as may best advance the object of the Club.

Seventh: A Finance Committee, of which the Treasurer shall be chairman, the duty of which shall be to provide the funds necessary for carrying on the work.

Eighth: A Committee on Membership, the duty of which shall be to secure and admit new members.

Ninth: A Committee on Decoration, who shall assist in the decoration of the church whenever such decoration may be desired.

Tenth: A Coat and Hat Committee, who shall take charge of those articles in the vestibule.

Eleventh: A Committee of Choristers, who shall take their places in the choir and assist in leading the congregation in singing.

Twelfth: A Census Committee, the duty of which shall be to canvass the neighborhood and ascertain the names of those who do not attend any place of worship regularly.

Thirteenth: An Executive Committee, which shall consist of the Pastor, the Officers of the Club, and the Chairman of the Committees, the duty of which shall be to look after the general interests of the Club.

ARTICLE VI. AMENDMENTS. — This constitution shall be amended by a two-thirds vote of those present at any regular meeting.

ARTICLE VII. MEETINGS. — A Business and Social Meeting, with banquet, shall be held on the first Friday evening of each month at eight P. M., in the Church parlors. Special meetings may be called by the President when necessary.

THE MEN'S SUNDAY EVENING CLUB.

It is at once apparent that this association of men has elements of real strength. In the first place it stands for a definite object, one that is worth the while: interesting the non-church-going men of the community and increasing the attractiveness of the Sunday services, especially the evening service. Men in the Church, as in business, must have something large enough to take hold of, something that will interest and occupy them. Give them a work worth doing, and a regular time in which to do it, and almost all men will respond and do their best.

Another vital element in the association is the equalization of labor and responsibility with the individual members. New officers are elected and committees appointed every three months, thus making provision for the distribution of places of responsibility. Every member of the club is, at some time of the year, given with others the responsibility for advertising and caring for some one Sunday evening service, and at all times is made to feel that he is responsible for his share in the work, and that he should do his best to make some non-church-goer realize that a warm welcome awaits him at any of the church services whenever he cares to claim it.

Another factor which plays an important part in the work is the nature of the organization. The feeling of fraternity is divinely implanted in men. What could more completely fill the want than a men's club? Here is something which belongs to them. It was made for them, and one element in its success is that men naturally take to the idea of a club. They want to be associated in a definite and distinct organization. They like the regulation of the idea, and the discipline appeals to them. If some church-members object to the term " club " as having a tone of " worldly ungodliness," it will be well to point out that its real meaning "is an organization in which each one bears his full share of the work or burden of expenses."[1] Several churches use the term "Men's League," but out of the two hundred or more clubs with which I have corresponded, only four have taken that name. The clubs place emphasis on the social life, and aim to produce a kindly acquaintance and goodly fellowship, not only among the members of the society, but also between the men of the church and the community. Provision is made for monthly or quarterly socials. Supper is served, and music, speeches, recitations, and other pleasant features are provided, as in the judgment of the Social Committee may seem best. Each member is usually permitted to invite one or two of his men friends. Most clubs have anniversary banquets, for which unusual provision is made, and members invite their families and friends. Still other clubs have these social gatherings when they have invited guests some two or three times a year. This social feature is deserving the stress placed upon it; it is important. Not only does it foster and develop an *esprit de corps*, but it meets one of man's deepest needs. He was ordained to be a social creature, and the Christian worker who will not recognize this either does not understand or else defies the nature of man and the laws of God.

But the work of the club centres largely upon the Sunday evening service; thus the social and club features are a means to the great end of bringing men within hearing of the Gospel. The nature of the Sunday evening service is determined by the Devotional Committee, together with the pastor. The evening

[1] "The Fishin' Jimmy Club," by Rev. John Clark Hill, D.D., p. 15.

meeting is a devotional service, with such pleasurable and helpful features as recover it from the unimportant service and render it a drawing power instead of a drag. The pastor presides, and usually gives a short, stirring address, — the very best he can put into twelve or fifteen minutes of time. The programme is bright, spirited, and varied with a considerable part for the people to share in by way of responsive readings, creed, prayers in unison, and singing. Not only is variety sought in each programme, but in the different programmes from week to week. The clubs have printed programmes giving the order of service and bearing the names of the officers and chairmen of the committees of the club; some clubs print the names of all the members as well as the chairmen of the committees, thus magnifying the importance of the individual member. The order of the morning service of worship is frequently indicated in the same bulletin, thus making the programme serve for both services. The make-up of the programme is frequently changed for the sake of variety. Sometimes the programme has only one page, but usually it has four pages, including notes relative to church and club news, and notes briefly stating the object of the club, its method of work by committees, the nature of membership, and other helpful information. The club also has charge of the advertising of the evening service.[1]

In starting a club the pastor must be willing to undertake it with small beginnings. Possibly only a few will be attracted at first by the idea. It may be possible that the board of ruling officers of the church will not take kindly to the new plan. There are always those who decry anything new, and stand in jealous fear lest some little place of prominence be

---

[1] For methods in advertising see Chapter XL

usurped. It will be helpful in the organization to tell what work has been accomplished by clubs elsewhere, discuss the needs of the community, and emphasize the importance of men working for men; and having presented the matter from the pulpit and worked personally, then announce the evening for the organization, and commence with those who are willing to begin. Many most successful clubs have had very small beginnings.

One thing that speaks strongly for the Sunday evening club is that it is a stepping-stone into the membership of the church. Many men in sympathy with the Gospel and the church are without its pale, feeling that they cannot (though it be for a poor reason) take the stand naturally expected of regular attendants of the church; but when a place is made for them in some auxiliary society they gladly fall into line. Must we not be willing to lead men one step at a time? Dr. Strong, in his "New Era," shows that a large proportion of those who have sat under the hearing of the Gospel have come into the membership of the church, and that little headway has been made towards bringing non-church-goers into the fold of Christ. Should we not make every effort possible, then, to bring men where they needs must hear the Gospel? — the word shall not return unto Him void.[1] One pastor writes me that the work of the club and the music attracted large audiences, but said that he preferred to have his regular services to preach to three hundred or so who *came to hear* the Gospel. Is that a broad-minded or right position? Rather should we not rejoice in any means which draws the people where they *must* hear the Gospel whether they want to or not? It is possible even for a minister to de-

[1] Isaiah lv. 11.

ceive himself and have jealous fear lest the people come to hear the music rather than to hear him. It is again the "capital 'I' crowned and enthroned in the place that belongs to Jesus Christ!"

Most encouraging reports are given by pastors relative to the work of the Sunday Evening Club. In my correspondence with over two hundred pastors who have such associations, but eleven reported failures. One of these ministers let the club drop because, as he wrote, "it required too much time on my part to look after it." It was a failure in another instance, the pastor writes, "because the officers of the club began to incur heavy expenses before any provision was made to meet them, and a radical difference of view as to what the club should attempt, with the presence of two or three Scotchmen who objected to almost everything." Three other clubs reported successful work for the first year, but did not continue the club thereafter, one feeling it not adapted to his community, another because the men "grew weary of working," another because too expensive. Another club did not continue because never resurrected by the pastor and officers after a summer's vacation. Such in general are the reasons given for the disbanding of the Sunday Evening Clubs. Regarding these reasons I would make but two comments: first, it is too much to expect of any organization that it will run itself; and, secondly, we may expect a certain percentage of failures here as in any enterprise, as all men are not gifted with business ability.

The following are extracts from letters received from ministers, telling of the success of their Club. I only regret that space does not permit the printing of all the letters written me relative to this work.

The Rev. William Carter, Sterling, Ill., pastor of the

MODERN METHODS IN CHURCH WORK.

First Presbyterian Church, among other things writes: "The Men's League has been an unqualified success with us. It was organized the 4th of November, 1894, and interested the men immediately. Its first year was marked by great enthusiasm, and its second year is starting out better than the first. Our charter membership was thirty-five; the second year we doubled it, and before the year closed we had almost one hundred members, and the list continually growing. Our Sabbath evening congregations have increased over one hundred per cent, and many are now in attendance that were not interested in any church before. As for practical results, we have a Missionary Society within the League, which is really constituted of all the League members, and a few Sundays ago a missionary programme was given in which all who took part were men. Certainly this shows an interest in spiritual things, and is drawing men nearer the Kingdom than ever they were before."

Rev. Frank Newhall White, associate pastor of the Congregational Church of Burlington, Iowa, writes: "We feel that the service has been very successful. A permanent congregation has thus been secured, and often we are privileged to minister to congregations varying from six hundred to a thousand. Scores of people, before habitually indifferent to the church, have been aroused to active attendance, interest, and co-operation. The willingness to be known publicly as members of such an organization is such an improvement on previous conditions, for a large number of men, that we feel much has been gained. The organization is now recognized as one of the positive forces making for the elevation and salvation of the city."

"Rightly used, the Club is an evangel," writes Rev. Dr. James A. Chamberlain, pastor of the First Congregational Church of Owatonna, Minn. Dr. Chamberlain says that three things are needed for a successful club. "First, a minister who can command the situation. A weak man should never have a club. Second, singers of sense, singers who will sing and let sing. Here we meet the greatest obstacle of the Sunday night service. Some singers want a 'holy opera;' some won't sing 'if so and so does.' Third, a Board of Deacons or Elders, who have been converted and have common-sense, to stand by the preacher and let him convert men with fiddle, trombone, flute, flageolet, etc., etc. Any instrument that will please men may and ought to be used for the glory of God."

Rev. J. H. Reynard, pastor of the Sprague Memorial Presbyterian Church of Tacoma, Washington, writes of his Club: "It is a good success, — no trouble to fill the seats and raise money to run the business end of it. The services are always evangelistic."

Rev. Joseph H. Seldon, pastor of the First Congregational Church of Elgin, Ill., writes: "Our League, well on in its third year, has proved from the first very helpful. The Sunday evening service has doubled in size under the work of the League, is larger than our morning audience, has averaged for over a year about five hundred in attendance, and a half-dozen times in the season will reach nine hundred. The League has reached and interested men in the church, and has made for itself an established place."

From the Presbyterian Church of Three Rivers, Mich., the pastor, Rev. J. H. McPherson, writes: "My primary object in organizing the Club was to feel that I had around me a band of level-headed, practical business men to whom I might go for advice, and also call upon for aid to bring many of our men into closer touch with the church and religious things. Towards this end the club has succeeded nobly. Our evening audiences when I came to the church, about sixteen months ago, had dwindled down to an average attendance of thirty. The evening audiences average to-day over three hundred (on special or extra occasions we have over six hundred), and the interest is still kept up."

Rev. Charles S. Hoyt, pastor of the Presbyterian Church of Oak Park, Ill., writes: "The evening audience has doubled, and much has been done to unify the church work, and to increase a spirit of pride in the church, and loyalty to its interests. We have succeeded in attaching to the church men who were indifferent."

Rev. C. A. Wight, pastor of the Congregational Church of Platteville, Wis., writes: "The audiences have filled the house from the start, and there is no decline of interest. Many people have been regular in attendance who did not go to church before. The financial cost is almost nothing in our case, and is met by the evening collections. Some have united with the church through the influence of the Club. Many men have gone to work for the success of the services who were doing nothing before, perhaps not even attending the services. For fifty years the evening congregation was a drag. A crowded house in the evening gives an impetus to all departments of work."

Rev. G. James Jones, pastor of the Presbyterian Church of Maywood, Ill., writes: "It has enlisted about one half of the men members of our congregation in practical work, visitation, and inviting and planning for the Sabbath evening service, which has increased in attendance very largely. It is the best help of a human kind that a pastor can have."

THE MEN'S SUNDAY EVENING CLUB.

Rev. Archibald Hadden, pastor of the First Congregational Church of Muskegon, Mich., writes: "We maintain a Vesper Service at 5 P. M. Sunday. The Club has charge of it, and it has become a feature of our church and of the city. A chorus of thirty or forty voices, accompanied by organ and orchestra, renders good music and leads in the hymns. The good results of the Club are: First, the creation of this service; second, giving the men a distinctive work to do; third, drawing into closer relations to the church a considerable number of men and women."

Rev. R. D. Scott, pastor of the Belden Avenue Presbyterian Church of Chicago, has a Men's Association which is carrying on various lines of church work. One result of this Association, the pastor writes, is "that the evening congregations fill the house so that extra chairs are needed. The music is attractive, and a deeper spiritual interest prevails. The Club is a pre-eminently good thing, and is capable of indefinite expansion. Making men know each other intimately is a great point gained, and one which we magnify."

Rev. Willis E. Parsons, pastor of the First Presbyterian Church of Danville, Ill., writes of his Club as follows: "There has been a large increase in attendance, and a growing interest on the part of the men of the League in the evening service, brighter and more helpful services, and the cheering of the heart of the pastor. The men of the League too are more interested in the general work of the church. In their meetings they consult concerning the church as a whole, and are willing to do work that hitherto they did not do. As I look at the Men's League in this church, I feel that there is no limiting its possibilities for usefulness if it be wisely directed."

Rev. E. L. Smith, pastor of the Congregational

MODERN METHODS IN CHURCH WORK.

Church of Walla Walla, Washington, writes: "Our Sunday Evening Club is now two years old, and has been of great practical service in enlisting the active co-operation of many young men for the church and in filling the church on Sunday evenings. The danger has been to drift too much toward entertainment in the evening music, but this has been bravely met and overcome. The result is more people hearing the Gospel and more at work for Christ and the Church."

Rev. Edward F. Goff, pastor of the First Congregational Church of Aurora, Ill.: "We have no difficulty in filling our audience-room every Sunday evening. We frequently need to place chairs in the aisles. Non-church-goers begin to cultivate a habit of church attendance, and place themselves within the sphere of pastoral influence." Mr. Goff adds: "I try to remember that the object of the evening service is spiritual and saving, — that whatever leads the people to the church, when I get them there, I must do them good. The most varied and attractive service may also be the most spiritual."

Rev. J. Monroe Markley, pastor of the First Congregational Church of Lee Center, Ill., writes in the following encouraging way about the work of a men's club in a small town. Lee Center is a country place of between two hundred and fifty and three hundred inhabitants, and Mr. Markley's church is composed mainly of country people, but he says: "I have proven most conclusively that the methods of the Men's Sunday Evening Club can be utilized successfully in the country church. Our church is crowded at every evening service, and often chairs are placed in the aisle; all available standing room is occupied. During the warmest weather last summer we turned people away by scores who were not able to gain admittance,

THE MEN'S SUNDAY EVENING CLUB.

and this matter of attendance is only one indication of an increased interest manifested in every line of church work. It has far surpassed my most sanguine expectations."

One of the most successful clubs in the country, and one that has done much to extend the movement, is that in the Presbyterian Church of Austin, Ill., of which the Rev. John Clark Hill, D.D., is pastor. He gives the following account of the results of the work of the Men's Club in his church: "The work of the Men's Club in our parish has forced the church and its work for the good of men and the glory of God upon the attention of the community in such a way that it has resulted in gathering a congregation on Sunday evenings that is limited only by the size of our building. It has done this without in any way affecting the audiences of other churches. It has brought together congregations at these services in which nearly seventy-five per cent are males; it has brought these men week after week under the influence of the preaching of the Holy Scriptures, read, preached, and sung; it has stimulated every department of our church work to greater zeal; it has brought the men of the congregation, and very many outside of it, into a closer sympathy with evangelistic work; it has brought these men into social contact that is a help to them and to the church. It has done this by persistent advertising, a great variety of good music, short discourses; and by giving the people a large share in the service, in congregational prayers, as well as in praise and responsive reading; and by the willingness to be led in all details by the Holy Spirit, that Christ may be glorified."

From the report rendered at the Fourth Anniversary of the Young Men's Sunday Evening Club of the First Congregational Church of Appleton, Wis., Rev. John

Faville, D.D., pastor, I take the following extracts, which show how the work has fared in one of the pioneer churches in this movement: —

"The results have more than justified the movement. The Club enters to-day upon its fifth year of work. It has grown in strength and usefulness each year. The membership of twenty at its organization has increased to five hundred and sixty. The average attendance at the evening service has increased from one hundred and fifty to six hundred and fifty. The Club has assisted in the morning service, increased the size of the parish, helped meet the financial demands, carried on for three years a successful lecture course, developed a better social life, identified itself with the local charities of the city, and in other ways has helped to make the church a house of life. Not the least of the many surprises in this movement has been the readiness with which so many men have responded when given something to do for the evening service." The anniversary programme of this club also bore the following large-hearted message: "The Club extends fraternal greetings to all similar associations, of which there are many, and is glad to give all the information and assistance possible."

Pastors purposing to organize a Sunday Evening Club will find, I am sure, that all clubs are glad to help and co-operate in extending the movement. A glance at the different Sunday evening programmes of different clubs will be found most helpful and suggestive.

CHAPTER X.

THE SUNDAY EVENING SERVICE.

The Church was founded by Christ as his great instrument in saving the world, and its great purpose should be to reach men and save them. . . . Teach the Church that it has a commission from the Lord Jesus Christ. Teach it that unless it puts forth every effort to reach men with the Gospel it cannot retain that commission, and it will learn that it must pay attention to the Sunday evening service, for with this definition at its heart and its spirit kindled with what it means, it will soon find that the Sabbath evening is the time of all others when the people can and must be reached. For instance, it will find that the laborer . . . having no religious principles to draw him to church remains at home, but in the evening it is otherwise. The long hours of the day have given a surfeit of mere rest, and the man and his family are on the lookout for some place to which they may go. They want to forget their work and their trials. They go out upon the street. They find one church with its doors barred. They find another with a few score of people assembled where there is room for thousands. Into the first they could not go if they would, and into the second they will not go if they can. They want to be where men are, and where they can feel the warm touch and glow of life, and so they pass by these doors and go to houses of entertainment that bid for their patronage.

REV. CHARLES S. MILLS.

MANY an anxious pastor has asked, "What shall we do with the Sunday evening service?" This has long been a serious question. Some have dropped this second service, others have shifted it to the afternoon, and others have permitted it "to struggle under the incubus of being a second-rate affair, holding it in the basement or back chapel."[1] Many churches which are filled in the morning are well-nigh empty at night.

---

[1] Rev. Charles S. Mills, Report of the Fifth Convention of Christian Workers, Hartford, Conn., 1890, p. 59.

MODERN METHODS IN CHURCH WORK.

The complaint has been a lack of interest on the part of church-members and no inclination on the part of non-church-goers to attend the evening meeting. But this state of affairs has not been looked upon, for the most part, with complacency, nor regarded as a finality by earnest ministers; they have faced the perplexing problem, and already beginnings have been made toward a satisfactory solution.

In the chapter on the Men's Sunday Evening Club, testimonies are given of most successful Sabbath evening services, showing a several-fold increase in attendance, and proportionate results in reaching the unsaved. This work of the Club is, I believe, one of the greatest helps as yet called to the assistance of the evening service. But there are many ways in which the second service of worship may be made helpful and interesting.

1. The Musical Service is always an acceptable variation from the usual formal preaching service. It is more than a pleasant change, — it is a change affording unusual possibilities for good. Many who will not come to hear the Word preached will come to hear the Word sung, and others who seemingly are not touched by anything else are reached by the sweet message of song. It was Henry Ward Beecher who said, "You are conscious when you go to an earnest meeting that while hymns are being sung and you listen to them, your heart is, as it were, loosened, and there comes out of those hymns to you a realization of the truth as you never heard it before." Ever since the morning stars first sang together, music has played a large part in worship.

The musical service, when wisely conducted, has proven to be a most impressive service. A prominent church in New York City, at the suggestion of the

THE SUNDAY EVENING SERVICE.

chorister, commenced giving a musical service once a month, and at once the attendance on the evening service increased from two hundred and fifty to an average attendance of over six hundred, and with an attendance of nine and eleven hundred at the musical service.

It is to be remembered that in a meeting of this kind there should be perfect harmony between the service and the pastor's own soul. Prayerful, spiritual, painstaking preparation is just as essential here as in any other service. The programmes of such services are varied according to the ability of the choir to render music, and the taste of the pastor who directs the service. The music which is the most spiritual, such as Gounod's "Sanctus" and selections from Handel's "Messiah," has always proven not only the most helpful, but also the most attractive to the people. This music is an uplift, presents the truth in a persuasive way, and also increases the interest of the choir, magnifying their importance and giving them music that readily commands their best effort. In addition to anthems, solos, quartettes, and duets, there is a programme of congregational singing, scriptural lessons or responsive readings, and such varied exercises as the pastor may arrange. The minister usually gives a short sermon of twelve or fifteen minutes, — the best that he can do in that time without one unnecessary or irrelevant word. Some ministers vary these services by an occasional brief lecture on music, again by having the burden of the programme consist of hymns by the congregation, the preacher giving a brief history of the hymns, — the occasion of the writing, and possibly some anecdote in the life of the writer, before the singing of each selection. For such information the busy pastor will find some good work on hymnology invaluable.

For worship in Berkeley Temple, Boston, the Rev. Dr. Dickinson prepared a series of Sunday evening services, which are somewhat different from those described. They are more in the nature of a liturgical service, and the readings and responses alternate by minister, people, and choir. It is interesting to state, in this connection, that the audiences of Berkeley Temple usually take every foot of available space.

2. This leads me to say a word as to the use of liturgy. Rev. John Clark Hill, D.D., pastor of the Presbyterian Church of Austin, Ill., recently, as a test, made a morning service somewhat liturgical in form. He says: "I found the people are in most hearty accord with this style of service. . . . I believe we have gotten out of touch with the people during the past generation, partly because they had so very little to do in church services. There is no reason why the people should not unite in a prose prayer in concert when there is no objection whatever to their singing a prayer in verse written by another." In the rebound from the formalism of the Catholic Church and other ritualistic churches, the Church generally has fallen into a different phase of formalism in allowing our worship to receive verbal expression only by the lips of another. There is a growing tendency with many ministers of nearly all denominations to bring more liturgy into the service, — at least enough to give the people to feel that they have a share in and are important to the service. And so far as I have learned, on careful inquiry, this tendency has been well received by the people and has been attended with most gratifying results. But again, let pastor and people expect nothing from mere method. "Wheels" are all right, but we must have the "living Spirit in the midst of the wheels."

THE SUNDAY EVENING SERVICE.

3. Another method which has met with good results in drawing the masses and in bringing the Gospel to bear on the hearts of the people is what is called the Brookfield Service. It originated with a number of neighboring pastors in Massachusetts, in 1889, as a result of a conference of Congregational ministers for devising ways of reaching the people with the Gospel. Opportunity appealed to them in the Sunday evening meeting. Accordingly a new order of service was carefully prepared, consisting of responsive readings, — interspersed throughout the programmes, — readings in concert, prayers, a varied programme of music, Scripture reading, and a short gospel sermon. A series of programmes were prepared on such fundamental gospel subjects as, 1. The Law of God (Its character and man's relation to it); 2. Penitence and Confession (On account of sin); 3. The Cross of Christ (The remedy for sin), and like themes. Every part of each programme bears directly and in a logical and forcible way upon the theme subject, and there is painstaking attention to detail, with ample provision for variation as may be demanded by the need of each church. The programmes are simply and comprehensively arranged, so that congregations not accustomed to liturgy can use them with enjoyment. The music, the evangelistic tone of the whole programme, and the large part given the people make the service attractive and helpful.[1]

4. Another way of varying the Sunday evening meeting, and one which the most conservative cannot question, is by having a Special Night Service. For instance, a temperance night, a young people's night, a business men's night, a women's night, a good-citizen-

[1] Further information can be obtained by addressing Hartford Seminary Press, Hartford, Conn.

ship night, a public-school night; and like important subjects. Our national as well as church calendar will also suggest timely themes, such as the anniversary of our national flag, victory at Yorkville, Landing of the Pilgrims, and so forth. The presence of the stars and stripes and other appropriate decorations at such times is helpful. "Timely" subjects always come to people with unusual appeal and interest, and afford opportunity for making deep and lasting impressions. It is not enough, however, that the simple announcement of a Special Service be given. It should be made special by the strongest programme within the resources of the minister. Let every wheel that will add an ounce of influence or power be set in motion. Advertise thoroughly. One thing should be guarded against: promise should never be made or implied through announcement or advertisement of more than an evening will give. If there is any disappointment, it is far better that it be a happy one, — for instance that more music and better music be given than was announced; that the service throughout be found brighter, pleasanter, and more helpful than had been anticipated. This does not preclude strong announcements, but compels strong services. Awaken high anticipation and meet it!

5. A series of special Sunday evening sermons is an old and ever-new attraction. The subjects of many such series, from pastors who have been especially successful in drawing large evening congregations, have come into my hands. I have been impressed that such series are usually on practical topics, such as "Christianity and a Life of Business," "Christianity and the Professions," "Christianity and the Teacher," "Religion and the Public Schools," "Chris-

THE SUNDAY EVENING SERVICE.

tianity and the Home;"[1] and on such evangelistic subjects as "Salvation — Man Needs It," "Salvation — God Provides it," "Salvation — Faith Secures It," "Salvation — Christ Assures it."[2]

In the First Presbyterian Church of Los Angeles, Cal., during the pastorate of the Rev. J. L. Russell, D.D., a series of Sunday evening lectures on sacred subjects was given by prominent laymen of that church and other evangelical churches in the city. Sometimes there were two brief addresses given during the same evening. The speakers were lawyers, teachers, and cultivated business men, and the series was received with great interest by large audiences.

The special service and the series of sermons have the advantage also of commanding, usually, the attention of the press. The reporting of sermons should be encouraged; it draws attention to the services, magnifies the work, and preaches the Gospel over again. This is not seeking notoriety; it is seeking to spread the Gospel.

6. The Illustrated Service. The Sunday evening meeting has also been improved in many churches by drawing spiritual lessons from objects of nature and by illustrating religious truth by use of pictures. This has proven an effective way of attracting the people and of appealing through eye and ear to the heart. These illustrated services are not given with the thought that "a substitute is needed for the old Gospel, or that pictures can take the place of preaching," but they are used as a means of preaching.

This method is not new. It is as old as God's rain-

---

[1] Rev. Elijah Horr, D.D., pastor of the Piedmont Congregational Church, Worcester, Mass.

[2] Rev. John Clark Hill, D.D., pastor of the Presbyterian Church, Austin, Ill.

bow covenant. Again, when God made covenant with Abraham, He addressed him through the eye as well as the ear. The covenant was consummated by the symbol of fire, and the "Friend of God" knew that he was under Divine favor. From the beginning this has been the Divine way of teaching. In the Old Testament there are upwards of seven hundred and fifty allusions to Christ in types, ceremonies, and symbols. The whole sacrificial system of the Jewish economy is on the principle of teaching the spiritual by things material. What but this was the meaning of the Passover, the Feasts, the Offerings, and the Sacrifices? Even the several parts of the Tabernacle had some special spiritual meaning. In like manner God taught Elijah, Elisha, Ezekiel, Jeremiah, and others. Our blessed Lord used natural objects for illustrating the truth which he preached, — not merely alluding to the objects, but drawing lessons from their visible presence. What is more forcible than his illustration to the woman at the well? Or his taking little children in his arms and talking to the people about receiving "the Kingdom of God as a little child"? Jesus, too, drew lessons from nature, the field, the flower, thus making simple and clear his meaning, and reaching hearts through eye and ear! Why fear and hesitate to follow his example?

The science of the mind has shown us much in recent years of the power of teaching through the eye as well as the ear. Teaching by illustration arrests the attention at once, concentrates thought, excites interest, and awakens imagination. When John B. Gough was appealing for aid in the building of the Five Points Mission, to a large audience in New York, after telling the sad story of a fallen woman, he called to his side a little girl from the front of the audience, and, lifting the child so that all could see her sweet face and tossing curls, said, "Now, how much will you give to save this child and hundreds like her?" The money was raised. No one thought him sacrilegious, and every week now hundreds of children gather in the Five Points Mission and sing of Wondrous Love. The Rev. C. H. Tyndall, former pastor of the Broome Street Tabernacle, New York, was very successful in drawing spiritual lessons from objects of nature, giving an object sermon about once a month. It was his experience that it increased the attendance at the service and crystallized the truth in the minds of his hearers by the association of ideas. In his book entitled "Object Sermons in Outline," he very clearly shows how such sermons may be undertaken. He gives numerous subjects that may be profitably illustrated, indicates the objects to be used, the lessons to be drawn from them, and shows in a very practical way how to arrange both the objects and the ideas of the sermons.

There are other kinds of illustrated services which have been used to advantage. The next to be mentioned is the Pulpit Paintings of Edwin M. Long and Son.[1] These paintings for the purpose of illustrating sermons had their origin, it is said, in the great revival of 1858. Since that time pastors have increasingly used these paintings, and strongest testimonies are given of their help in getting and holding Sabbath evening congregations, and of their educational and evangelizing force. The paintings are illustrations of Bible history and teachings, and are arranged in series, with three paintings for one sermon and four rolls (twelve paintings) for a month's course. The

[1] Address Edwin M. Long & Son, S. E. corner 12th and Berks Streets, Philadelphia, Pa.

subjects covered include Scenes in the Life of Christ, Great Questions of the Bible, Scenes in the Lives of the Apostles, Old Testament Biography, and the Gospel of the Pentateuch. The paintings are rented. Illustrated chart sermons (engravings), said to be copies of the pulpit paintings, are considerably cheaper.

Another method of illustrating sermons is by use of the stereopticon. Like the innovation of the Sunday-school, Mission Societies, and the Young People's Movement, this new method of presenting the Gospel has received severest criticism. I fear that some share the prejudice against the stereopticon for the preaching service without a careful canvass of the situation and the work it has accomplished, or without having ever been eye-witness to such services. Is such a judgment a considerate one? Preaching by means of stereopticon pictures is no longer an experiment. And from every quarter there come testimonies that the new method is successful in bringing the unchurched masses into the church, and is being blessed of God in preaching the Gospel with converting power. Many come, doubtless, through curiosity or interest in the pictures rather than the Gospel. Paul rejoiced that Christ was preached, even "of contention, not sincerely,"[1] as well as of love. Let us rejoice that people come where Christ is preached, though not constrained by the motive of love. God has promised to bless his Word.

The stereopticon service, when taken hold of with painstaking care and prayerful preparation, is a deeply impressive, spiritual, and beautiful service. The heart is reached through the eye, the Gospel is simply told, and many are brought into saving knowledge of Jesus Christ. Rev. W. A. Mason, D.D., Baptist, Minneapo-

[1] Philippians i. 16, 18.

lis, Minn., is authority for saying that sixty conversions attended a minister's illustrated lectures on the life of Christ, and that "there are in the world to-day thousands who associate the stereopticon with their most precious religious hopes."[1] We must admit that the method of preaching is somewhat unusual. But when we remember that one-half our country's population is estranged from the church, that every two persons out of three of the world's population have never heard of the Gospel, it seems time for something "unusual." Mr. Moody has said: "When God works, many things will be done 'out of the regular order.'"[2] When some way of working, though unusual, has been blessed of God in winning souls to Christ, is it not time that we question our prejudices rather than the methods?

In many parishes, no doubt, such illustrated Sabbath evening services would not be advisable. We must be governed by the law of adaptability. In other parishes the best way to begin is by first using the stereopticon in the prayer meeting or a lecture on Missions, or by giving a series of three or four lectures, week-evenings, on such subjects as "The Life of Christ," "Pilgrim's Progress," "The Story of Ruth," "The Holy Land." Views illustrative of some of the popular and standard hymns, such as "Rock of Ages," "Nearer my God to Thee," or "Onward, Christian Soldiers," should also be given; while these views are being presented, the hymn may be sung as a solo, or in concert by the congregation. In addition to this, other hymns with words in full may be thrown upon the screen from time to time for congregational singing.

---

[1] Reprint from "Open Church," in pamphlet, by Riley Brothers, on "Solved: The Sunday Evening Service," p. 29.

[2] To the Work, p. 14.

For the Sabbath evening service, in addition to the hymns and views illustrating the sermon, other things, giving variety to the service, may be thrown on the screen, such as the Apostles' Creed and Psalms for unison and responsive reading.

Stereopticon views and lantern can be rented from any one of a number of opticians in our various cities. Where the lantern is owned, the cost is, of course, much less. The increase in collections ought to cover the increase in expense.

7. Special features. The Rev. Henry H. Stebbins, D.D., pastor of the Central Church, Rochester, N.Y., regards the following as among the features of the successful evening service in Rochester: —

1. Personal work at hotels, through letters and calls.
2. The provision of a bright, attractive Order of Worship, circulated at the door, and in sufficient quantities to allow every attendant to have one.
3. Singing, — popular, rather than artistic.
4. Sermons, — evangelistic in tone, but addressed to men where they live.
5. Amiable and vigorous competition among the churches, stimulated by what some had done, that fed the conviction that the same could be done elsewhere.

The prelude is another feature employed by some pastors, and questioned by as many more. The prelude is a five or eight minute address before the sermon, on some popular subject or issue of the day. In speaking of it, Dr. Stebbins said: "I am bound to say that I think the prelude has perhaps attracted some. I am not in sympathy with that sort of thing, for various reasons. I do think, however, it has attracted people who would not otherwise have attended the service. I do not employ it myself, and it is a question whether it will serve permanently as a magnet."

THE SUNDAY EVENING SERVICE.

In Bethany Presbyterian Church, Philadelphia, it is the custom from time to time to place the advertising of the Sunday evening service in the hands of some one of the societies of the church, as the Christian Endeavor, Andrew and Philip, or Sunday-school. The society chosen uses every effort, by cards and personal work and through friends and supporters, to advertise this service. At times the work of the various organizations of the church is magnified and brought prominently forward by having the officers of such society sit on the platform, reference being made to the work of the society during the exercises of the evening. This church aims always to have something special for the Sunday evening services, but never aims to be sensational. Occasionally the church uses the stereopticon for the opening song service, then following with a sermon.

CHAPTER XI.

THE AFTER MEETING.

The after meeting, held at the close of the last preaching-service of the Sabbath, is for various purposes: To ask God's blessing as a seal to deepen and quicken the spiritual impressions of the day, to hear requests for prayer, and to make appeal to the impenitent and the wanderer to accept Jesus Christ as their personal Saviour. The dominant purpose of the meeting must, of course, be determined by the circumstances of the time and the prevailing conditions of the church and the community.

The after meeting is not merely for large congregations. Wherever there is a church, there is reason for this service. It gives opportunity for the people of the church to come together informally when their hearts are warm and aglow with Divine truth, and when inevitably they must come closer together in sympathy and Christian feeling, and closer to Him who is the Great Head of the Church.

There are several features of the successful after-meeting which through experience have come to be recognized as essential to it.

That the meeting may be informal and a marked change from the preaching service which has preceded, it is usually held in some smaller, adjoining room, such as the Sunday-school room or chapel. When no such room is available, the need is met by the pastor coming from the pulpit and taking a chair on the floor in front of the pulpit.

There are several ways of giving the invitation to the after meeting. It is frequently given thus: "After the benediction we will pass to the closing service of the day, held in the adjoining room for fifteen minutes, to ask God's blessing upon the labors of the day, and for general conference, testimony, and prayer. We invite you all to come to this service. It is frequently the best one of the day, gathering up the blessings of them all." The doors opening to the room should be clearly indicated, always, that any stranger present may not suffer any excuse to turn him away. The invitation at another time may be to different classes of people, as, first, to all those who desire to draw nearer to God and to unite in prayer for his abiding blessing upon the services of this day; second, any one who desires to request the prayers of Christian people for himself or friends; and third, all who are personally interested, and feel that the Holy Spirit is urging them to a decision for Jesus Christ.

When the meeting is held in a room contiguous to the main auditorium, arrange with the organist and two or three singers to open the after meeting, *just as soon as* the preaching service closes, with some familiar, heart-stirring hymn. The singing will do much toward drawing the people in. This plan presumes that the congregation will largely pass to the second service. Another simple way is to ask all who will to pass into the after-meeting room during the singing of the last hymn, it being understood that the benediction will be pronounced for those who cannot stay to the after service. A familiar hymn is then announced. If but few pass out, it will be well to stop at the close of the first verse, and again urge people to pass into the meeting while the hymn is being sung, but adding, "If you prefer to wait here for the benediction, you, of course, are privileged to do so."

There is no difficulty in getting the people to attend the after meeting. It is one of the sweetest and most helpful services of the day when wisely conducted, — and to this end the leader needs well to pray for the controlling and guiding presence of the Holy Spirit. Many an after meeting has been shorn of blessing for the want of prayerful preparation. Much depends upon the leader. He may open the meeting, after the singing of a hymn or two, by some single heart thought, or by prayer, or illustration, or "exhortation," for which the Rev. B. Fay Mills says, "a wise preacher has kept one of his best illustrations or strongest entreaties." The leader should especially remember that this is no place for a talk or address, not even a short talk. The leader, as all others, should be *brief* in what he says. Many an after meeting has been talked to death.

Great care should be exercised in the selection of hymns. Under no circumstances should new ones be selected. So far as possible the hymns should be appropriate and familiar, although it is better to sacrifice appropriateness to familiarity. There is little time for music in the after service, but there should be a hymn or two, or a stanza from each of two or three hymns. The singing may be varied by asking the women to sing the verse and all to come in on the chorus. Again, if a good soloist is present, it can be made effective to have the soloist sing the lines and all join in the singing of the refrain and chorus. Repeating the singing of the chorus is always spiritually helpful and suggestive. The meaning is emphasized by sometimes reading the verse in concert before singing it. Most effective

THE AFTER MEETING.

appeals can be made at times between the singing of the verses of a hymn.

A common way of conducting the after service is to say that the meeting is open for testimony, conference, and prayer, and invite all to take part, as moved to do so by the Holy Spirit. To relate occasionally the circumstances which suggested the writing of a hymn, or to give some experience or conversion connected with a hymn, is always helpful and of interest. Should any one make request for prayer, when the thought of the meeting has been on other lines, it is well, usually, to call on some one immediately to pray for that particular case.

The after meeting, at other times, may be held especially for the spiritual quickening of Christians. Opportunity is then given for confession of failures and shortcomings, by word or by rising. Prayers, of course, will follow. It is helpful at the close of a service to take some consecration hymn, like that of Frances Ridley Havergal, "Take my life and let it be," and urge all who desire to make the hymn the prayer of their hearts to sing.

A bright and helpful feature of any meeting is the reciting in concert of some verse of Scripture. Silent prayer, too, is always solemnly impressive. This, varied by *short sentence* prayers, can be used with frequency and helpfulness in any after meeting. Until the people come to understand that prayers are *only sentence* prayers, it may be well to arrange previously with a number of younger and older people for them. Sentence prayers encourage many to take part who would otherwise not do so. All heads are bowed, no one is conspicuous, a sentence does not appear to be a large effort; and so the people gladly share in this part of the service, are helped and warmed by so doing, and others are awakened and quickened by the interest which seems to pervade all.

Another way of leading the meeting is to open with requests for prayer and then have several pray for these requests. After a prayer or two, an appeal may be made to the unsaved. It is a simple way, and appropriate, to stop and say, "Now, before the next prayer, is there some one who desires to take Christ as a personal Saviour, and by raising the hand will say, 'Include my name in your prayer, pray for me'?"

Whether the appeal be made briefly at this time, or the after meeting as a whole be given to it, there are several ways of making openings to penitents for confession and of drawing the net for the unsaved.

After short prayers, testimonies, and an earnest appeal, as the case may be, the penitents may be urged to come forward and kneel during the singing of a verse of some hymn. This is a method quite common to one of the leading denominations. Another way, used by other denominations, is to invite those who have manifested a personal interest to come forward and stand in a circle about the pastor. At the conclusion of the singing of the hymn he joins hands with them, and offers prayer.

With a more formal people other plans may be necessary. Christians may be asked to bow in silent prayer; then the leader says: "Now, while all heads are bowed in prayer, is there one here who will say, 'I desire to lead a Christian life, pray for me'? — raise your hand." But some people have honest doubts and difficulties. They need encouragement to make some kind of a start, though a small one. One of the leading evangelists of to-day frequently gives an invitation as follows: "How many of you will say, 'I am willing

THE AFTER MEETING.

to be made willing to lead a Christian life'? — will you raise your hand?"

Again the leader of the meeting, after opening by illustration or entreaty, may ask all who are church-members to rise; then all who are not church-members but are trying to live a Christian life; and third, all who have an honest desire to live a Christian life. This may be varied, at another time, by first asking all men who are church-members to rise, then all women who are church-members to rise, and proceeding as before.

It is hardly necessary to say that the leader in making the appeal should be warmly sympathetic and tender, patient and persistent, and with a divine confidence and supreme faith in God. Such a minister will meet with great victories where another would only find a losing cause.

But the results of the appeal should be gathered into real and tangible form. The names and addresses of the inquirers should be obtained, that they may be followed up promptly and helped as there may be need. For this purpose the following card may be passed by ushers:

....189.....

I desire henceforth to lead a Christian life.

Name,...

Address,...

Street and No.,..

Church Preference,..

The ushers, men capable of doing personal work, should be on the lookout for all who in any way manifest personal interest. There too should be a number of personal helpers, — the wisest men and women of the congregation. The above card is that used by the Rev. B. Fay Mills. In speaking of this card, the evangelist in the "Independent" for March 14, 1895, said: "I do not think it well to print a theological formula on the card, nor to make its expression more positive in determination. The reason for this is that while this simple card will be very helpful in aiding those who are clearly decided, and are ready to 'subscribe with their hands to be the Lord's,' it will also develop interest in those who are not theologically educated, and will give to you the addresses of those who are somewhat impressed, but who might not be sufficiently interested to sign a statement of a more unequivocally decided expression. The helpers should write on the back of each card some little statement about the individual signing it, such as, 'Young man, very much in earnest,' or, 'A middle-aged woman, almost but not quite persuaded.' This will be very helpful in assigning proper people to follow up these inquirers later."

The last thing to be remembered by the leader of the after meeting is to close on time. Do not prolong the meeting. The preaching service should close promptly, and sufficiently early to encourage attendance upon the after service, and the closing time of this meeting should be guarded with jealous care. It is better to send the people away hungry, and when the meeting is at its height, that they may desire to come again. At this last service people are tired from attendance upon the services of the day, — more so than they usually realize, — and unduly adding to the service, even by two or three minutes, may make the after meeting a burden rather than a mount of privilege.

It is the opinion of some pastors that to hold the after meeting for three or four weeks and then to drop it for a similar period increases its attractiveness.

CHAPTER XII.

THE PLEASANT SUNDAY AFTERNOON.

AFTER hearing so much of the estrangement of working-men from the church, it is refreshing and encouraging to learn of successful efforts in bringing them within the fellowship of the church. And this has been the result of that movement known as the "Pleasant Sunday Afternoon."

That working-men have not attended church has, I believe, been more from failure of adaptation of method to condition than from the want of heart welcome on the part of the church. Sunday morning the working-man has chosen for rest. At other hours of the Sabbath, the concert, amusement hall, beer-garden, and the socialist or the labor agitator have recurrently claimed his attention. The counter-attractions to the church are always strong.

To provide an elevating hour for laboring-men, with sufficient attractiveness to draw them in, to win their hearts by these means to Christ, is the object of the Pleasant Sunday Afternoon. The movement which bears this name was started in England about four years ago.

The character of the meeting is indicated by its name. It is simply a very bright gospel service, with high-class instrumental and chorus music, solo singing, and a talk which "deals directly with gospel topics." The following are two sample programmes: —

MODERN METHODS IN CHURCH WORK.

1. 3.30 Hymn.	1. 3.30 Hymn.
2. 3.35 Prayer.	2. 3.35 Reading Scriptures.
3. 3.38 Instrumental Music.	3. 3.38 Anthem, or hymn, with chorus.
4. 3.43 Reading Scriptures.	4. 3.43 Prayer and Lord's Prayer.
5. 3.45 Hymn Solo.	5. 3.45 The First Solo.
6. 3.50 Instrumental Music.	6. 3.50 Notices by Secretary.
7. 3.53 Hymn.	7. 3.53 The Chairman.
8. 3.58 Address.	8. 4 Hymn.
9. 4.20 Instrumental Music.	9. 4.05 Speaker for afternoon.
10. 4.25 Hymn.	10. 4.25 Second Solo.
11. 4.30 Benediction.	11. 4.30 Exhortation to sign Pledge.
	12. 4.35 Short Prayer.

The music is always in charge of a director who is a thorough Christian, so that the choice of pieces may safely be left entirely to him. He, too, is one who can gather musical helpers around him, those who will not fail to appear on Sunday and who will give time to practice during the week. There is usually an orchestra or band, which gives instrumental selections of a sacred character, and also plays the accompaniment to the hymns. Sometimes the music is rendered by a prize choir consisting of men who have been especially trained, and they lead in the singing or give special selections.

The address for the afternoon is a matter of deep moment. Platitudes and religious cant will not succeed here, though it is sometimes tolerated in churches. What the men demand is a "bright, brotherly talk on things spiritual." Different speakers are obtained for different Sabbath afternoons. Representatives of the various professions, business men, and other available laymen who are fairly good speakers are drawn on for this service. The members enjoy seeing new faces and hearing new voices. This plan is adopted by so gifted a preacher as the Rev. F. B. Meyer, B.A., pastor of Christ's Church, London, who as president of his Pleasant Sunday Afternoon presides at all meet-

THE PLEASANT SUNDAY AFTERNOON.

ings. And this is the usual custom: different speakers, but the president to preside always. Here, as in other departments of Christian work, success depends in a measure on the personality of the leader. He should be a man of strong character, popular and winning, bent on saving souls, and "able to fill the gap on every emergency and to pull the meeting through if the speaker fail or the address be unfortunate." The time for the address is limited to twenty minutes, and is, as are all the other exercises, strictly confined to the time allotted to it. This is very satisfactory to the men, and prevents all dragging and dulness.

The Rev. F. B. Meyer says, at the first meeting of his Pleasant Sunday Afternoon he determined that five committees were necessary: "Visitation, especially of the sick; the promotion of teetotalism; of stewards; and markers; and benefit societies."[1] He then pointed out certain parts of the hall where those interested in each should gather. He says: "The whole group of men immediately broke up into five large groups, each making for his own special hobby, and found himself surrounded by those like-minded. Each group then elected their chairman and secretary, in which selection I confess to have had a great deal to do, as the men were strange to one another and I was very anxious that suitable ones should be chosen at the outset. These two from each group, together with myself, a few Vice-Presidents, and the Treasurer and Secretary of the society, formed a first Council. These five groups dwindled as time went on, but the residuum became the committee in each case, with power to add to its number and with full warrant to carry forward its own work, subject to the general approval of the Council."[2] Mr. Meyer has two

[1] Christian Treasury, February, 1895, p. 37. [2] Ibid.

corners in the church which are respectively named the Teetotal and Consecration corner. Those who want to sign the pledge are invited to one, whilst those who are willing to help in any special work or desire to become Christians are exhorted to the other.[1] As the men go out after the Sunday afternoon meeting, they put contributions into boxes for the Benevolent Fund, which is administered by a special committee and devoted to the relief of the needy and the sick in the brotherhood.

All who become members of the Pleasant Sunday Afternoon subscribe an English penny a Sunday; it has been suggested that in America probably a nickel would be best. This is put into the Book Fund. At the end of the quarter this money is spent in books to be given as prizes to those who make a good record in attendance. Those who are present thirteen Sundays get a first prize; those who are present ten or more Sundays, a second prize. As only the money subscribed is spent in this way, the value of the prizes varies according to the money in the fund and the number who win prizes. The books are bought at a low price from some bookseller interested in the movement, and are a great incentive to regular attendance. The prizes are distributed at some weekday gathering, the next week after the quarter ends, by some influential lady. The men are asked to bring both their men and women friends to this entertainment, and the new men who come are urged to join at once, so as to begin the quarter with the others. The sight of the book prizes and the pleasant gathering induces many of the visitors to join the society. A part of the Pleasant Sunday Afternoon plan is to have a Registrar to every hundred members. The

[1] Christian Treasury, April, 1895, p. 90.

THE PLEASANT SUNDAY AFTERNOON.

Registrars sit in the vestibule at little tables, each with a rubber stamp, prepared to stamp the cards of members and also the attendance sheet which is before them, and to receive the pennies of those who are members of the Book Club. This record enables the Visitation Committee to tell who is not present; and if a member is absent without explanation for two weeks, he is visited with a view of seeing what brotherly kindness can do for him. It is from this record that the list of those who are entitled to prizes is made up. Certain exempt classes, as local preachers, railroad men, postmen, and policemen when on duty, are allowed to send their penny for registration. In any other case that has special features, the Council decides as to what allowance shall be made. In fact, the men are made to feel in every way that it is their meeting. The Council is consulted as to the speaker, and about any other matter that affects the welfare of the Club.

Some Pleasant Sunday Afternoon Societies conduct various other lines of work during the week and year, — educational classes, an ambulance corps, a band or singing practice, annual excursions, walks and teas on holidays, a Benefit Society, a Working-Men's Institute, a midweek prayer meeting, and a men's Bible-class on Sunday.

Two things have been emphasized in this movement. The first is that the work shall be absolutely self-supporting. The men must raise their own funds, if money is needed.

The other principle emphasized is that " the first and last object of the P. S. A. is to win working-men for Christ."

The success of this institution is unquestioned. In Hanley, England, there is a branch numbering 1,680, of whom not more than three hundred were found in any other place of worship when they joined. At Liverpool, St. George's Chapel, Congregational, there is a branch of between three thousand and four thousand members.[1]

A work similar to this was begun in 1887 by the Baptist Church which worshipped in Tremont Temple, Boston, Mass., until the work was arrested by fire in 1893. This service, however, was open both to men and women. There was an orchestra of twelve pieces, but no chorus except the great congregation. At every service solos, quartettes, and so forth were given. It was customary to have an after meeting, and in the fifth year of the movement as many as 491 rose for prayers during the year. The meetings were also very helpful to the church. The evening services were better attended, and large numbers were brought into the Sunday-school. In addition to the spiritual results mentioned, that the movement was satisfactory from a financial standpoint the following figures will show: —

	Receipts.	Expenses.	Net Gain.
1888	$ 820.09	$ 556.35	$ 263.74
1889	1977.45	1012.36	965.09
1890	2141.63	791.37	1350.26
1891	2269.67	1007.87	1361.80
1892	2923.23	1017.78	1905.45

The Reformed Church of Harlem, New York, has an afternoon Bible-class which they call the Pleasant Sunday Afternoon. This organization meets separately at the time of the Sunday-school, has appropriate opening exercises, and then an exposition of the lesson

[1] Rev. H. N. Kinney, Report of Christian Workers' Seventh Convention, Boston, 1892, p. 137.

of the day. It is attended by both men and women, and enrols large numbers of young people and also parents who bring their children to Sunday-school. It has several social features, among which are social meetings during the year, an annual excursion, and other gatherings which increase the acquaintance and good-fellowship of the members.

In the Central Metropolitan Methodist Episcopal Church of New York, there is an organization of this kind called the Pleasant Hour Bible Class. It is similar to the one in Harlem, but holds its sessions immediately after the Sunday-school in the afternoon, and studies the lesson for the following Sunday. This is done for the benefit of Sunday-school teachers. This class has been in existence for three years, and has increased from an attendance of eleven at its first meeting to an average attendance of about five hundred. The entire collection goes to the church funds, as there are no expenses. The exercises are opened by a varied musical programme which is furnished voluntarily by the musical friends of the movement, and consists of both instrumental and vocal selections. This is followed by a short exposition of the lesson, studying directly from the Bible. Then there are ten minutes allowed for questions on the lesson only. On Review Sunday the class studies the subject of temperance. There is an evangelistic side to the work, and there are professed conversions every Sunday.

Thus we see that on both sides of the sea new efforts have been made to improve the hours of the Sabbath afternoon. It is to be hoped that the movement will be more and more general, until the churches shall vie with the Young Men's Christian Association in the efforts they make to " redeem the time" in these fruitful hours of the week.

CHAPTER XIII.

YOUNG PEOPLE'S SOCIETIES.

In considering the subject of Young People's Societies, it is not necessary to mention their mode of working. Many and valuable works have been written, abounding in accounts of work already done, and helpful suggestions for future effort in this great field of Christian usefulness.

The movement comprehensively known as the Young People's Society is the miracle of modern times. What has been done in the past by this powerful engine for good, what is being done by it, fills us with wonder and awe. What will be accomplished by it in the future opens up a vista so far-reaching, an avenue so crossed and intersected with branching paths to every field of Christian duty, that imagination cannot follow. What will be the effect on the Church when all these trained workers assume the full responsibility of mature manhood and womanhood? How cordiality and hospitality will reign in the churches when the social committees of the present become the owners of homes and possessors of influence and ability to welcome in a practical way the stranger of the future! How missions will thrive when the cultivated intelligence of men and women trained from youth in the spirit of *giving* and *going* becomes the ruling genius of the churches! How the prayer meetings of the future will differ from those of the present, when free-

YOUNG PEOPLE'S SOCIETIES.

dom of speech, enthusiasm of endeavor, and a high spirit of consecration take the place of the formalism and half-heartedness that too often characterize the midweek meeting of to-day! How the Church will grow in numbers and efficiency when loving hands are stretched out to gather souls into the kingdom, and the *look-out* spirit prevails with all the Church, to keep and guard and cherish those who come into her sheltering fold!

The Young People's movement is carried on by the undenominational organization, the Young People's Society of Christian Endeavor,[1] the Epworth League[2] of the Methodist Church, the Baptist Young People's Union,[3] and other denominational societies. The membership of the Christian Endeavor Society is about 2,500,000; that of the Epworth League about 1,250,000. In the Baptist churches, the Young People's Union have about 4,000 societies, while there are about 3,511 Baptist Christian Endeavor Societies.

A glance at the principal committees and departments of the three leading societies shows the scope of the work undertaken by each respectively. The Christian Endeavor Society works through several committees. The principal ones are the Look-out, Devotional, and Social, to which are added in most cases Temperance, Missionary, Sunday-school, Visiting, Flower, Good Citizenship, and Literature. In the Epworth League there are the following departments: the Department of Spiritual Work, of Mercy and Help,

---

[1] Mr. John Willis Baer, Secretary, 646 Washington Street, Boston, Mass.

[2] Rev. Edwin A. Schell, Secretary, 57 Washington Street, Chicago, Ill.

[3] Rev. Frank L. Wilkins, D.D., Secretary, 122 Wabash Avenue, Chicago, Ill.

of Literary Work, of Social Work, of Correspondence, and of Finance. The Baptist Young People's Union, in many of their societies, group their work into Devotional, Social, and Educational Departments.

Within these societies are often found working branches organized to meet special needs. In connection with the Epworth League there are Reading Circles formed for the study of religious topics. On completion of a given series of readings a certificate is given, to which seals are attached from time to time as the prescribed courses of reading are completed. In the Baptist Young People's Union there are Christian Culture Courses which cover in the main missionary topics. The subjects are discussed at monthly meetings called Conquest Meetings. The course extends over four years. At the close of each year an examination is held covering the ground gone over, and on completion of the course a diploma is awarded. The Society of Christian Endeavor in addition to the regular work of the committees does a vast amount of missionary and philanthropic work. Among the sailors and light-house keepers, Bibles, helpful literature, and comfort bags are annually distributed. Some societies have opened parlors for men and boys; others do active work in the hotels in distributing invitations to the meetings of the Society and other services of the church; others have instituted savings-banks; still others have opened newspaper exchanges for the interchange of religious reading. Some societies band themselves into "working circles" to help on the general work of the church. Accounts of different work undertaken by the societies may be found in the pages of the "Golden Rule," the official organ of the United Society.

A book that gives many practical suggestions as to

the methods of Young People's Societies is "Ways and Means," edited by Rev. F. E. Clark, D.D., President of the United Society of Christian Endeavor. It fully describes the organization of Young People's Societies, speaks of the best manner of conducting devotional, business, and consecration meetings, and treats of the work of the committees. It also gives many practical suggestions as to maintaining and arousing interest in the Society, and in every way is a perfect handbook of information. The chief value of the suggestions lies in the fact that they are experimental. Every plan commended has been successfully tried in some individual society.

An important factor in the work of young people's societies is the monthly, or bi-monthly social, held in the parlors or Sabbath-school rooms of the church, or, as sometimes, at a private residence. These social gatherings meet the need of young people for a social good time, promote Christian fellowship, and ought to be encouraged. The brightest minds should be placed upon the Social Committee, and a programme of entertainment should be carefully prepared for each social. A book invaluable for its descriptions of games and ways of entertainment for socials is "Social Evenings," by Amos R. Wells.

A great deal more might be said of Young People's Societies, but a knowledge of the scope of the methods of this endeavor for humanity has already been widely disseminated through the reports of the great conventions held yearly, and still more through the personal efforts of individual members of this vast body of workers "for Christ and the Church."

CHAPTER XIV.

THE PRAYER MEETING.

Can anything new and helpful be said in the interest of the midweek meeting? Probably no one church service has received so large attention from writers and workers as the weekly prayer meeting. Yet all has not been said. Certainly, the combined experiences of earnest and thoughtful pastors each year ought to be fruitful of many helpful suggestions for the weekly prayer meeting. This does not imply that we shall outgrow all the old ideas of the prayer meeting, or all the old ways of working. The idea, for instance, that the prayer meeting is the family gathering of the church is constantly emphasized, and is a principle that must always prevail. When, as a church, we realize that ideal, our prayer meetings will be shorn of stiffness, long stereotyped prayers, and stilted formal addresses; rather there will be the brief, simply worded petition, the tender or practical remarks, or the bit of helpful experience or counsel. But in addition to holding "fast that which is good," in conducting our midweek service, we welcome all that is helpful, though new.

The Rev. J. M. Patterson, pastor of the Westminster Presbyterian Church of Detroit, Mich., issues a little card to his people, in which he first urges their prompt and regular attendance on the prayer meeting, and asks the following questions, after each of which there is left a space for reply: —

THE PRAYER MEETING.

1. May I regard you as an attendant upon one or both of the weekly prayer meetings (General and Young People's) (if but one specify it), and place your name on the list of such which at present I am making out?
2. May I occasionally call upon you to read passages from the Bible?
3. May I occasionally call upon you to speak in prayer meeting?
4. May I occasionally call upon you to offer prayer in public?

These cards are returned to the pastor, and from them he gathers helpful ideas about his prayer-meeting force, if one may so put it.

The Rev. J. M. Meeker, D.D., pastor of St. Paul's Methodist Episcopal Church, Cincinnati, O., circulates a pledge card embracing the following points: —

1. I will pray for the meeting every Wednesday evening.
2. I will attend the prayer meeting at least twice each month if possible.
3. I will occupy a seat nearest the pulpit.
4. I will, if opportunity is given, take a brief part in the service.
5. I will tell others of our prayer meeting and invite them to attend.

This simple system in St. Paul's Church has proven very helpful. Some of the features of the above plans could, if desired, easily be incorporated in the enlistment card mentioned in Chapter V.

The Rev. Frank Russell, D.D., pastor of Bridgeport, Conn., Congregational Church, addresses a circular letter to his people urging them to come with special preparation, also to come early and occupy front seats on their own part, and to encourage the attendance of others. Another pastor, in a similar letter, which, however, is more personal, as it is addressed to but one or two at a time, invites the person to whom the letter is sent to take part in the meeting without being called upon, tells him that a similar request has been made of others, and that the prayer or remarks may be brief, and that too close adherence to the scheduled subject is not necessary.

The Rev. Abbott E. Kittridge, D.D., pastor of the Madison Avenue Reformed Church, New York, has a very large and interesting prayer meeting. He has some original methods. For instance, there is no instrumental accompaniment to the hymns, but they are started by the pastor himself, while the congregation is turning to the hymn announced. In advance of every meeting the pastor speaks privately to two or three members and obtains their promise to speak on the topic of the evening. It is the practice of Dr. Kittridge to merely open the meeting without extended remarks or by giving only a brief exposition of Scripture. At the close of the service he sums up the points that have been brought out, and makes the concluding remarks.

The Rev. Washington Gladden, D.D., tells of a pastor who arranges the theme of the meeting under several heads, putting the subdivisions into the form of questions. He then selects answers from the Bible and distributes them among the people. The pastor, having asked the question and received the answer, briefly comments on it, proceeds to the next question, and the meeting is thus pleasantly opened.[1]

The Rev. H. M. Scudder, D.D., makes the following suggestions: that the pastor make several lists, including all the persons in the church who can speak and pray in public; that he select a leader from each list and ask him with his fellow-members on the list to

[1] Parish Problems, p. 265.

THE PRAYER MEETING.

be responsible for one meeting. This will secure several participants at every meeting.[1]

A somewhat simpler method, and one that has proven very successful in encouraging the attendants to take part in the meeting, is to give out slips of paper bearing Scripture references and to ask the persons to whom they are given to read the passage (without being called on), and if they will, to comment on the passage in its relation to the subject of the evening.

The Rev. Thomas S. Hastings, D.D., President of Union Theological Seminary, when pastor of the West Presbyterian Church, New York, had most successful and largely attended prayer meetings. Among other features, Dr. Hastings occasionally had Question Box Meetings. The meetings were always announced in advance, and the congregation urged to hand in questions; it being understood that all questions must reach the pastor before the day of the service. To encourage personal interest in the service, the pastor, as questions were asked of him when making pastoral calls or at other times, frequently said, "Won't you please hand in this question in writing for our Question Box Meeting?"

In the Metropolitan Methodist Temple, New York, Rev. S. P. Cadman, pastor, the people are divided into prayer circles, which meet for prayer and testimony in the class rooms before the regular prayer meeting. Afterwards, they assemble in the main room for a twenty-minute exposition of the Scripture.

The Rev. Elijah Horr, D.D., pastor of the Piedmont Congregational Church of Worcester, Mass., scores a very good point when he invites people "to come in at any time during the meeting." He adds that "no one is asked to take any part. All are invited to do so, but

---

[1] Dr. Gladden's Parish Problems, p. 256.

all know that there will be no constraint or restraint." This last plan emphasizes the family idea. The intimate fellowship that appreciates the fact that Mr. A. has to be at the store late and cannot get to prayer meeting at the beginning, or that Mrs. B. must get the children settled for the night before she can come, and that makes it possible for these and other tired people to slip into their seats at any time during the service without shame or confusion, is one of the things that makes the prayer meeting the home gathering-place of the church. Then the informal speech without being called upon is suggestive of the home life.

Music is one of the best aids to make the prayer meeting attractive, but it is too much neglected even in those churches which have excellent music at other services. The minister is afraid to give out an unfamiliar hymn, and so the old hymns are droned out month after month. To improve the music, it may be well to get a precentor and occasionally have the meeting convene a little earlier and the time be devoted to singing new, bright tunes. It will increase the attendance and put new life into the service.

The prayer-meeting topic is also a matter for thought. Groups of subjects unfolding different phases of the same theme may be studied on successive evenings, or consecutive portions of the Bible may be subjects for study. Whatever the plan, it is always best to have the topic of the evening and the Scripture reference understood in advance. In the preparation of these topics, a variety may be introduced by inviting the congregation to hand in subjects that they would like to have taken under prayerful consideration. From the topics handed in, the pastor selects the list for the quarter, announcing that it was impossible to include all.

THE PRAYER MEETING.

In former times, it was customary in several denominations to devote one evening in the month to a missionary concert, and it is a pity that so excellent a practice should be abandoned. With care in arranging the programme, with some special music, these evenings may be made attractive and most helpful. Oftentimes persons who will not ordinarily take part in the weekly meeting may be induced to do so by having papers assigned to them on missionary subjects, and thus a knowledge of this great work spreads among the congregation, genuine interest is elicited in missions, and new voices are heard in the prayer meeting.

The question of participation in the prayer meeting by both sexes may seem to Western readers one settled long ago; but it is still very seriously believed in some Eastern churches that Paul's injunction to women to "keep silent" is to be literally taken. Such churches are great losers. Personally, I believe this to be a form of that ignorance that God in former times winked at, but now commandeth all men everywhere to repent of.[1] In the large formal gatherings of the church, there may be two opinions as to the advisability of woman's voice being heard; but in the family meeting, she should be at liberty to take such part as her conscience dictates.

The practice of having the pastor lead the midweek meeting seems to be most satisfactory to the majority of churches, but the plan of having it conducted by officers of the church and gifted laymen in rotation has been successfully tried in others.

But whoever leads, whoever takes part, or whatever adjuncts or methods be employed, the prayer meeting will not fill up the measure of its usefulness unless it is the place where "friend holds fellowship with

[1] Acts xvii. 30.

friend." In some churches arrangement is made for a pleasant tarrying on the part of the attendants. There is a convenient grouping of chairs or arrangement of settees, and everything possible is done to encourage sociability and to suggest an informal reunion at the close of the meeting.

There are other things that ought to be remembered of the prayer meeting. Though the suggestions may not be new, they are vitally important. First, every prayer meeting should commence promptly on time, though no one is present but the pastor, and should close promptly on time. A careful observation of this principle always encourages attendance, and is otherwise helpful.

Second, the meeting is deserving of the most painstaking and prayerful preparation on the part of the pastor. Is this preparation always given? The people, I believe, will come when they find the spiritual help which their souls crave. Having made careful preparation, another danger confronts the minister, — and one which, according to common fame, is often yielded to, — that of taking up too much time. The meeting then gives way to a lecture, and the nature of the service as a prayer meeting and as a people's meeting is lost sight of.

Third, the prayer meeting should be the place where plainness of dress is the rule, where there is no haste to go away, and where the humblest church-member is met and greeted with heartfelt interest in his welfare, where the story of trouble is heard with sympathy, and where the news of good fortune awakens sincerest joy. No formality can exist where such feeling reigns. The heart of the toiling and sorrowing will then turn to the prayer meeting as the child to its mother. No effort will be needed to draw the people

THE PRAYER MEETING.

together, and stormy nights will see the room well filled. Here the burdened pastor will find the reward of his labor, and the stranger the green spot in all the arid week, and each succeeding gathering will slip away into eternity only to bring nearer the glad reunion of the household of God.

CHAPTER XV.

THE COTTAGE PRAYER MEETING.

WHEN Peter had been released from prison by the angel of the Lord, he went straight to a cottage prayer meeting in the house of Mary, the mother of John. The homes of many Christians have been glorified by such gatherings for prayer; meetings that have ever been a means of grace. The informality of the gathering appeals to the heart, and many of those who will not attend the regular midweek meeting of the church may be won to the neighbor's fireside and thus be brought under spiritual influences. There are two reasons why these prayer meetings should be held: first, on account of their influence on the church. Such meetings increase the heart acquaintance of the church-members with each other and with those whom they would reach, and deepen the common interest in the spiritual life of the church. Then, by means of the cottage gatherings, the prayer service may be taken to those members who are unable to attend the regular midweek prayer meeting. There are in every congregation those who through age or infirmity are unable to get to church. And there are others who have the care of invalids and young children and consequently cannot attend the usual services of worship. With many churches the cottage prayer meetings are not held twice in the same place, but are carried to different parts of the parish in succeeding weeks. Second,

THE COTTAGE PRAYER MEETING.

cottage prayer meetings should be held on account of the influence on the outside world. These meetings stand to the people around the church as the social settlement does to the community. Such meetings attract attention, and from them flow streams of influence which permeate the remotest parts of the community. A woman in New York City gathers into a prayer meeting held weekly at her home from thirty to forty working men and women, to whom the prayer circle would otherwise be unknown. She obtains the help of some of the members of her church in carrying on the meetings, and their work has been wonderfully blessed: many of the people who come to the meetings have been brought through its influence into the fellowship of the church; others have been brought into the Sunday-school and church attendance. If such a meeting could not be conveniently held continuously in one home, it might be held for a month or three months at one house, and then for a like period in another.

A similar plan should be in operation in every church in addition to the work done in the churches and missions. Besides the fraternal and spiritual benefits which accrue from such gatherings, they have the merit of being inexpensive. When we read of the tremendous average cost of each convert in this country, and on the other hand read the pitiful appeals for money and men from fields where the millions have never once heard the Gospel story, we realize that there is something wrong in our methods, and that we ought by all means to do this thing also and not to leave the other undone.

Cottage prayer meetings have been successfully conducted for many years by the churches of Oberlin, O., that centre of religious activity, where the life-work of the sainted Finney still goes on. The congregations of the principal churches of Oberlin are divided into prayer circles somewhat after the plan of the "classes" in the Methodist Church. Cottage prayer meetings are also being carried on by many other churches throughout our country.

This return to the simple ways of the early Church has a wonderful hold upon the heart. It was the custom of the early Church to meet for prayer at the homes of the adherents to the new faith. The seventy, as they went out two by two, must have gathered the families to whom they brought the message of life into many an hour of quiet prayer. And this home prayer service was hallowed also by the presence and prayers of our blessed Lord.

CHAPTER XVI.

OPEN-AIR PREACHING.

Open-air preaching is not a new thing. It is as old as the Garden of Eden. Scripture abounds with allusions to open-air preaching, and records many such a sermon. The holy prophets of old, on the streets, or wherever they found the people, lifted up their voices in warning. We associate John the Baptist with great sermons and the open skies of the wilderness. There was the open-air sermon of Pentecost, the ringing open-air messages of the seventy, and Paul's address on Mars' Hill. Our blessed Lord went out through the dusty highways and taught the crowd that followed him, or spoke to them from the little craft anchored off the shore. He preached to the one woman at the well, preached in the streets of Jericho, Jerusalem, and Capernaum, and preached the great Sermon on the Mount under the open skies and from the commanding heights of the hills. The most of his preaching was out of doors. Coming down through the years, we find that some of the greatest teachers of the centuries, John Knox, Roland Hill, Spurgeon and Moody, Whitefield and the Wesleys, have preached in the open air.

In England services have been carried on out of doors to an extent that has never been undertaken in this country. There are one thousand open-air preachers in London, and they are not only of the Salvation Army and the City Mission, but the leading ministers of the city, numbering such men as the Bishop of Bedford and Lord Rodstock. St. Mary's Church, Whitechapel, the scene of so many murders, has a pulpit built into its outer wall, and clergymen preach every Sunday to the people that crowd to hear them in that district renowned for wickedness.

The Presbyterians in London have a committee devoted to this special work. The famous preacher, Rev. John McNeil, D.D., when a pastor in London, often preached in the park. Rev. Newman Hall, D.D., has a service in front of his church every Sunday night in summer. Rev. Mr. Woffendale, a Presbyterian minister, goes out with a company of young people to some distance from his church. There they pause and sing, while others distribute hand-bills containing invitations to the services; a few words are spoken, and the company passes on. Another minister in London sends out his young men in different directions. They bring in all they can gather, and go out again. The service begins at half-past seven, and continues for two hours and a half, and it is estimated that of the thousand members of the church two thirds were converts from open-air preaching.

Rev. Mr. Stewart, a rector of London, sends four bands of young men to occupy different stations. The next Sunday they occupy four others, so that he has the Gospel preached to every man in his parish during a month. The Christian Evidence Society conducts Gospel services from a platform erected in one of the parks. Numerous cases are recorded of the triumphs of the Cross and the silencing of those who came to scoff.[1]

Rev. E. P. Hammond says, "The rule or law of the

---

[1] Edwin H. Byington, Fifth Convention of Christian Workers, Hartford, Conn., 1890, pp. 357-360.

OPEN-AIR PREACHING.

Presbytery of Glasgow is that every minister shall once a month, at least, preach in the open air." [1]

Open-air services have been conducted with great success in this country. Rev. Frederick Campbell, pastor of Jefferson Park Presbyterian Church, Chicago, says that during the summer of 1895 he conducted outdoor services for three months with marked success. In each case an after-service inside the church was held, and a large per cent of the crowd, of the very class he most wanted to reach, followed him into the meeting. They were attentive, respectful, and evidently deeply impressed.

The Broome Street Tabernacle, New York, has an out-of-door meeting, notice of which is placed in the church bulletin, and is as permanent as any other service of the church. This meeting is usually held some distance from the church. When the workers at the meeting return, bringing with them such as are impressed, a pleasant tea is served them by the ladies. After tea a prayer meeting is held in special interest of those who have asked for prayer in the outdoor meeting. In this way the church holds together the workers, who are converts from the class which the church is trying to reach.

The Fourth Congregational Church of Hartford, Conn., has preaching from its church porch. After this service the people are invited to go to church. Their attention is called to the different churches in the neighborhood, and they are assured of a hearty welcome from any of them. For this work there is a band of four pieces, and they hold, in addition to the service mentioned above, another at the baseball grounds, and yet another in the rougher part

---

[1] Second Convention of Christian Workers, New York, 1887, p. 154.

of the city. The Bethany Presbyterian Church of Philadelphia has open-air services, conducted by a brotherhood of young men. In St. George's Episcopal Church, New York, the Brotherhood of St. Andrew holds open-air services in front of the mission on Sunday afternoon. The Boston Baptist Tabernacle holds a variety of open-air meetings,— at the wharves, among Sunday workers, and at many points where men congregate in idleness.

The most familiar example of outdoor worship was, in the past, the camp or tent meeting. This has, in later years, been adapted to the town by the erection of tents for holding religious services on some vacant lot. Here the people may be gathered night after night, during the heated term, when it would be impossible to get them to go into a hot, close hall. Then, too, those who would not go to a religious meeting may, perchance, in passing, pause to hear a sweet Gospel song, or may catch some word of entreaty that will strike home to the conscience. In the summer of 1896, tent meetings were successfully held in New York, and resulted in many conversions.

Still more effective in reaching the masses, who will not go to the place where the Word is preached, is the Gospel wagon, since it may be moved into densely populated neighborhoods, where there is no chance to put up a tent. Two or three audiences may be addressed on the same night, and a large number of people reached. Besides the crowd that gathers around the wagon, there is an invisible audience within the houses in the vicinity.

In Washington, D. C., they have a Gospel pushcart, which can get still closer to the people, as it can be moved by hand into narrow alleys where a wagon could not be drawn. The Gospel wagon is manned

OPEN-AIR PREACHING.

by a corps of earnest workers who are able to sing or speak in the power of the Holy Spirit. A portable organ is of great assistance in the music. In some cases a number of volunteer workers accompany the wagon on foot. The office of these is to notice those who seem affected by the talk, and to enter into conversation with them and strive to bring them to Christ. After the speaking and singing, opportunity is given to signify the desire for a better life, and an after-meeting is held, when personal work is done. The wagons also distribute tracts and sell or give away Bibles and Testaments.

The Gospel wagon may very profitably be used in the village or city park, by the beach or common outing-place, and services conducted for the benefit of those who throng such places during the hot evenings of summer. By Gospel wagon I do not mean any particular wagon, although wagons are made for that distinct purpose. Gospel wagons are improvised. Any vehicle serving the purpose of elevation and transportation is made use of every year by many ministers for this purpose. There is never want for a congregation. People are attentive, and there are reports of many conversions.

The work spoken of above has been largely that of the city church; but let it be remembered that the country church has as large opportunity for successful outdoor preaching. The country church, too, may carry its aggressive work into its outlying districts in the summer time, and thus the busy farmer will not have too far to go to reach and enjoy the privilege of Gospel services. Whether, then, the message be told in the city, by the restless sea, or in the quiet country, it shall be told, and the summer days be no less filled with work for God than the working months of the winter.

CHAPTER XVII.

CHAPELS AND MISSIONS.

I AM persuaded that the religious work of chapels and missions can be less expensively, if not more successfully, conducted than is usual in such branch-work of churches. There has been room for improvement. The Gospel services of some chapels and missions have suffered a dragging existence, and the spiritual results have not been, according to the confession of men in charge, as large as they believed that they had reason to expect. On the other hand, while the churches with institutional departments have met with unusual spiritual results, yet the number of such expensive plants, until the wealth of Christians is more consecrated than now, must necessarily be limited. Therefore, instead of the parish-house displacing missions and chapels, there promises to be an increasing demand for them, especially in the cities; for it is here that the great tide of population is coming, in high and mighty waves. "In one century the population in cities of 8,000 or more has risen from one thirtieth to nearly one third of the whole, the rate of increase being much greater from 1880 to 1890 than ever before."[1] Not only is the population massing in cities, but those parts of the cities where the population is densest have the fewest churches. This fact is so

---

[1] The New Era, by Dr. Strong, pp. 164, 165.

proverbial that it is not necessary to give statistics proving the statement. All this goes to show that there will be an increasing demand for chapels and missions. There are simple, practicable ways of conducting such missions, reached by long and costly experience, which are being blessed to large increase in efficiency and results of the spiritual work.

First, as to the religious services. How can these meetings be most successfully conducted? The plan of the McAll Mission, as that of the Pleasant Sunday Afternoon in England and America, is marked by variety. Different speakers present the gospel message, though some one is recognized and is always present as permanent leader, known, possibly, as the superintendent of the mission. In the McAll Mission two persons frequently give short talks the same evening. It is the genius of the Pleasant Sunday Afternoon that some new face address the meeting at every service. *It gives the opportunity for the use of a large number of lay workers.* The plan has been tried by some chapels and missions in the United States with the most gratifying results. It is true, almost without exception, that the most successful missions in our cities are those following the plan of frequently having different speakers. The plan of different speakers for short talks is the plan, too, advocated by so thoughtful a writer and experienced worker as the Rev. Dr. Josiah Strong.

Care should be exercised, of course, to have the best available speakers. But the testimony or short talk from stammering lips is often used by the Spirit with great power. If there is loss in the flow of speech, there is gain in the endless stream of living witnesses. Not only should there be different speakers, but different meetings, also, should be differently conducted. It is a principle of Mr. Moody, I understand, so to conduct meetings as not to be anticipated in any part of the programme. Variety in music — quartette, vocal and instrumental solos, chorus, and responsive singing — will add to the brightness of the meetings. Dryness is not essential to orthodoxy, and truth that runs in ruts is not the most effective. Minds are kept alert by varying the programme from time to time: responsive readings, readings in concert, quoting individually verses of Scripture, quoting passages in concert, give pleasant variety. Another successful plan is to assign some chapter, and pass little slips on which the members of the audience are to place the number of their favorite verse in the chapter; then the cards are collected by the ushers and classified; all the verses chosen are read in order, when the number of persons selecting the verse is announced. The artisan classes, for the most part, think differently, feel differently, and are moved differently from their more "well-to-do" neighbors; and unless we can put down our formalism at the feet of Jesus Christ, and adapt ourselves to the conditions and methods that will prevail, an innumerable company will continue to live Christless lives and die Christless deaths.

But it is not enough that the meetings be special and specially good; there must also be a personal interest. Some missions send, as often as once a month, a circular letter to the attendants of the gospel services. This makes the invitation special and individual. A mimeographed letter or a neatly printed circular can be sent. If a mimeographed letter is used, the expense will be but a trifle, save in the mailing of the letters. But the increase in attendance gained will, by an increase in the collections, usually more than cover the expense. The plan is an invaluable aid in gaining attendants and regular attendance on the gospel services. There is something in the fact that Uncle Sam brings the letter that makes it appreciated. We all know that! It is a secret little pleasure that we never outgrow. It is to be said that one address will answer for a family, but such envelope address should be as inclusive as possible. For example, if the family consists of father, mother, and children, address Mr. and Mrs. H. C. Smith and family. These little things are not more closely noticed or appreciated by the richer than by the poorer classes. All this is helpful, but there is still more that can be done to magnify the importance of the individual.

It is desirable that each attendant feel that he is a part of the chapel; that he is responsible for and in a measure essential to its success. Those who unite with the church, of course, will appreciate their privilege and duty, but others enjoy belonging to something, and a gain of attendance and interest will be made by having an "attendants membership." The word "attendant" is used, that such enrolment may not be confused with membership of the church. To be enrolled as an attendant, application is made by signing a little card which bears the simple statement, "I desire to be enrolled as a regular attendant on the gospel meetings of —— Chapel." The back of the card usually states the advantages of such enrolment and the duties which will be expected of the applicant, such as regular attendance as far as practicable upon the Chapel meetings, helping its interest in any way possible, also speaking well of the chapel and its members, and so forth. When the card is signed, a pass-book is handed the applicant which may bear some thoughts similar to the following: "This book will admit the bearer to the socials, the annual supper, and special services at the chapel. This book will also insure the member all the privileges of the chapel and its several societies under the usual conditions." The pass-book is made of red leather, with gold lettering on the outside, and containing a little leaflet of four pages within, bearing a list of the meetings, hints for helping in the work, and the following significant statement: "This pass is available so long as the superintendent of the chapel is kept informed as to your address. If you change your address, send word to the superintendent of —— Chapel." The pass-book idea was suggested by the pass-book of the Auxiliary League of the Salvation Army. When the expense of the book (about ten cents) may not be warranted, a neat card will serve the purpose.

The same effort to reach strangers and obtain their names should, of course, be made in the chapel as is made in the churches. There is nothing complex about this system. All is very simple. I do not see how less could be done, save the whole work be conducted in a loose and haphazard way.

But in addition to making much of the attendants, they should be made to do much. Every one enjoys being of use, enjoys realizing that he is of some aid in the work, is regarded as of sufficient worth to be used. To give all something to do must be one great study of the superintendent.

Second, as to the expenses of conducting the gospel services of chapels and missions. For fear of being misunderstood, and at the risk of appearing to repeat, I wish to say that the practicability of any plan must be determined by local conditions. The method of having lay speakers is a large saving of expense. The superintendent in charge, by this method, is spared the burden of preparing many addresses, and aside from the details of the work (about such as rest on the superintendent of a large Sunday-school), only presides at the meetings and acts in the capacity of pastor to the people. The labor is not so arduous as to demand all of the leader's time. A capable man, therefore, for a small compensation, can often be secured, and sometimes a volunteer leader can be obtained.

Now let us see how this plan works. There is a gospel and testimony meeting one evening every week, in which the attendants and members of the mission take part. One prayer meeting a week means fifty-two prayer meetings a year. The superintendent, though a day laborer and an uneducated man, in addition to presiding at every gospel service, will address the meeting as many as four times a year. The pastor of the home church and the superintendent of the Mission Sunday-school will each address the meeting as many as four times during the year. This leaves forty meetings to be provided for by a board of ten officers of the home church. These officers, in alphabetical rotation, are present at the prayer meeting, and give the opening address, — each officer appearing four times during the year, and at the considerable interval of ten weeks. In addition to the interest awakened by the new faces and the helpfulness to the people of the personal presence and interest of different men, there is a reflex influence upon the church which is felt for good in its every part. This work, in being an outlet for the energy of the members of the church, cannot be over-estimated. Our church work has lacked, in some measure, the balance and support of the man influence and interest; but bring men into touch with great needs, poverty of spirit and life, and they will see that there is something practical and real that they can do, and will respond as steel to the magnet. This plan provides for the weekly prayer meeting of the mission. The Sunday-evening services may be similarly conducted. There is always a goodly number in the church to draw upon for such meetings, such as members of the Young People's Societies, Missionary Societies, Men's Club, Sunday-school teachers, and others. Then, too, the community can be drawn upon; addresses can be secured from lawyers, physicians, business men, and other laymen. This plan of developing and using lay forces by placing the chapel in the charge of lay workers is in successful operation in the Ninth Street Baptist Church of Cincinnati, O., Rev. W. G. Partridge, pastor. This church has six chapels in different parts of the city, and the work has been greatly blessed; through the efforts of the missions many souls have been won to Jesus Christ, and brought into the membership of the church. By using many lay speakers, the McAll Mission "can conduct a hundred missions at a total expense for salaries of only $18,000. With us, a hundred city missions would mean more than a hundred paid missionaries at the expense of not less than $200,000." [1] In commenting on this difference, Dr. Strong says: "Of course salaries are larger here than in France, but that is only an added reason for adopting cheaper methods." [1] Should the demands for the services of an ordained minister at the church proper be so large that he could not meet them, why not place the several chapels under the control of one minister, giving him

[1] The New Era, p. 336.

CHAPELS AND MISSIONS.

the assistance of lay workers, as in the plan outlined above. It would soon be found, I believe, that various lines of work, in addition to the gospel services, could be carried on for the benefit of the residents and their associates.

The foolish objection, often urged, by which many churches excuse themselves from assuming mission work, is that their church is in a fashionable part of town. So much more reason for such a church carrying on mission work! for it has both the means and the ability; nor is that church which is less fortunate financially, exempt from such missionary work.

A most comprehensive plan, and one but recently formulated, is known as the "Buffalo Plan," whereby many churches of Buffalo, including Congregational, Methodist Episcopal, Presbyterian, Roman Catholic, Baptist, Lutheran, Hebrew, Unitarian, and other denominations have blocked out the city, assigning a section to the care and supervision of each church, whose duty it is "to look after all needy persons in it who are not otherwise helped, and to aid them in any way possible, and in connection with the Charity Organization to keep close watch upon the condition of the people in the district. Sometimes the district assigned to a church is in its immediate vicinity; but if it is a strong church, and located in a well-to-do quarter of the city, it is more likely to receive a district in the poorer portion of the city."[1] This scheme does not preclude the church working in districts other than the one assigned; it but insures that the church will look thoroughly to the interest of that district. As a result of this co-operative plan, a large work on institutional lines, such as classes, clubs, educational and social work,

[1] The Independent, July 23, 1896, p. 13.

has already been commenced, and the plan gives great promise for the future.

All this goes to show what a large work can be accomplished, and how the members of the church can be made of real service. We must make larger use of lay workers or suffer the world to be lost. It is all nonsense for any church to assume that it has not capable workers within its membership. All can do far more in the work for Christ than we usually think; the thing that we as pastors need to do is to give the people a chance and encourage them to do. Neither pastors nor people have a right to stand on excuses.

"It is not by might, nor by power, but by my Spirit, saith the Lord." [1]

[1] Zechariah iv. 6.

CHAPTER XVIII.

COUNTRY EVANGELIZATION.

It is the farm and the village that yearly furnish our municipal and national life, civic and religious, with a great part of its new blood and best working force. Statistics show that the greater proportion of the young men who enter the ministry received their early religious instruction in some country parish, and it is well known that the greatest men of our nation have been, for the most part, those who came from the farm or smaller town. Dr. Mark Hopkins said, "You might sweep the whole of the city of New York into the ocean to-morrow, and the country would recover quicker and come out of it better than if you should destroy a similar number of men and an equivalent amount of property in the country towns."[1] If this be true, and the value to the nation of the men and institutions of the country is so great, it must also be true of the church, which is the very heart of any community, and indicates by its pulsations the ebb and flow of the life blood within. In view of the great importance of the rural church as a conservator of our country's weal and of the principles of the Church at large, indifference to its welfare is greatly to be regretted. City evangelization, the home church, missions, and other worthy causes have

[1] Quoted by Rev. S. W. Dike, D.D., Christianity Practically Applied, p. 417.

claimed our attention to the exclusion of country evangelization.

Now, what are some of the opportunities for country evangelization? It is said that one-half of the people of the State of Vermont never go to church;[1] and when we remember that Vermont is essentially a rural State, with no great cities of large foreign population to swell the number of the unchurched, the statement is astounding. Here, then, right at the door of the country ministers of that State is a field which rivals that surrounding any church in the larger cities. The Rev. Samuel W. Dike, D.D., says that the non-church-goers in the fourteen northern States east of the Mississippi consist largely of those who live more than two miles from the nearest church, the proportion being fifty per cent greater outside that limit than within it.[2] Is it not as clearly the duty of the country church to carry the Gospel outside the two-mile limit as it is incumbent on the city church to overflow into "tenement districts"? Dr. Josiah Strong, after careful investigation, estimates that more than one-half of our entire rural population are non-church-goers. He says: "A large proportion of those who do attend live in the villages, while probably seventy per cent of those who live two miles from church (which of course means farmers) do not attend. As two-thirds of our entire population live in the country, it is evident that farmers constitute a large proportion of the non-church-going class."[3] Clearly, then, here is a great field, unworked, and within reach of the village and town churches.

---

[1] Prof. G. Frederick Wright of Oberlin College, Interior, June 19, 1890.

[2] Quoted by Professor Wright, Ibid.

[3] The New Era, p. 207.

COUNTRY EVANGELIZATION.

And if this great country population is not reached, it is due to the criminal neglect of those churches. 'Go,' says Christ, 'and disciple the world, and I will give you the omnipotent power.'[1]

It may not be possible to bring the people beyond a few miles' limit into the church, but it is possible to take the church to the people. The village church has the best of opportunities for doing a large *missionary* work. Many churches conduct services regularly in school-houses of the out-lying country districts. These places of working are called "Stations," and are regarded by the parent church as an organic part of its work, the meetings being conducted, and the largest part of the pastoral work done, by laymen under the direction of the minister. Rev. Newton W. Cadwell, pastor of the Presbyterian Church at Westfield, N. J., has four such stations in districts outside his parish. Each is in charge of a superintendent, who, with most of the teachers in the station school, are members of the home church. The following excellent points give an outline of his work in his own words: —

"1. Always a Sunday-school on Sabbath afternoon.
2. Always a Christian Endeavor meeting once a week.
3. Always a Christmas and Children's Anniversary.
4. Always invited to the home church festivals and special services.
5. Always invited to go with us on our annual summer excursion to seashore, and share in the profits.
6. Always consult the Superintendents every few days.

"Results: Many additions to the church. New people developed and trained for church workers. Most loyal adherents found in outside schools."

A similar movement was started in Oberlin, O., in the fall of 1890. Meetings were held in sixteen out-

[1] Matthew xxviii. 19, 20.

MODERN METHODS IN CHURCH WORK.

lying country districts, some of them several miles from the village. In less than a year one hundred and ninety conversions were reported. What has been done in one country parish may be accomplished in another. The plan of working is simple. In the home church some one usually is found living near the objective centre of the new work who will act as superintendent. If not, a little of the enthusiasm that sends a citizen out in that direction to hunt up voters in the fall may be aroused in the church-members by the minister who wants to see righteousness carry by a good large majority. The Christian Endeavor or other Young People's Society is of great aid in this work. Pledged to active Christian service, the members of this Society will lend themselves to carrying on aggressive work if the pastor co-operates with them and directs their energy. A committee of the Endeavor Society of the home church may have in charge the organization of branch societies in the stations, and may go out on Sunday afternoon to assist in carrying on the Sunday-school. The work of the station once well organized, the Christian Endeavor Society is naturally cared for by the attendants from the district; the same interest and readiness for prayer and testimony prevailing here as characterizes such meetings everywhere. The Christian Endeavor meeting may be the weekly prayer meeting of the station. And when impossible to have a gospel address or sermon each week, the Christian Endeavor meeting is, for the time being, the centre of their Christian work and worship. In this way a great many workers are developed.

To reach those in the country who from ill health or lack of facilities to get to the station are kept away from the meetings, the Home Department of

COUNTRY EVANGELIZATION.

the Sunday-school has been found to be of great service. When to this is added the invitation to help in such enterprises of the church as may be participated in at home, such as help with the missionary box or furnishing supplies for the picnic or church festival, so much interest and enthusiasm for the church is aroused that obstacles deemed at first insuperable are overcome, and the non-attendant developed into the regular church-goer.

How shall this work of evangelizing the country be inaugurated? In the first place, the ministers of villages and smaller cities must realize their responsibility for country evangelization. They must preach Christ, the Saviour of the WORLD, and work for a MISSIONARY church. Is this possible with a church so feeble that it is barely holding its own, the number of yearly accessions scarcely counterbalancing those who pass away? If so, what is the first step? Organize the Christian Endeavor, Epworth League, or a society with similar principles, but do not limit the membership to the very young. The prestige of these societies has penetrated to the remotest hamlet, and the people will be glad to join them. With this organization at the heart of the church, with the hearty co-operation of the officers of the church (which the pastor must by all means secure), with his personal influence and preaching, the smouldering church may be made a "burning and a shining light."

A series of revival meetings for the benefit of the church itself is always helpful. When there is an aroused interest and consciousness of spiritual blessing, then come with strongest message on the duty of the church to the unsaved around them. God's people will not prove unfaithful; but every church,

MODERN METHODS IN CHURCH WORK.

I believe, will cry out, "What can we do to help them?" Some one has said that the way to carry a reform is so to labor that people will say, "Why, this is our reform." That is the wise way of conducting every good movement. Guiding, but avoiding all appearance of driving, the pastor will lead his people to suggest the effort to gather in the people in the surrounding neighborhoods. A committee can then be appointed to see the trustees and obtain the use of a given school-house or to secure other suitable place for services, and get permission to announce in the day school a series of meetings. A week's meetings, with every effort being made to get all the people of the vicinity to attend, may close with the organization of a Sunday-school and a Christian Endeavor or other similar society, as may be practicable. The work of one station would then be strongly inaugurated. Let not the home church grudge the money to buy Gospel Hymns; it will come back in a harvest of treasure and souls. Other stations may be occupied as time goes on, and soon the church will be the centre of a large, aggressive work.

All this presupposes hard work, — work that may be regarded as beyond reason by some members of the country church, though not exceeding that performed without question by workers in a city church, amid all the demands upon the time incident to life in town. It is a matter of education as well as spiritual fitness, but the pastor who himself yearns to extend the kingdom will best succeed with his people in this work.

A house-to-house canvass of the field (as indicated in the chapter on "Reaching the People Outside the Church") will prove of incalculable aid in reaching the country people.

COUNTRY EVANGELIZATION.

Efforts to evangelize the territory circumjacent to the country church is one of the conditions, I believe, of the spiritual growth of that church. Little wonder that rural churches dwindle away when many of them do no missionary work of this kind! "He that abideth in me, and I in him, the same bringeth forth much fruit."[1] So long as the country churches fail to go with the Gospel, so long will they be cursed with barrenness and suffer a struggling existence.

> "Faith, simple faith, the promise sees,
> And looks to that alone;
> Laughs at impossibilities,
> And cries, It shall be done."

[1] John xv. 5.

CHAPTER XIX.

MEN'S CLUBS.

GRAND as is the work of the Men's Sunday Evening Club, it is evident that this society is not adapted to all churches. The Sunday evening service may already be under successful management, or the need of the field may demand a comprehensive society for various lines of work.

1. A society of men, organized for general church work, and one of the largest and most successful of its kind, is the Westminster Club, in the Westminster Church, Buffalo, N. Y., of which Rev. Samuel Van Vranken Holmes is pastor. The Club holds monthly meetings at the private residences of members, when a literary programme is followed by refreshments and a social good time.

The Constitution and By-Laws of this Club are model ones. According to the Constitution the object of the organization is to secure the associated services of the men of Westminster Church and Congregation in religious, philanthropic, and social work. The officers are a president, three vice-presidents, a treasurer, recording secretary, and corresponding secretary. These officers with the pastor *ex officio* constitute an executive board for the governing of the Club. There are three general standing committees, of each of which one of the vice-presidents of the Club is chairman, viz.: 1. Committee on Religious Affairs; 2.

MEN'S CLUBS.

Philanthropic Committee; 3. Social Committee. In addition to these, there is also a Topic Committee, Membership Committee, and provision for such other committees as the executive board may direct. The work of the Topic Committee is by no means a small one. It is their duty to provide topics for discussion and suitable speakers, at the regular meetings, and to furnish the Corresponding Secretary the material for his announcements at least two weeks in advance. While it is the special duty of the Social Committee to promote the social interests of the Church and of the Club by welcoming strangers and by providing suitable entertainments, yet it is the thought and purpose of the Club that this *social spirit* should prevail with all the members of the association. The annual dues of members are three dollars; each member has the privilege of inviting one gentleman to any regular meeting of the Club (except annual meetings) provided he secure the permission of the host at least three days in advance.

In answer to an inquiry as to the result and influence of the work of this Club, Rev. Mr. Holmes writes: "Two years of deepening interest and growing work have served to establish the Club as one of the most important factors in our church life. Men hitherto unidentified with any form of organized church effort are now enthusiastic workers; men of different interests and from different relations in society have been brought into close and friendly contact; and one detects a spirit of loyal attachment to Westminster Church, which before was lacking. The large success of the Club in these regards has been due, I think, to two causes. First, the care that has been taken by the Topic Committee to make each meeting one of interest and profit to thoughtful and cultivated minds.

Prominent men, many of them specialists from out of the city, have been secured to speak at the monthly meetings; and in no instance have we been disappointed. Men will attend the Club meetings only when they can be sure that the effort will be repaid; and without such regular and general attendance, a church club will quickly languish and die. In the second place, work of far-reaching importance has been undertaken, giving each member something to do. Westminster House, our Social Settlement, has been supported and managed entirely by the Club. In the past year $3,000 has been raised for its maintenance, and many of the men have given an evening each week to the care of the various clubs and classes incident to settlement work. The good thus accomplished can hardly be estimated, while its reflex influence upon the men of the parish has been enormous. Westminster Club is just entering on its third year of life with membership of one hundred and fourteen, with prospects brighter than ever before, and with a philanthropic fervor among the men of the church which could have been quickened in no other way. I can cordially commend the organization work of our Club to other churches. Especially to those churches which, like Westminster, have among their number men from different walks of life, and some wealth at their command, I am convinced that our methods are suited to accomplish the largest and most lasting results."

With organization almost identical with that of the Westminster Club, the Men's Society of the Church of the Covenant, Washington, D. C., is doing a large and aggressive work. Rev. Teunis S. Hamlin, D.D., the pastor of this church, writes: "The Men's Society of the Church of the Covenant has been very useful during its two and a half years of existence, in enlisting the interest and services of men not before actively identified with any form of the work. Our Religious Committee conducts evangelistic services from time to time at our mission, takes part in our midweek service, and is generally useful. The Philanthropic Committee does much good among the poor, maintains a reading-room at the mission, etc. The Social Committee prepares our monthly programme, always excellent, serves refreshments at each meeting, calls on strangers, etc. The total effect of the Society has been a marked accession of *esprit de corps* throughout the ranks of our men."

2. LABORING-MEN'S CLUBS. When we come to provide for, and aim to reach, working-men, it is evident that our plans must again be modified to meet the changed conditions and different personalities with which we have to do. Great masses of laboring men live in cramped apartments of one or two rooms that are gloomy, dirty, and filthy ; especially is this true of our tenement population. What is called " home " is a cheerless, depressing place. The men go to the street for diversion. But the policemen and lamp-posts are not companionable. What are they to do? The church is closed. But the saloon is open, and for five cents they can find fellowship, be on a footing of equality, have a mug of beer, smoke, talk, and share a room that is warm, lighted, and cheery. It is plain that the social side of the life of the laboring-man must be taken into account in our dealing with him. There are some churches that have appreciated this fact and have organized men's week-day social clubs. These clubs, while not distinctly religious, have proven helpful to the men and to the church.

In Pullman, Ill., such a club was organized under the auspices of the Greenstone Presbyterian Church.

It is called the Young Men's Institute. There is no charge for membership, and the privileges afforded are very great. A reading-room, gymnasium, bowling-alley, and large lecture hall are a part of the equipment, while lecture courses, scientific classes, and an ambulance corps are being arranged for the future.

In connection with the Chapel Clergy House of Grace Church, New York, there is a Men's Social Club, which holds weekly meetings. The first meeting in the month is for business, the third is social, and a great variety of entertainment is given, comprising music, recitations, and lectures. On the other club nights, the men meet informally. Rev. Melville K. Bailey, assistant minister, says, that while the club-room is supplied with newspapers and periodicals and has a fine library, the men make very little use of these things. In the main they come to meet each other, the clergy and lay helpers, so it is along this friendly line that the members of the Club are reached. No distinctly religious feature is introduced into the meetings of the Club, but the members are invited to attend the church services in general, and a special invitation is given on occasions of particular interest to them. Mr. Bailey further says that the Men's Club is found to be the most effectual means in the chapel for attracting mature men to the church, and that by the visits of the clergy to the men in their homes, the members of the Club and their families are often led to confirmation, the communion, and other services of the church. He sums up the benefits of the Club as follows: —

"An advantage to the members in finding work.

"A stimulus to their mental life.

"A strengthening of the spirit of fraternity.

"A deepening of their religious life."

MEN'S CLUBS.

This social side of the working-man's nature, that part of him that wants companionship rather than culture, that prefers the plain room with his mates to the finely appointed one without them, is not taken into account always. And yet we ought to rejoice in it, for it is proof that he has a heart to reach, though he conceal it under much roughness of talk and uncouthness of behavior.

In speaking of the Pleasant Sunday Afternoon, Rev. F. B. Meyer, B.A., of Christ Church, London, tells how he carried out a business social for the benefit of the members of that brotherhood. He says: "At the end of two months, so many had joined that I felt it desirable to apportion the work amongst them, and therefore invited them one evening to a meat tea. This was a great occasion. The ladies of my congregation cooked the joints, which disappeared with surprising swiftness; and after the tables were cleared, the men arranged themselves around the platform for business. Then there took place an episode which to my working brothers cemented our union as tenaciously as salt does the Bedouin and the traveller. Every one who knows me knows that I neither smoke nor enjoy smoke, much less tobacco-smoke. But I knew that to a workingman smoke is more than food, and that if they could not smoke in the hall, some of them would be itching to get out to the street or public house. So I had invested ten shillings in the purchase of tobacco of a special quality, highly recommended by a friend on whose judgment I could rely. This was handed round amid the cheers of the men, accompanied by my explanation that I had no wish to impose my feelings in the matter on them, and that I could forgive the smoke if they would renounce the beer. 'To what purpose was this waste?' says some critic. But I refuse to consider that money wasted which enables you to weave a bond between another soul and yourself, forming a strand which will presently draw in the rope and that the cable and the twisted iron."[1]

Mr. Meyer certainly has had great success in welding the hearts of laboring-men to himself; and if the Church at large can get hold of them on their social side, she also may draw them to her by the "cable and the twisted iron" that had its origin in this simple strand. It is in appreciation of this fact, doubtless, that the 63d Street Mission of the Fifth Avenue Presbyterian Church, New York, Rev. John Hall, D.D., pastor, has a men's club-room with papers and periodicals, which is accessible at all hours of the day and evening, and where the men are permitted to smoke at any time. There is also a bowling-alley in connection with the club-room. St. Bartholomew Mission of the Church of St. Bartholomew, New York, also has such a club-room; and many other churches make the same provision for the laboring-man.

A somewhat different organization from the above mentioned, and one that may now be called a movement, as it has been and is being adopted by a large number of churches, is the Christian Industrial League.[2] This is a society *within* the church or mission, and its object is to organize the men of the church for the purpose of reaching men, especially those who are engaged in industrial pursuits, and train them to do personal Christian work among their fellows; to promote the domestic, social, and spiritual life of its members; to promote patriotism, and to give help in sickness by providing watchers, nurses, etc. In connection with

---

[1] Christian Treasury, February, '95, p. 37.

[2] For literature, constitution, and by-laws, etc., address, Christian Industrial League, Springfield, Mass.

MEN'S CLUBS.

the League is the Christian Industrial Benefit Association, the object of which is to provide for the temporal wants of its members and of family or friends in case of death. This association gives laboring-men the benefit of a society conducted on Christian and philanthropic business principles, encourages providence, and meets the need of providing for one's family in case of sickness or of death. It should be remembered that the Benefit Association is a voluntary step open to the members of the Industrial League. Strongest testimonials have been given by ministers as to the value of the League in organizing the men of the church, developing a spirit of Christian service, and winning men to Jesus Christ.

CHAPTER XX.

REACHING AND HOLDING YOUNG MEN.

IN the progress of the kingdom, no one thing in recent years is more significant than the aroused conscience and increasing interest and activity of young men in Christian work. The tide has turned. It is beating at the doors of our churches. All that it asks is a chance, — the open door. Wherever entrance has been given, the flow of a new life has come surging through the church, and with irresistible power. The following, from a pastor of one of the largest churches in Buffalo, N. Y., is illustrative of many messages received by me: "It is my conviction that the movement of the young men of our country toward supporting the Church at large and its interest has been marked of recent years; and instead of fewer young men attending service, a larger number are attending than ever before. Certainly, if my congregation is any indication, there is a far greater proportion of young men than young women in attendance, and I believe such may be found to be the case in most centres of population."[1]

A canvass of some of the colleges shows that the number of church communicants in the student body, Department of Liberal Arts, is as follows: —

Northwestern University	75%
Yale University	66%
Princeton University	64%

[1] Rev. Henry Elliott Mott, pastor of the Central Presbyterian Church.

REACHING AND HOLDING YOUNG MEN.

Cornell University	37%
University of Pennsylvania	50%
Oberlin College	85%
Michigan University	45%
Ohio Wesleyan University	85%

There is no doubt that the number of church communicants in most of the western colleges is much larger. When we remember that a hundred years ago Yale University had but four or five Christians in its entire student body,[1] we at once perceive the increasing hold of Christianity on young men. In Young Men's Christian Associations and other societies there is evidence of the same Christian awakening and aggressiveness. A church which is not reaching young men and holding them within its fellowship may well question the spirit and methods of its work.

The purpose of this chapter is to speak of four organized movements among young men of the church for aggressive Christian work. There are other societies doing a large and successful work, but their several methods are practically covered in one form or another by the following societies: the Brotherhood of St. Andrew,[2] the Brotherhood of Andrew and Philip,[3] the Young Men's Sunday Class, and the Young Men's Club.

I. The Brotherhood of St. Andrew is an organization of young men in the Protestant Episcopal Church. It was the example of this society which inspired the organization of the Brotherhood of Andrew and Philip for work among the non-Episcopal churches. A study of the Brotherhood of St. Andrew, therefore, will not

[1] Dorchester's Problem of Religious Progress, p. 107.

[2] Mr. John W. Wood, General Secretary, 281 Fourth Avenue, New York.

[3] Mr. Edgar M. Folsom, General Secretary, 93 West 103d Street, New York.

only inform us as to the work of that society, but will also help us to understand the work of the Brotherhood of Andrew and Philip. The following is from the Constitution of the St. Andrew Society: —

"*Object.* The sole object of the Brotherhood of St. Andrew is the spread of Christ's Kingdom among young men, and to this end every man desiring to become a member thereof must pledge himself to obey the rules of the Brotherhood so long as he shall be a member.

"*Rules.* These rules are two: The Rule of Prayer and the Rule of Service. The Rule of Prayer is to pray daily for the spread of Christ's Kingdom among young men and for God's blessing upon the labors of the Brotherhood. The Rule of Service is to make an earnest effort each week to bring at least one young man within the hearing of the Gospel of Jesus Christ."

The Brotherhood was organized in St. James Church, Chicago, on St. Andrew's Day, 1883. It takes its name from the apostle, who, when he had found the Messiah, went at once for his own brother Simon and brought him to Jesus. The work of the society from its inception was so successful in bringing non-church-going men into the services, that other chapters were soon started having the same object and two rules. Now, "by the influence of young men upon their fellows," and of one church upon another, the movement has grown until there are about fifteen hundred chapters with sixteen thousand and more members. There are one hundred and eighty-five chapters connected with the Church of England, forty in Australia; also chapters in English and American churches in various parts of the world, — Germany, West Indies, Barbadoes, British Honduras, New Zealand, and other places. This is a wonderful showing when we remember that the Brotherhood of St. Andrew is limited to one denomination and to one sex. It is a society of *young men* working for young men. The members are under a solemn obligation to pray and to work, and to pray every day and to do something definite *every week* " to bring at least one young man within hearing of the Gospel of Jesus Christ, as set forth in the services of the Church." The effort of the society is not for numbers, but for efficient workers. No drones are allowed within its busy hive. Those who join the Brotherhood do so not for what they can get, but for what they can give, as men whose minds and consciences are aflame with a holy desire to spread the Kingdom of Jesus Christ. Every man is a pledged worker, a pledged personal worker, a pledged praying worker, and a pledged definite worker, to reach some new man each week.

One thing that has long put off the millennium has been the shifting into the future what ought to be done to-day, instead of saying, "This one thing *I do*." It is only the men who are ready to do who are admitted to the membership of the Brotherhood of St. Andrew. This qualifying for membership by heart communion with God, and passionate heart longing to reach the lost, gives the Brotherhood of St. Andrew a somewhat unique position. It is positively refreshing to know of such a society, and it is an object lesson to every Christian worker. Its influence in time ought so to rattle the bones of sleeping organizations as either to shake to the dust the "rest-easies" or awaken them to the consciousness of Christian privilege and responsibility. Another good of the St. Andrew Society is the prevailing spirit of prayer which possesses the young men in their work and in their daily walk. The record of the chapters and their growth in numbers, and the deepening spirit of consecration in the members, speaks of the "quiet hour" and of the presence of the Holy Spirit.

MODERN METHODS IN CHURCH WORK.

Different lines of work are covered by the committees of the various chapters. Last year 1,072 chapters reported that their members regularly invite to church services friends and acquaintances who are irregular church-goers; 966 chapters reported regular efforts to bring men to baptism, confirmation, and holy communion; 1,174 reported work in welcoming men to church services and Bible classes; 725 reported Bible classes and a total membership in the neighborhood of 1,200; 350 distributed regularly, at houses and on the street, cards of invitation to service; 825 made special efforts to visit men in their homes; 540 did hotel work; 360 did work at hospitals, prisons, and other public institutions; 627 men were reported as acting as licensed lay readers; 370 chapters maintained or assisted in maintaining mission services.[1]

II. In thus detailing the work of the Brotherhood of St. Andrew, I have practically given the genesis of the Andrew and Philip Brotherhood, which was organized in 1888 by the Rev. Rufus W. Miller, D.D., of Reading, Penn., for churches of all denominations. It comprehends the essential features of the St. Andrew Society, but is inter-denominational. The Andrew and Philip Brotherhood, too, is not quite so stringent in requirements for membership. Some chapters, anyway, admit persons who have little more than a willingness to come. Such chapters argue that we must take young men as we find them, and lead them one step at a time into a larger and grander service. All that has been said in favor of the St. Andrew's Society is also to be said of the Brotherhood of Andrew and Philip.

The following committees are suggestive of the work which the chapters are covering in the several churches: Devotional, Social, Reading-Room, Adver-

[1] Statistics furnished by Mr. John W. Wood, General Secretary.

tising, Invitation, Vestibule, Flower, Visitation, Rescue, Strangers', Ushers', and Reception. The number and kind of these committees is determined, of course, by the needs of the chapter. The work of these brotherhoods has been far-reaching. But every society has its limitations, and no one plan avails for all.

III. Another way of working for and reaching young men is organizing them into Sunday Classes. These classes have a twofold object: the study of the Bible and the cultivation of brotherly intercourse and mutual benefit. The class usually meets at the regular Sunday-school hour and studies the appointed Sunday-school lesson, but the principles and methods of class organization and procedure at once distinguish it from the ordinary Bible class. A class which admirably sets forth the new methods is the Alling Class, which was organized by Mr. Joseph T. Alling in the Central Presbyterian Church of Rochester, N. Y.

The growth of the Alling Class is indicated by the following table. Note the rapid growth of the class from 1888, the time when the class was reorganized under the new methods.

Year.	Total Number Enrolled.	Average Attendance.	Largest Attendance.
1884	8	6	
1885	19	10	
1886	19	11¾	15
1887	20	11	17
1888	24	13	20
1889	66	26	70
1890	97	56	82
1891	276*	78	221
1892	363*	153	345
1893	575*	206	456
1894	872*	227	363
1895		246	425

* This number includes registered visitors.

MODERN METHODS IN CHURCH WORK.

By the permission of Mr. Alling I take the following extracts from a pamphlet relative to his class: —

"The first step towards building up a Young Men's Bible Class is to arouse a strong class spirit, an enthusiasm for their own organization, and pride in its success; in short, that very effective something which the French call *esprit de corps*.

"Everything, in itself harmless, that will conduce to that end has been encouraged, and the first step was the formation of a class organization, officered entirely by members of the class.

"There is some difference of opinion among class workers as to how completely the teacher should divorce himself from all the business affairs of his class, but the opinion is practically unanimous that on no account should he be its President. Very possibly the young men, out of deference, will offer to elect him to that office, but we should make no exceptions whatever in saying, 'Do not accept.'

"ORGANIZATION. — A very simple organization answered our purposes for some years. The officers were a President, Vice-President, Secretary, and Treasurer, and the Executive Committee, made up of the three officers just mentioned, three other members of the class, and the teacher, *ex officio*. This organization has been added to as the needs developed, the teacher retaining at all times his *ex-officio* position as member of the Executive Committee.

"The officers at present are a President, Vice-President, Treasurer, Corresponding Secretary, Recording Secretary, Chairman of Attendance Committee, Chairman Social Committee, Chairman Employment Committee, Historian and three Librarians, and an Executive Committee."

Large numbers of men join the church from this class every year. As the result of special meetings at one time, one hundred and twenty members of the class indicated their interest in personal religion, and out of that number sixty soon joined the church.

A consideration of the duties of the officers and

committees of the class will give an idea of the work which is carried on by it. The President, Vice-President, and Treasurer perform the duties that fall to such officers everywhere. The duties of the last officer are by no means so light as usually fall to the Bible class treasurer. During ten years over five thousand dollars passed through his hands. Part of this was raised by special entertainments, part by special pledges, and part by the morning collections, which average ten dollars a Sunday. The class pays twenty per cent of their collection to the Sunday-school, and divides the remainder into two funds, benevolent and expense. The class contributes to various forms of religious work from its benevolent fund on recommendation of the Executive Committee. The Corresponding Secretary is a busy man, since to him falls the duty of mailing notices to members and others which are sent out at least twice a month the year through. Invitations are sent to visitors and those who are not members of the class. The following is an example of the invitations.

Dear Sir,— We were glad to find your attendance card among those of the Alling Class last week, and on behalf of the class we cordially invite you to come again, get acquainted, and join us if you feel so inclined. It is the aim of the class, in its different departments of work, to interest and help men as much as possible, and if we can be of any service to you, or if you feel willing to give us the help of your presence and effort, we shall be most glad to have you become one of our members, provided you wish to do so, and are not connected with any other class.

Yours very sincerely,

.................................*President.*

.................................*Teacher.*

MODERN METHODS IN CHURCH WORK.

If the stranger wishes to join the class the following card is sent him: —

ALLING CLASS MEMBERSHIP CARD.

Date, ... 189....

Name, ...
Address, ...
Business Address, ...
Age, ...
Occupation, ...
If "Student," where? ....
Is your home in city? ....
Are you a member of Y. M. C. A.? ....
Are you a member of Y. P. S. C. E.? ....
Are you a member of any other class? ....
Are you a member of any Church? ....
If so, what one? ....

The above questions are not asked with any intention of being inquisitive, but that the teacher of the Class may become better acquainted with each man who becomes a member.
Every member is expected to sign this card.

The Recording Secretary makes up his attendance roll from cards (like the one on the following page), which are presented at the door to every man who comes to the class. They are afterward collected, and from them the attendance is made up.

These cards are afterward passed on for the information of the chairman of the Attendance Committee, and a careful record is kept of the attendance of every member. It may be helpful to state in this connection that the plan of Mr. John Wanamaker in keeping record of the members of his large class in Bethany Church, Philadelphia, is to divide the class into groups of ten members, over each of which is appointed a leader who immediately visits all absentees, and reports weekly on his "ten." Thus all cases of need, spiritual and material, are promptly met, and the class spirit is deepened.

ALLING CLASS.

VISITORS.

We are glad to have you with us. Come again.

....

Address, ...
Are you a member of any Class? ....
If "Student," where? ....

NOTE.—Visitors are always welcome. If you are not a member of any class, we would be glad to have you join us. Apply to President or Secretary for membership card.

MEMBERS.

....

Address, ...
Have you signed Membership Card? ....
Have you read the Lesson? ....

The chairman of the Attendance Committee of the Alling Class with his colleagues looks over the record weekly, follows up the new-comers, and looks up absentees. The chairman of the Social Committee and those who are associated with him act as ushers at the Sunday meetings of the class, and also arrange for social gatherings. They have a Reception Committee badge and greet the men, especially new-comers, and try to make them feel at home. They are greatly assisted in their duties by the custom which prevails of devoting five minutes before the lesson to hand-shaking. The class thus becomes for the time a social "committee of the whole." The chairman of the Employment Committee and his associates do everything in their power to obtain employment for members out of work. The whole class are urged to co-operate with this committee by giving early information of vacancies of which they may hear. The librarians have charge of Bibles and singing-books, and distribute the attendance cards.

The class, in addition to the work under the charge of the various committees, has undertaken other forms of effort for young men. There are under its auspices baseball, basket-ball and bicycle clubs. They have also a debating club and an orchestra, and give entertainments and hold excursions and picnics during the summer months. One of the greatest occasions of the year for the class is the annual banquet. This is held at a time when the largest attendance is obtainable, and is served with all the accessories and accompaniments of such occasions. Scores and hundreds of men have been brought into membership through the influence of these annual gatherings.

Such are the Alling Class methods, the general features of which, says Mr. Alling, were inspired by those of another Young Men's Bible Class in the Central Church, Rochester, and by the class of the late H. S. Hull of Bath, N. Y. There are now similar classes in other parts of the country. Wherever tried, reports are that the work has been attended with gratifying results.

IV. The Young Men's Club is the fourth means of reaching young men. Its aim is to meet their demands for healthful diversion and social pleasure. It is usually conducted as a part of the work of the brotherhoods above mentioned, but sometimes the Club is independent of these, having its own officers.

We can appreciate the value of these clubs only as we appreciate the need of young men. The desire for pleasure is manifest very early in life. A baby is first taught through its desire to be amused; and a child is best taught in the same way. It was recognition of this principle which gave rise to the kindergarten system. It may further be said that the desire to be amused is never exhausted. The objects of our immediate desire may change, man may put away childish things, but in doing so he instinctively puts something in their place. Now how are we to meet this demand of young men? In their homes there is not always the fellowship of young companions, and in some churches there is neither companionship nor opportunity for diversion. What are the young men to do? They have abounding energy and needs that must be satisfied; they have worked all day at study, or in the store. The club is too expensive or, if in a smaller town, there is none. Energy and desire have been gathering, and they are ready, like the waters of Niagara, for a plunge of some kind. Alas! how often it *must be*, per force of circumstances, the wrong kind. Then, too, in addition to the young men who have homes, there are in all our towns and cities crowds of intelligent young men who are in boarding and lodging houses. They find but little social life there, and feel the necessity of going where exercise and diversion may be found. The club, the lodge, the armory, the saloon, — these meet deep needs; and these institutions get all the young man's energy (outside his business) and all his time, save an hour or two a week given to some church service. Thoughts are turned from the church, and the young men who in time are not weaned from it are the exception. How much larger their gain, how much larger the gain to the church, if this diversion, exercise, and amusement can be given, not only apart from all temptation, but also *where there* are *positive influences for good*. Then young men will feel the influences of the church, will recognize that it is their friend, and will be receptive of its spiritual ministries.

There is another reason for providing amusements. Drawing young men through such attractions is the only way of ever coming into personal touch with many of them. There are young men working at such occupations as preclude all opportunity of speaking with them during the day, and you may seldom find them at home during the evening. How then are we to get hold of these young men to tell the story of infinite love? The world allures, unfurls its banners of hospitality, offers bright, absorbing amusement. If the church is to cope with this tide of counter-attractions, something must be provided to take its place. We must "overcome evil with good." [1]

Social needs may be met in many ways. A clubroom contiguous to the main auditorium of the church may be easily arranged at comparatively little expense. This can be supplied with books, magazines, illustrated weeklies, daily papers, and games. Give the rooms an air of comfort; make them bright, cheery, and attractive, and have easy-chairs, "not straight-backs-in-a-row." A coffee-urn in the corner, or hot chocolate at pleasure, will add to sociability and good cheer. This provides a place where young men may meet one another, come together socially, and find restful recreation after the day's toil. In this way the holy and persuasive influences of the church gradually enwrap a young man's life; his sympathies, his thoughts, are with the church, and soon his effort and heart and life are given to the great cause for which the church stands. This is taking the young man a step at a

[1] Romans xii. 21.

time. "What we need," says Dr. Edward Judson, " is a kind of a halfway house on the road leading from the saloon to the prayer meeting. Nowadays you cannot swing religion into a young man's consciousness prayer-meeting end to."[1]

But some pastors who believe in this work, urge that their equipment is not sufficiently large and that the club-room is too expensive. But the club-room pays for itself. A nominal fee should be charged. When under the direction of a Brotherhood like that of St. Andrew or the Andrew and Philip, the expense can be covered from annual dues, possibly only five cents a month. As to the room, if there is no parish-house, one of the smaller Sunday-school rooms may be used. This is the practice of many village and even of many city churches, where architecture of a few years ago made no provision for a young men's club.

Ten dollars will buy sufficient games to entertain fifty young men. As for papers and periodicals, members can usually be found in a church who are glad to contribute yearly to reading matter or in full for some one periodical. The coffee and chocolate will be of little expense. So the club-room is within reach of all, and when in operation becomes the rallying point for a large work for and by young men.

The Rev. Milton S. Littlefield, when pastor of Mizpah Chapel, New York City, had among other things in his successful work an annual supper for the men and young men of his congregation. The women of the Chapel prepared the tables and prettily arranged them with lamps and decorations, and made the room bright and cheery in every way possible. The supper was donated in part by the women of the congregation, the remaining expense being met by the small

[1] The Judson Memorial, p. 10 (reprint from "The Examiner").

charge of twenty-five cents a plate. The supper was followed by "after-talks," and the result of the occasion always was an increasing hold of the Chapel on the interests, sympathies, and fidelity of the male attendants.

CHAPTER XXI.

ATHLETICS.

We are learning that the religion of Christ touches us in all the parts of our lives. Physically, mentally, and spiritually we need strength and development. . . . Nothing helps more to make a man thoroughly equipped and prepared for the battle of life and usefulness than a strong, vigorous, and well-balanced body. We cannot overrate the importance of athletics. . . . As Christian men and women, as Christian citizens, as Christian parents, it is our duty and our privilege to sympathize most heartily in all this athletic work which is making our race stronger and more vigorous and giving better life for the future. It has very often been said that a great deal of bad theology has come from bad digestion. The time has long passed when it was necessary that a man should be narrow-shouldered and sallow-complexioned and sad-looking in order to do any work for the Master. God has given us our body as a magnificent tool to do his work with, and it should be equipped and strengthened and made vigorous in every way.

WILLIAM E. DODGE.

ATHLETIC exercise is one of the chief and natural interests to a boy from the time he leaves the toys and picture-books of the nursery, to the time when he is ready for the serious business of life and often far into the latter period. As Professor Henry Drummond says: "Sport commands his whole leisure and governs his thoughts and ambitions even in his working hours. And so striking has been this development in recent years, and especially among the young men of the larger cities, that the time has come to decide whether athletics are to become a curse to the country or a blessing. That issue is now, and in an almost acute form, directly before the country."[1] If, then, our

---

[1] *Christianity Practically Applied*, p. 209.

boys and young men have their hearts centred on this thing, which one of the clearest thinkers of the times warns us is liable to be a "curse to the country," it becomes the duty of the Church to focalize attention on it that happily she may turn the threatened "curse" into the possible "blessing."

Athletics are here to stay; of this there can be no doubt. They have taken a prominent part in our American life, and promise to take a still larger part; the increasing use of the bicycle is at least suggestive of that. And so long as man is "in the body," he will have need of exercise. What then is the Church to do about it? Crowd out and shut out athletics beyond its holy influence and restraints, or recognize that her duty and concern is for the whole man, — *body* as well as soul and spirit? "Know ye not," said Paul, "that your body is the temple of the Holy Ghost?"[1] It is because the devil so often gets "the body" of men that he also holds sway over soul and spirit.

The Young Men's Christian Association by its fine gymnasiums has done a great deal to gain a hold on young men along this line. One of the requisites for a Physical Director in the Young Men's Christian Association is that he shall be an earnest Christian man and prepared by personal contact to win young men for Jesus Christ. Some gymnasiums have a corps of volunteer helpers. When a strange young man comes in, he is approached by one of these volunteers. If not familiar with the exercises, the helper tells him which ones he will do well to undertake first and gives him all the assistance possible until he can have the services of the Director. The acquaintance and feeling of good-fellowship thus established between the two young men gives the Christian the best of opportunities to win

[1] 1 Corinthians vi. 19.

the stranger into the Christian work of the Association. In like manner, the church may get hold of the young man, by going with him into, and helping him to the means of enjoying, his favorite pursuits. Show your interest in a young man in things which innocently and of necessity interest him, and you have direct approach to his heart. It is the open door divinely placed in every man's nature. And yet I suppose some church-workers will continue to shut their eyes to that door, to cry " unholy," and thank " God that they are not as other men are"!

Christian influence in athletics would have another effect, — a purifying effect. When young men come under the guiding influence of the church in their athletics, we shall hear no more of brutality, betting, or the introduction of the professional element. Julian Hawthorne, in an article entitled "The Building of the Muscle" in Harper's Magazine for August, 1884, expresses himself most admirably on this point. He says: "The peril of all muscular cultivation is professionalism. . . . Blackguards are always ready to rush in where angels will not take the trouble to be present, and brutality can be banished from our palæstræ just as easily as from our drawing-rooms and by precisely the same methods." It is the presence of good people that will purify the games, not their money, nor even their good wishes, but they *themselves.*

In our discussion of the subject, let us remember that there is real need of aid for physical improvement. We at once realize this when we look out upon the poor of our cities, where we find little provision for physical exercise and bodily improvement. Jacob Riis says, in speaking of child life in the tenement houses: " Sometimes they ask me, ' What is this all about, with your infant slaughter in the tenements? The children are bright and strong to look at.' A doctor once was asked that question, and he gave the only reasonable answer I ever heard. He said: 'It is a clear case of the survival of the fittest. Only those who are strong as cattle can stand it.'"[1] We may well believe that this is so. Born to an environment of filth, surrounded by everything that can be a menace to health in the overcrowded slums, the little bodies must indeed be of the strongest to withstand the insidious foes on every hand. In the homes of the well to do, the hours from four to six P. M. are spent by the children, usually, in play, and such play takes the form, at least in part, of active physical exercise. In the country, at the school recesses there is more or less of vigorous play, but the city child gets neither the one nor the other in the tenement districts. Dr. Felix L. Oswald declares that "nine tenths of our city children are literally *starving* for want of recreation."[2] But both Church and State have paid little attention to that kind of hunger. Now, aside from the account the Church must render for the bodies and souls of these "little ones," we need for the sake of our country and our race to give the children that physical equipment essential to highest thought and service. The church may provide some place for recreation for boys and girls during the hours of the day when they are out of school. A large well-ventilated room may be furnished with games that require active exercise, or possibly a play-ground might be secured, upon which improvements of a temporary character could be placed. Children are easily amused. It takes little to fully equip their playground. Never were greater returns realized on so small an investment. They consist in roses on pale cheeks, firm

[1] Sixth Convention Christian Workers, Wash., D. C., 1894, p. 296.
[2] Popular Science Monthly, August, 1881, p. 455.

ATHLETICS.

muscles developed from flabby ones, bent backs made straight, and an aggregate of happiness such as only childhood knows.

But this work of the church will be conducted chiefly among the lads and young men. In the preceding chapter we have seen the need of diversion by our young men. Many of them in our towns have occupations which do not call for active bodily exercise. Even among the working-men the invention of mechanical appliances has done away with much of the need for muscle. The cheapness of transportation and the lack of physical vigor combine to make the working-man prefer to ride to and from his daily toil. The result is that nightfall finds him without proper physical exercise, though one set of muscles may be weary with the day's labor. The sport instinct is there, nevertheless, and is gratified vicariously, as he reads the brutal details of the prize fight or bets on his favorite champion. It is just here, in the need of harmless recreation and physical development, that the church may find the working-man and meet his need and reach his heart. The gymnasium in point of usefulness is to be mentioned first. It can be enjoyed at all seasons and can be equipped at small expense. Dr. Oswald tells us the following appliances may be made at the aggregate cost of not more than fifty dollars: —

> Spring-board and leaping gauge.
> Inclined ladder.
> Horizontal bar.
> Swinging rings.
> A vaulting horse (rough-hewn).
> Chest expander (elastic band with handles).
> Buckets filled with shot or pig iron, for health lifts.[1]

[1] Popular Science Monthly, August, 1881, p. 455.

MODERN METHODS IN CHURCH WORK.

An infinite variety of exercises may be performed with these simple appliances, and they may be added to and improved upon as the needs of the gymnasium grow, and men are drawn in to share in its expense.

Swimming is good athletic exercise, and nothing that the church can put within the reach of boys and young men will be more appreciated. Swimming-tanks have been put in operation in the People's Palace of the Jersey City Tabernacle, New Jersey. Long lines of boys waiting for their chance to go in attest their appreciation of this neighbor of godliness. In the People's Tabernacle (Congregational), Denver, Col., a part of the world where water has a decided market value, they also maintain free baths. In the beautiful new mission-house of Grace Episcopal Church, New York, is a very complete arrangement for plunge and shower baths for boys and men.

There are many among our young men, however, who do not see the advantages of physical development, to whom sport as sport appeals. We must find some way to include them in our plan, to sanctify the young man's necessity for physical amusement. T. Gold Frost pertinently remarks: "Christianity does not consider amusements, either indoor or outdoor, to be the plaything of the devil. The real Christ is a wise counsellor, a lovable companion. He will not rob you of a single cricket match."[1] This is the true attitude of the church toward athletic games, and the introduction of this idea among the manly young fellows of our country is bringing hosts of them into the Kingdom. The reflex influence, too, on sport is already being felt. "The athletic men are learning to carry their Christianity with them into their sports, and as a conse-

[1] Andover Review, November, 1888.

ATHLETICS.

quence these are becoming more and more characterized by Christian behavior and deportment."[1]

Bicycle-riding is another form of athletics that is in great favor with young people at the present time. Harmless in most cases and of positive benefit in others, the bicycle is a great source of Sabbath-breaking. Christian young men may do a great deal of good by organizing bicycle clubs which by their rules either prohibit Sunday riding or at least restrict it so that it shall not interfere with church duties. Tennis, golf, baseball, football, rowing, swimming, gymnastics, and other innocent and manly exercises and diversions may become weapons in the armory of our God. The presence of good people will banish the evils which now threaten athletics. No betting or gambling can take place where the spirit of Christ reigns, and even professionalism will perish for lack of countenance. The reign of pure athletics will be begun, the kind that Paul tells about through all his epistles: elevating, for it makes the "man temperate in all things," and "brings the body into subjection;" conscientious, for it has due regard to the "cloud of witnesses" in earth and heaven, and "runs with patience the race that is set before it;" thrice blessed, for the end is coming "into a perfect man, unto the measure of the stature of the fulness of Christ."

[1] Andover Review, November, 1888.

CHAPTER XXII.

CHURCH LIBRARIES, READING-ROOMS, LITERARY SOCIETIES, AND ENTERTAINMENT COURSES.

"READING maketh a full man." Did Bacon mean the ephemeral literature of the newspaper or the sensational novel? Verily, the diet of the prodigal son in the far country contained as much nourishment. And yet, unless good people help the world to a taste for something better, the great majority will continue to feed on "husks," leaving untouched the better portion, even, of the daily press. What are the means the church may use to cultivate a better taste?

1. LIBRARIES AND READING-ROOMS. It is appropriate that the church have a library and reading-room; something more, too, than the Sunday-school library; appropriate that the church encourage her people to read, and to read that which is "worth while." To this end let there be a wise selection by a competent committee of the best fiction, scientific research, travels, history, biography, and other standard works. A book on animals or the steam-engine, with attractive letter-press and captivating illustrations, will prove a treasure to a bright boy, from which not even the "Adventures of Tom Sawyer" can draw him. The same rule applies to children of a larger growth. Another feature which increases the usefulness of a church library is to make of it a working library. Every family is not well equipped

with atlases and encyclopedias. Every household has not an abundance of missionary literature, and some have not any. Such a collection of books may be of great value in the preparation of articles for the missionary meeting or young people's society. There should be a committee whose business it is to keep advised as to new and useful books.

Many churches have a reading-room connected with the library, open certain hours of every day, as the library is open certain times during the week. Along the reference line these reading-rooms have subscriptions to various missionary and general religious papers. To foster the taste for the educational books on the shelves, the best scientific and literary magazines are supplied, while bright-colored prints and reputable newspapers are not excluded.

In some States there is little need of church libraries. In New York and Massachusetts, for instance, many a hamlet has its public library, while in California the admirable provision made for school libraries supplies an abundance of first-class reading matter. But all States are not so fortunate, and the church has the opportunity of meeting this need.

The location of the library and reading-room is a matter of importance. It will be shorn of much usefulness if tucked away in some garret corner. The reading-room should, if possible, have a street entrance, and be adorned with a modest sign proclaiming its useful mission. It is a mistake to believe that people know all about *our* church. Both *we* and *ours* are not always of consequence to other people.

Rev. Russell H. Conwell, D.D., thus tells of the development of the reading-room in his church, Grace Baptist Temple, Philadelphia: "Our reading-room consisted of one room and one paper in the first place, and it is entirely a case of Christian evolution. Years ago, after our prayer meeting, it was our habit to put out the gas at once and send the people home. We forgot that Christ's way of teaching was largely a social way. . . . Now we keep the whole church open as long as people wish to stop and carry on a Christian conversation. We had then a little room, to which I referred, open, with one paper in it; afterward some friends brought it some other papers, because people liked to stop and read the Christian news who did not take a Christian paper, among the poorer people as well as among the better classes. From that one paper, by adding one at a time, without any plan laid or great committee, but steadily adding one more and one more, we have gone on till now we have five different reading-rooms. . . . It is just simply going on doing the next thing, till now our reading-rooms are open all day and in the evening, and the men and women come and go as they see fit, and nearly all are accumulating quite extensive libraries." [1]

In the Episcopal churches there are Church Periodical Clubs. In the 1894 Annual Report of St. George's Church, New York, we read: "There are now twelve hundred clergymen, besides numerous laymen and missionaries who are the beneficiaries of the Club, most of whom are receiving regularly one or more magazines or papers which they could not otherwise enjoy. Most of these are living in the West, or no less destitute South, far away from any contact with the fresh thought of the larger cities. The arrival of an attractive current magazine is one of the greatest pleasures of their lives, — lives so meagrely supplied

[1] Seventh Annual Convention of Christian Workers, Boston, 1892, p. 98.

with intellectual pleasures." This society also sends out Bibles, Prayer-books, and Hymnals, with scrap-books, calendars, text cards, Christmas and Easter cards. Is not here an example worth following, — this sending the benefits of the reading-room beyond the bounds of the individual church?

2. LITERARY SOCIETIES. Literary societies form a very suitable part of the forces of a well-organized church. The Chautauqua Circle is a very practicable plan to follow. No better course of reading for the purpose can be obtained anywhere. The books are by eminent writers, the cost is reasonable, and a high moral and religious tone breathes through all. Several sets of the books can profitably be placed in the reading-room, and at the disposal of the members of the Circle for their daily hour's reading. This relieves those who do not feel able to purchase the books. There may be one or more sets on the library shelves to be loaned under certain restrictions for prompt return, but the better plan is to confine most of the books to reading-room use.

In the Delaware Avenue Baptist Church, Buffalo, N. Y., is a literary society, called the Gradgrind Club. It has the following quaint substitute for a constitution: —

The Appellative Fact: The name of this Club shall be the Gradgrind Club.

The Intentional Fact: The object of this Club shall be the search for facts, — historical, literary, artistic, social, political, moral, and intellectual.

The Administrative Facts: The officers of the Club shall be a President, a Vice-President, a Secretary, and a Treasurer, elected annually, whose duties shall be such as are usually performed by such factotums.

The Dictational Facts: An Executive Board, consisting

of five members appointed by the President, shall have entire charge of the programme for the year.

The Personal Facts : The membership of the Club shall be limited to all members of the congregation of the Delaware Avenue Baptist Church, and twenty-five outside members.

The Necessary Fact: The annual dues shall be one dollar.

Additional Facts: By-laws and changes to the Constitution may be made as becomes necessary.

This Club meets from October to March, having twelve meetings, at intervals of two weeks. Two of these meetings have a social character, — the midwinter meeting and the annual meeting, held the last of March. The other ten are devoted to some subject of study. The season of 1895-96 was devoted to the study of America, with papers, talks, and discussions. Here is an example of real live educational work under the direct charge of the Church.

A debate is also a pleasant feature of literary societies. It fosters intellectual growth when mind meets mind in discussion, and there is nothing better than a debate to bring out the best in our young people. The Chatham Literary Union of Grace Church, Philadelphia, is the largest debating society in this country. It has an average attendance of seven hundred and fifty, and holds public debates with free admission. To quote from Dr. Dager: "There is a work to be accomplished by such societies that is needed in every church. . . . Many a young man would testify for the Master more frequently if he were more confident of his language and his self-control before people. What can help them along this line like the literary society? Experience everywhere attests that the literary society benefits the cause that is dearest to our hearts by teaching the young men, who are too often accustomed to sneak away in silence

ENTERTAINMENT COURSES.

from the shallow statements and flimsy arguments of unbelief that meet them in daily life, how in word to meet life's common scepticisms, how to express the claims of their Divine Master. If the Church of Christ needs trained intellects and ready speakers, let her foster the literary societies."[1]

Many churches in cities are conducting large and successful literary societies; but the village and country church is usually, I believe, more successful in this work. The work of the Winter Night College, Ravenna, O., an account of which is given in Chapter XXIII., is an illustration of what the village can do. The country and village church does not suffer the counter-attractions that the city church suffers. Literary work is a happy diversion, gives something to do, feeds and stimulates the mind, trains and develops. Public exercises of a varied programme, recitations, essays, and debates, will add to the interest and the helpfulness of this work.

3. ENTERTAINMENT COURSES. Educational work is further prosecuted by means of lecture and entertainment courses. This work, which is now being so helpfully carried on by many churches, is not the old-time entertainment for revenue only. Truly, we have had quite enough of that. Pity it is that some churches have reasoned, "How much money can we make out of this thing?" rather than "How much good can we do this people? What are their needs? Can we direct their minds to nobler things, give them pure and helpful enjoyments, lift them by any and all means to a higher life?" It is a travesty on religion and common-sense to preach, "Don't go to the theatre, don't play cards, keep away from the ball," and not put something better in their places.

[1] Modern Temple and Templars, by Robert J. Burdette, p. 239.

It is well that we remember the story told by Jesus of the evil spirit which was driven out of a man, but returned again, and finding the house of the soul swept and garnished entered in, taking with him seven other spirits worse than himself, because the house was empty. The ideal church lecture and entertainment course excludes the idea of profit. The proposition is to give to the congregation and to the community the very best possible entertainment at the least possible expense.

The value of entertainments of an uplifting order has long been admitted. The question is how to bring them closest to the lives of the people. A course of entertainments scattered through the winter at regular intervals, each advertising all the others, is better than sporadic efforts that spring up occasionally. The announcement of the course also enables people to plan ahead to attend them. And the people will attend if the lectures are of such character as to make it worth their while. The greatest care, therefore, should be exercised in the selection of the lecturers and entertainments. Keep the standard high! But let it be remembered that there is a difference between keeping the standard high and presenting a programme that is dry. It is not surprising that a New York Fifth Avenue Church which secured a scientific lecturer for *a course* of "scientific" lectures, and announced that the lectures would be free, had an audience of from twelve to fifteen people. The wheat of summer under one breath of sun may burst into dashes of gold; but scientific minds are like rare flowers that demand peculiar climate and long training.

How can good entertainments be given at small cost to the public, and still keep the expense within the reach of the church? Several churches in one

ENTERTAINMENT COURSES.

city, in different parts of town, or several village churches in neighboring towns, may combine to have the same course during a season. This plan is now in operation in a number of places. The result is a great saving of expense. The talent from abroad, by reason of securing a series of engagements, and where proximity reduces expense, are willing to come much cheaper. Again, some of the best talent will cheerfully be contributed for the asking. There are many benevolent men like a leading college president, who said that "wherever in the United States a goodly number of people wanted him to come and address them, he felt it his duty and privilege to go, simply on condition of having his expenses paid."

The stereopticon lecture is always instructive and enjoyable. With the list of views and conveniences furnished by opticians, even the busy pastor can easily prepare a fascinating and instructive lecture which can be given at little expense.

The Madison Avenue Presbyterian Church of New York, and Berkeley Temple, Boston, have given a very high grade of entertainments, perfectly self-supporting, for ten cents admission, even, sometimes, six tickets for fifty cents. The course of entertainments, in addition to meeting a real need, is invaluable in reaching non-church-goers, and so helping to win them to Christ. Dr. Dickinson thus explains the Berkeley Temple plan: "We have a system of complimentary tickets, and have distributed, in the aggregate, to thirty thousand people, and have found by this means that six thousand did not attend church anywhere. . . . We know where our tickets go, and can tell, almost in detail, the history of some of the families. . . . For instance, Tuesday night we send out from three hundred to five hundred complimentary tickets:

we receive some of these tickets at the door, and some one will be set to keep track of the users of these tickets, and of the families, and how they are sent. It is one of the students of the theological seminary who takes charge of this, and Wednesday he finds, approximately, who used them. Let us take one. It was numbered '2' on the back, and was issued to John W. Elcline, the register shows, because his name is opposite No. 2, in the corner. . . . As a result, we have reached more non-church-going people, and have received them into the church doors, and into our church-membership, than by any other means. We did not suppose it would work at first, but we reached their hearts, and we have got some of our most active Christian men and women into the church, who were first attracted by the entertainments and complimentary-ticket system." [1]

The Madison Avenue Presbyterian Church, New York, distributes complimentary tickets to non-churchgoers through the medium of the church-members. Each is requested to give a ticket to some one who is not a regular church attendant. The ticket gives the dates and subjects for the entire course, and bears the following note: "This ticket will admit the bearer to any one of the above entertainments. By writing your name and address below, a ticket will be mailed you, free of charge, admitting you to all the entertainments of the above course." The return of the ticket shows that the recipient is interested, and, following up the case, often results in securing him as a loyal adherent to the church.

Thus, concert, lecture, stereopticon entertainment, or reading may become powerful in the hands of the consecrated servants of the Lord in winning souls to

[1] Christianity Practically Applied, pp. 29, 30.

him. It is not so much the means as the spirit that is back of them. It takes time, patience, and grace to perfect and carry out an entertainment course and follow it up with personal effort. But when a church and pastor are so endued with the Spirit as to be willing to undertake this great labor of love, the fulfilment of the promise follows as night the day, — "in due season we shall reap, if we faint not."[1]

[1] Galatians vi. 9.

CHAPTER XXIII.

TEACHING BY MEANS OF CLASSES.

There is no wealth but life: life including all its powers of love and joy and admiration. That country is richest which nourishes the greatest number of noble and happy human beings; that man is the richest who, having perfected the functions of his own life to the utmost, has also the widest helpful influence, both personal and by means of his possessions, over the lives of others. — RUSKIN.

THERE are many reasons why the church should enter upon the work of teaching. It is one way of "doing good." Then, too, there is sore need of it in almost every community. Even the Bible is of little value to those persons who cannot read. Every one is the better for education, — we all know that. But the fact is that many people are not able to secure the advantages which education gives. They have not the means to pay for instruction, neither have they the courage, when old enough to realize their deficiency, to undertake the task of self-improvement. The time of compulsory attendance on the schools is not long, and thereafter many children must help to sustain the meagre home. Many a poor boy, like George Stephenson and David Livingstone, cannot study without the evening school; and many in moderate circumstances will not be persuaded to improve the mind unless the chance to study be given at little cost. Why should not the church help them? To aid them in their education is doing no more than every minister and college graduate has had done for him, since tuition is a small part of the cost of college instruction. To help the poor to something of an education is one of the best ways, also, of helping them to help themselves. Clearly, this is a benevolence above criticism, as well as a work of urgent need. Again, the church may obtain great influence over both old and young by serving them in this way. When the church shows a hearty interest in the people around her, it is sure to be appreciated, and will enlist returning interest, sympathy, and effort, in Christian work.

Night classes for adults may be held where the common branches — reading, writing, arithmetic, geography, grammar, and spelling — are taught. Other branches, too, should not be neglected. To furnish a young person with a working knowledge of book-keeping or typewriting, and stenography, puts him in a position where he can make his own way, and therefore is as much better than a gift of money as anything that is a part of one's mental furnishing is better than any external thing. Drawing, too, may be used in so many of the vocations of life that a knowledge of it is one of the best gifts the church can bestow. When a church earnestly sets herself to this work, the way will open before her. She will find among her members and friends those who will lend themselves to promoting the enterprise. Volunteer teachers will appear, and many in the congregation, who appreciate what education has done for them, or how they have been handicapped by its lack, will help on the good cause. In Berkeley Temple, Boston, there is such a work. Dr. Dickinson, the pastor, in speaking of the various branches taught in his church, says: "Every one of these classes at present is under the instruction of our own church people. We insist that when a teacher takes a class he takes it with the understanding that he is expected to bring a part or all of his class to Christ."[1]

This is but the beginning of a work that may be carried on almost indefinitely, even to the extent of founding an educational institution, as some of the churches have done. Under the charge of Bethany Presbyterian Church, Philadelphia, is Bethany College. This college, through its six comprehensive departments, offers "a liberal and practical education to all that are desirous of availing themselves of it." Then there is Armour Institute, of Chicago, with its six departments, the outgrowth of Armour Mission, "founded for the purpose of giving to young men and women the opportunity of securing a liberal education." Grace Baptist Temple, in Philadelphia, has founded the Temple College, — a splendid educational institution of ten departments. This college has also six academies in different parts of Philadelphia, and one in Camden, N. J., so that the college is in walking distance, practically, of all Philadelphia. This is a great saving of time and car fare to the poorer students, and enables and encourages many to attend who otherwise could not. The night schools connected with this institution give a much more liberal education than the ordinary night school, as they prepare young people for college. The day schools have a higher rate of tuition than the night schools, but any person who works at night, a night watchman, for instance, is admitted to the day school at night-school rates.

The description of these colleges for higher education may bring little comfort to churches which are

[1] Fourth Annual Convention of Christian Workers, Buffalo, N. Y., 1889, p. 57.

only in moderate circumstances; but the Rev. W. G. Schloppe, pastor of the Congregational Church of Ravenna, O., has proven that an educational institution of a high order can be carried on successfully at little cost. Mr. Schloppe calls this institution the "Winter Night College." It was started in the fall of 1895. The following prospectus, which was printed and posted in the shops and stores of Ravenna, gives an outline of the plan of the college:—

THE WINTER NIGHT COLLEGE OF RAVENNA.

Sessions are held each Wednesday evening in the parlors of the Congregational Church from 7.30 to 9 P. M.

Circles have been organized in French, German, Civil Government, English Literature, and Current Events.

Four members can start a circle in any branch of study.

Weekly sessions will be held until April.

Entrance fee to any circle, fifty cents.

Every one invited to join us.

The best literary minds of the little city volunteered to lead circles in their special line. The dining-tables of the church were covered with bright cloths, and each circle gathered around a table, and, under the guidance of its leader, discussed the topic previously announced.

At precisely half-past seven o'clock, the session is opened by music given in an informal way. This is followed by a twenty-minute essay on a subject of interest, by some person of known ability in the town or vicinity. These preliminary exercises are open to the public, who may retire at the close or remain to join a circle, or to read at a long table near the entrance, which is loaded with the best magazines and periodicals loaned by the people after a week's use at home. The regular session is from eight to nine o'clock. The discussions are as free and informal as possible without disturbance of the work. Often crowds of young men are at the reading-table, but all is quiet and orderly.

The college, though started by the Congregational Church, and having its pastor as president, is undenominational, and the other officers were chosen from different churches. The President, Vice-President, Secretary, and Treasurer, and three members at large, appointed by the President, form the Executive Committee. They secure the leaders and attend to the general business of the college.

The plan of the Winter Night College, so simple, so flexible, so economical, cannot but commend itself to the church, especially in smaller towns and cities. In fact, committees from towns near Ravenna have visited the college, and have been so favorably impressed with it that similar institutions have been planned for another season.

Mr. Schloppe gives us the following points in favor of this movement. It has organized the literary forces of the place. It has inspired a literary taste where before it was unknown. Its popular features are fitted to make it a success. And he adds: "Not least among the results in our town is a common admission that never before have so many of the business men been so favorably disposed toward the work of the church. . . . And many people say they have established the habit of coming to the church building, and the desire has grown upon them."

Such institutions may be equally successful in any community where the poor are, — and where are they not? — and in any place where the literary ability is not organized but undeveloped. In the country and smaller villages a reading-circle may enroll all who could be induced to study; but in most places there will be found a great need for this kind of work, and the church should prove herself equal to the emergency.

In conclusion, we would quote the strong words of Mr. Schloppe: "It is a part of the church's work to promote broadest Christian culture, and the best method of controlling frivolity is to put something better in its place." It may also be said that by this means we shall beat paths to our church doors, "establish the habit of coming to the church building," give the people to feel that the church is their friend, — ready to meet their varied needs, — and so, step by step, we shall win and lead them unto Him "in whom are hid all the treasures of wisdom and knowledge."[1]

[1] Colossians ii. 3.

CHAPTER XXIV.

WOMEN'S WORK.

A LARGE and constantly increasing part of the work of the church is being done by women. "Phœbe, our sister, the servant of the church," is being multiplied many times in these latter days.

The work of the women, ever before the eyes of the church, showing a faithfulness and competence which men may well emulate, needs but brief mention and outline here. In most churches woman's work covers three distinct branches: Ladies' Aid Society, Women's Home and Women's Foreign Missionary Societies. In many churches, however, there is but one comprehensive women's organization, the various departments of work being covered by committees, which are in the nature of auxiliary societies.

In the First Congregational Church of Detroit, Mich., there are four committees, — Foreign and Home Missions, Church Aid Committee, and Committee on Local Charities. One Tuesday in the month is the business meeting, when Church Aid has the largest place; one Tuesday is devoted each to the Foreign and Home work, while the remaining Tuesdays are devoted to such work or entertainment as may be planned by the Executive Committee. The Immanuel Presbyterian Church of Los Angeles, Cal., pursues a different plan. The Aid Society continues as a separate organization, but the Home and Foreign Missionary Societies have been made into one general missionary society. The work is done by committees, — Home, Foreign, Freedmen, Literature, Mission Boxes, and Social Committees. The chairman of each committee, with the President and Treasurer of the contingent fund, constitute the Executive Committee. Each committee has its own treasurer, as the funds are to be kept separate, and each member of the society subscribes to the work of as many committees as she feels able. No fee is required for joining the missionary society. It is an understood thing that every woman in Immanuel Church belongs to it. The meetings are held during an entire day once a month, the Home work alternating with the Foreign in the morning or afternoon exercises, a half-day being devoted to each. The Social Committee has charge of providing out of the contingent fund coffee for the midday lunch, and each lady brings lunch for two; this provides for new-comers and strangers who may be present.

Whatever plan is adopted, one thing must be clearly borne in mind: the work of missions is *one*. Every Home-mission worker should be in heart also a Foreign-mission worker, and every Foreign-mission worker a Home-mission worker. For convenience and stimulus through a reasonable competition, it may be well to have different societies for Home and Foreign missionary work. But we must not forget our responsibility for *all* this work. Jesus Christ said nothing about home missions, and said nothing about foreign missions. His command to his disciples was to go into all the world and preach the gospel to every creature. That is our commission, nothing less. Any method that unifies missions and prevents that feeling of rivalry which sometimes exists between the two branches is to be welcomed.

MODERN METHODS IN CHURCH WORK.

Interest in missions may be cultivated in several ways. It is of great value to keep in touch with the Boards of the Church by following the news and needs of the field. To this end subscriptions to missionary publications should be encouraged. Again, much more will be accomplished by having some definite object to work for. This is within reach of the very poorest church when a native teacher in Ceylon may be hired for $25 per year. Even the poor Christian natives of that country are supporting thirty missionaries.

2. The Aid Society work has such scope that every woman in the church may share in it, and the society is an excellent introduction for a new-comer into the church life. In the Park Congregational Church of Grand Rapids, Mich., this society is called "United Workers." There are two hundred in the organization. They are divided into tens. Their work is that of the ordinary Aid Society, but they have also undertaken to provide the salary of the pastor's assistant. This plan of dividing the women of the congregation into circles of ten is in operation in a goodly number of churches. Sometimes these circles alternate in taking general charge of suppers, sociables, and meetings. This plan still keeps the work under the control of one executive head, and yet stimulates by reasonable and healthful competition. It is also of advantage in that it gives all the women, at various times, some leading responsibility. The First Congregational Church of Appleton, Wis., calls this body of church-workers "The Ladies' Parish Society." All members of the congregation are members of this organization. They are assigned to divisions in alphabetical order the better to carry on their social and financial interests. There are ten divi-

sions with about forty in each. Each division has a month for an entertainment of some kind.

3. We may here make mention of the Unity Church League of the Church of the Unity, Los Angeles, Cal., for the model constitution and working plan that this society presents. It is a women's league, but men may become members of it by the annual payment of one dollar. The constitution declares that the object of the League is "to promote the welfare of the Unity Church in Los Angeles, spiritually, intellectually, socially, and financially." One article says that the League shall consist of as many branches as may from time to time seem necessary, and another declares "that every member of the League shall manifest an interest in each and every branch." Any woman may belong to as many of these branches as she likes. The branches at present in the society are: —

The Philanthropic Branch, which assists the poor and sick and encourages the struggling, especially strangers.

The Channing Branch, which promotes the spiritual welfare and ethical culture of the members by study.

The Sunday-school Branch, which aids in the work of the Sunday-school.

The Parish Extension Branch, which aims to increase the membership of the church.

The Library Branch, which buys and keeps stocked both the Sunday-school and League libraries.

The Unity Aid Branch, which makes garments for the poor, and assists in church enterprises financially and otherwise.

The Young Woman's Branch, which assists in the last-named work.

The Music Branch, which maintains a musical

organization in the League, and attends to other musical matters in the church.

The Children's Branch, which works for children.

The Post-Office Branch, which distributes literature and endeavors to extend the influence of the Unitarian Church.

Might not other churches copy, with profit, an organization which permeates with its influence every interest and activity of the church with which it is connected?

4. The Helping Hand is a society conducted by the women of the church for the poorer women of the community, chapel, or church. The women come one afternoon in the week at half-past two o'clock. The first fifteen minutes are spent in devotional exercises. After this the women begin to sew. Meanwhile a talk is given on some practical topic. They remain until five o'clock, and during the afternoon are instructed, if necessary, in the best methods of doing their work. They are paid ten cents an hour for their time, thus making about twenty-five cents an afternoon. The materials are bought at wholesale, and the women fashion them into garments for themselves, the object being to provide clothing for mothers who neglect themselves to provide for their children. The women are paid for their work in garments, but they are sometimes allowed to take ten cents of their money in groceries instead. This is a very practical form of benevolence, as it combines instruction with help, and brings the women under the influence of the church for three hours during the week in a close and intimate way. In some Helping Hands there are as many instructors as one to each ten women. There should be enough teachers to give needed advice and instruction, and they should be the prac-

tical and spiritual women of the church. The Helping Hand is usually held only during the winter months, but it is often continued with great profit as a mothers' prayer meeting during the summer.

Another work closely allied to the Helping Hand, but combining, also, some of the features of an employment society, is that in the Marble Collegiate Church of New York. It is called the Women's Employment Association. This work differs from the Helping Hand in the fact that the women are given work to the amount of forty or sixty cents, to take home and do, with the privilege of buying the garments at a nominal cost. There is no compulsion to take the pay in clothing, and the work is disposed of to outside parties. In other churches carrying on a similar work, sewing is obtained from public institutions and done at a low cost in order to furnish employment to the women.

It is a mistake for village and country churches to regard this work as beyond the need of their communities. Why excuse yourself by saying your field is too small, and sin as did the man with one talent? Mrs. William G. Frost has recently demonstrated what can be done in so small a place as Berea, Ky., — known through the college, of which Rev. William G. Frost, Ph.D., is president, for the large Christian, industrial, and philanthropic work of that institution. A small town filled with students would apparently have little need of a *women's* sewing-circle. But Mrs. Frost started one; and one hundred and fifty women from the country and mountains rode into town on horseback to attend the class. Berea has been working with limited means, and the only available room would accommodate but seventy-five women. Mrs. Frost then announced that she would have two divisions, alternating each week. But all the women wanted to attend both sessions, and begged the privilege to come and stand during the opening exercises of worship and prayer. Thus the poor mountain women are being practically helped in their struggle with poverty; and He who provides the "seamless garment" is being disclosed, to the joy and comfort of their souls. The expense of this work need not be great, and should not stand in the way of a church with limited means. The instruction will be voluntary, and, if necessary, — where the expense cannot be covered by subscription or an entertainment, — sufficient charge may be made for the garments to cover fully the cost of the cloth. The Mothers' Christian Endeavor Society [1] is often conducted in connection with work like the above. Whether conducted in conjunction with other work or independently, this society has proven most helpful.

5. The list of these societies may fittingly be closed with one that epitomizes the ideal of woman's work in the church, though it is found among the humble attendants of Grace Chapel, New York. The Woman's Friendship Club is an association of women banded together by "personal self-denial" to pay ten cents a month toward the new work of the church. "She hath done what she could" was the Master's tribute to the self-denial of one woman; and as the personal element in the gift of the "widow's mite" made it outweigh the benefactions of the wealthy, so the sacrifice of time, personal comfort, and individual enjoyment of the women of the Church will receive the blessed approval of Him who "looketh on the heart," and be enriched with His blessing unto great ends.

[1] Mr. John Willis Baer, General Secretary, 646 Washington Street, Boston, Mass.

CHAPTER XXV.

WORK WITH GIRLS AND YOUNG WOMEN.

The object of this chapter is to indicate in a brief way how pastors have been helpful to young women and how young women have been helpful in church and Christian work.

It has long been the custom of the Rev. F. B. Meyer, B.A., pastor of Christ's Church, London, to hold a meeting for the young women of his congregation at regular intervals, for their instruction and aid, and to plan with them for the great work of the kingdom. "Let every minister," says Mr. Meyer, "have a weekly or monthly meeting for the young women of his church, teaching them the deepest truths he knows, and banding them together for holy service." In speaking of his experience in this work, the pastor of Christ's Church says: "I have always tried to be a big brother to the girls of my charge. . . . And as I look back on a fairly large experience I feel sure that in numberless cases I have saved my young sisters from making irretrievable mistakes. I have helped with counsel, rejoiced in the first tidings of their gladness, strengthened them to bear heart-breaking disappointment, and in return for such brotherly sympathy I have had untold devotion. . . . The young girls of Christ's Church are banded together on the basis of devotion to our Saviour, total abstinence, modesty, self-sacrifice, and sisterliness. We meet once a month at the Lord's Table to repeat our vows, and have originated many societies and meetings of one sort and another for mutual help, benefit, and service. This is a real sisterhood, and out of it all kinds of good things have come, are coming, and will come. It is not a mere form which leads us at the end of our meetings to stand round the room with hands linked and sing, —

"'Blest be the tie that binds
Our hearts in Christian love.'

One of the best results of that sisterhood has been the establishment of an Evening Home for Girls, in the thickly populated neighborhood near by." [1]

This personal interest and definite systematic helpfulness by the pastor of Christ's Church to the young women of his congregation is significant, and a worthy object-lesson. Too often ministers through negligence or prudish timidity permit young women's societies " to go as they will," without a guiding hand or helpful word. Their work may be well done; nevertheless the opportunity is lost of helping them to larger plans; of counselling them and establishing such mutual sympathy as shall make for incalculable good; of aiding in things of vital interest, where a pastor's wisdom and sympathy would be most helpful, and when his influence would be formative of the years to come.

In most churches there is but one Women's Aid Society, which all women are expected to join. This simplifies the work; and when we consider it from the standpoint of unity, there are arguments in favor of but one organization for this kind of work. But when we remember that the ways of working of the older and young differ somewhat, and that the time at

[1] Christian Treasury, May, 1895, p. 110.

which they can conveniently assemble may not be the same, we see room for a Young Women's Aid Society. This may be conducted, if practicable, as auxiliary to the main society. Certain things will naturally fall to the juniors, such as supplying the pulpit with flowers, decorating the church for entertainments, serving refreshments at church gatherings, and teaching in the sewing-school and other educational enterprises under the charge of the church. Equally applicable are the arguments in favor of having the young women banded together into Home and Foreign Missionary efforts. The work of young women is incomplete save it include missionary effort. The missionary meetings of young people more often have a social feature than those of their elder sisters. Occasional evening meetings open to young men have been held with good results. Interest in missions has thus been awakened. If there should be more of this missionary work "at home," perhaps the future years will not show such a disparity between the sexes in missionary zeal.

There are other things that the young women can do. Some young ladies' societies in cities do a large work each year by raising money by means of musical entertainments, suppers, and sales for the "fresh air fund." Thus many hundred children each summer have respite from their poor and crowded homes in the hot city, and receive the health and happiness of a little outing in the gladsome country. Just here, too, is where young women's societies and others in the country can assist. They may do a grand work by co-operating with friends in the city in providing places for children either in private houses or by assisting for their care in larger numbers. A small house together with a tent will accommodate a hundred or more children. This plan is in operation in a number of places.

MODERN METHODS IN CHURCH WORK.

Friends in the village or country visit the children, make gifts of fruit and food, and thus the expense is largely reduced, and a few dollars is made to care for many children. If friends in the country knew of the poor sad homes where thousands of city children live, where foul air, ignorance, vice, and crime abound, they would, I believe, gladly rally to this work.

The Young Woman's Christian Temperance Union [1] presents opportunities for usefulness in many ways. The Daughters of the King [2] is another open door to service. This is an organization among Episcopal young women. It was started in 1885. It has for its object the spread of Christ's kingdom among women. It is a noble order, and has accomplished much good.

Similar to this is the order of the King's Daughters.[3] It differs from the former, however, in being undenominational and in the fact that it uses its efforts for the betterment of every class of society. It is the broadest of all existing societies in the scope of its work. Its members are pledged as individuals and as an order to help the poor, to aid the suffering and needy, and to help in *any* good work. Each circle chooses its own work. The one obligation for membership is service.

This order was organized early in 1886, and during the ten years of its existence, the little silver cross with the knot of purple ribbon and its legend, "In His Name," has been carried into many lands. As now combined with the order of King's Sons, the good

---

[1] Mrs. Katherine Lente Stevenson, Corresponding Secretary, The Temple, Chicago, Ill.

[2] Miss Elizabeth L. Ryerson, Secretary, 520 East 87th Street, New York City.

[3] Mrs. Isabella Charles Davis, Corresponding Secretary, 158 West 23d Street, New York City.

accomplished so quietly and unostentatiously is beyond all reckoning.

The following are some of the different kinds of service that have been undertaken by the circles of King's Daughters and Sons. This enumeration must prove suggestive to other young women societies. The Countess Circle of New Glasgow, N. S., strives for more sociability in the church with which it is connected. A circle in Richmond, Vt., where the people are poor, has not only seen that the pulpit was filled, but has also undertaken to see that the supply was paid. Once when there was no minister, the leader of the Circle herself held a praise service. A member of the Montreal "Whatsoever Circle" held an "at home," and sent an invitation to every King's Daughter and Son in the city with their friends to come and bring something for the poor. From the supplies and money contributed, thirty-seven families received Christmas boxes of groceries, clothing, and toys. In Wakefield, R. I., the village milliners give the Circle hats to be trimmed. The Circle trims them, gives them to the poor in the Sunday-school, and also sends a box to needy ones in New York. The Kingston, Ont., Charity Circle has a "Food and Fuel Club." This was organized to help the poor to save during months when work is plenty. The matter was explained to the people in a meeting called for the purpose, and those who did not come were called upon and given the opportunity to join. Collectors, members of the Circle, volunteered to call every month on those who joined the Club. Each collector was provided with a book in which the names of those in her district were entered. The members, on the other hand, had cards signed by the officers of the Circle. At each visit, the collector entered the money paid by the club-member in her book and also on the card of the member. The season for saving was from April to October. When winter drew near, it was found that $176.86 had been collected. The Circle had made arrangements for coal, so that the members had the benefit of the reduced summer prices. Arrangements were also made for moderate prices in groceries. The members, of course, drew their money out as they needed during the winter. But preference was generally shown for the Circle's orders on the food and fuel supply, for which the savings were made. The Circle also paid out of its own fund five per cent interest on the money paid in. In Philadelphia, near the great brickmaking yards and oil works, stands the "R." It was established by Miss Mary Schott, a King's Daughter, and the young men of her Sunday-school class. It is under the care of the King's Sons. "The 'R' is a restaurant or place of resort where men may rest and partake of refreshment, and afterward find recreation in reading, while the King's Sons work for their reformation by means of religion." It has a thoroughly equipped reading-room and library. Lessons in drawing, music, and carpentry are also given. It does an incalculable amount of good in the quarter in which it is located. The "Silver Cross Club" of Chicago has furnished a cosy lunch-room where girls may furnish part of their lunch, may rest in the easy-chairs and lounges and enjoy the books and magazines provided. The Circle in Germantown, Penn., has a Boys' Parlor open every evening. It contains, in addition to reading-room and games, a shop where are found carpenters' tools, jig-saws, and other similar tools. Anything the boys finish they may take home. There are also classes in drawing, hammock-netting, and so forth. One member of the Circle gathers the boys around her and teaches them Natural History by means of a cabinet of specimens, which she and the boys have collected. At nine o'clock a hymn is sung, and the boys depart. At times, the stereopticon is produced for their entertainment or a little talk is given. There is another Circle in New York called the "Happy Sunday Afternoon." About half-past three, the children come, all girls, with the exception of baby brothers who have to be brought along. The children sing several hymns, the words being on paper and hung on the wall. Then they gather around the story-teller and are entertained for an hour. After singing, they are dismissed, each child being given a magazine or paper.

Some other things that circles have done may be briefly told. One circle bought a saddle for a home missionary; another a sewing-machine for a poor woman; another a music-box which they sent around among the institutions of the city to entertain the inmates. Other circles have made comfort bags for sailors and light-house keepers, have paid regular visits to the Old Ladies' Homes and hospitals, to cheer with their bright faces, to read or to take some dainty dish or article, or to play or sing for the aged. Another circle gave a Christmas tree to the Free Kindergarten. Another furnished each two sheets and a pair of pillowcases to the Bethany Home for Working Girls in Boston. One circle, even, did a washing for a poor woman, and another circle sent milk daily to a starving baby. Many circles dress dolls to send to babies' hospitals and nurseries, and make scrap-books for the babies. One circle made a bright screen for a child's hospital. The screen was decorated with picture cards, and served a double purpose of keeping off the draft and amusing the little sufferers. Another circle

MODERN METHODS IN CHURCH WORK.

has invented the Envelope Library, which consists of selections cut out and pasted on strong manila paper. Each envelope contains stories, poetry, comforting words, and the Gospel invitation. The cuttings are light and easy to hold, and the variety the envelopes contain makes a break in the monotony of the sick-room or the hospital. Another circle has for one of its plans *thoughtfulness for workers.* The members of the circle are careful to give exact change to conductors on street cars, make it a rule to be decided in shopping as to what they want before going to the counter, and never to shop late in the day. Still another circle totally discourages gossiping, and calls itself the "Silent Circle."

Some circles are paying the expenses of children who are learning a trade; others buy appliances to straighten crippled children's limbs, or crutches for the lame, or an invalid chair for the helpless. Many circles subscribe to Ramabai's School for Child Widows in India, and others assist in the work among the lepers in the East, while others help in the missionary work of the churches with which they are connected. Many circles are helping in the Clothing Bureau established in New York in 1892 by the Central Council of the King's Daughters. It has been found that the deserving poor would rather pay a small price than to receive clothing as a gift. Some of the clothing is of so excellent a character that the Bureau has been able to help that class most to be pitied, the refined poor, the nature of whose ability demands that, in seeking work, they shall be able to present a respectable appearance. Other circles send clothing to the babies at the Children's Hospital and gather soft fine old handkerchiefs for use at hospitals. The circles in New York take especial pains to have vacation trips for tired mothers, who, bearing the heat and burden of the house-work, have been the last usually to be thought of. They also assist the "Little Mothers" to vacation trips and outings. The circle in Wilmington, N. C., have a pleasant home at the beach called the "Shelter of the Silver Cross," to which they send people for a summer outing.

These are but a very few of the kinds of Christian work this noble organization is doing both by itself and in connection with other societies whose aim is the betterment of mankind and the spread of the Gospel. Everywhere they are working, — through the Fresh Air Fund, the Charity Organization, the Missionary Society, and the Church. No service too menial, no labor too arduous; it is fitting that they call themselves sons and daughters of the King. They are closely following the footsteps of Jesus, saying, "I must be about my Father's business."

> "I would not wait for any great achievement;
> You may not live to reach that far-off goal;
> Speak soothing words to some heart in bereavement,
> Aid some up-struggling soul."[1]

[1] Ella Wheeler Wilcox.

CHAPTER XXVI.

THE SOCIAL PROBLEM OF THE CHURCH.

Behind the social problem lies the key of what should constitute the impulse of all our work, if we would reach the unchurched masses, — it is this, we must realize the power of the Indwelling Presence which the Holy Spirit was sent to reveal, and which is the heritage of every redeemed soul; and as we lean upon this help, we shall learn more and more how to take the hand of strangers and bid them welcome in our churches, and they will know by the very way we look into their faces, that they have met a friend, and they will be convinced of the reality of the religion of Jesus Christ. — Mrs. GIDEON FOUNTAIN.

1. THE work of the women of the church has always been so thorough and far-reaching that a new society which finds place for itself and, instead of encroaching upon, proves to be the open door to other societies, commands our closest interest.

The Mary and Martha League is a new society which simply and comprehensively solves what has long been a perplexing problem; namely, the social relation between the richer and poorer members of the church, and the relation of new members to the older members.

The fact that the poorer people have not always felt comfortable with the "well-to-do" has not always been the latter's fault, though they have commonly borne the blame. There is a sensitiveness to social distinction, which is more consciously felt by the poorer people than is remembered by the Christian well-to-do classes, and as a result very few calls are made upon the latter, though a most cordial welcome is given. Under such circumstances the helpfulness of large acquaintance in the church is not realized, at least for a considerable length of time. On the other hand, with many of the strangers coming into church, running the gantlet of "return calls" is not a coveted process. Again, some are so situated that they cannot make the calls, while others would not, even though they could.

What, then, is to be provided in the way of social life for these people? The men have associates in business and diversion in the club, but the women are like Ruth in Bethlehem, with *one* friend. What is needed from the church is the Christ touch of a kindly welcome. Many hearts ache for sympathy and for fellowship with the people of God. The church must supplement the home, and this cannot be done alone by pastors and church officers. Such welcome is always appreciated, but in itself does not extend the acquaintance very far, and is incomplete, as "there is a touch of welcome that can come only from a woman. As woman is the hostess in the home, so she must become the embodiment of a Christlike hospitality in the church. As individual Christians, we are called upon to bear witness to the power of Jesus Christ to save; are we not also called upon to bear witness to his loving kindness, to his cordiality, to his gracious welcome?"[1]

Here is woman's opportunity. And the Mary and Martha League is trying to realize the ideal of expressing this hospitality, to promote the Christian fellowship of the church, and by this means to bring homes into living union with Jesus Christ. The society was organized in the Madison Avenue Pres-

[1] Paper by Mrs. Gideon Fountain, read before the Open and Institutional Church League, Philadelphia, November, 1894.

byterian Church, New York, in January, 1894, as a result of many gropings to meet what many a church has found to be a peculiar need. The following is the Constitution of the society: —

This organization shall be called the "Mary and Martha League of the —— ——."

The League is a part of the church itself, and like all the other societies is subject to the wish and general direction of the pastor.

The object of this League is for the spread of Christ's kingdom in our midst.

To this end those desirous of becoming members are asked to observe two rules, viz. : prayer and service.

The rule of prayer is that each member promises to pray daily for the spread of Christ's kingdom and for special blessing upon this society.

The rule of service is to make an earnest effort to bring persons where they shall hear the Gospel preached, or in any way to emphasize the regular appointed services of the church of which this is a part.

Any one may become a member of this society by paying the annual fee of ten cents and signing the Constitution.

The members shall consist of two classes, — active and associate.

Active members shall consist of those who are already church-members. The associate members are entitled to all the privileges of the association, may work on committees, but shall have no voice in voting.

This League shall consist of the following officers, and shall be elected annually, — President, Vice-Presidents, Secretary, and Treasurer.

The annual meeting shall be held in January.

This Constitution may be amended at an annual meeting by a two-thirds vote of the active members.

This Constitution, like that of the Andrew and Philip Brotherhood, which suggested it, is simplicity itself. There are two distinguishing features in the work of this society. The first is that of the Calling Committee, and the second is that of the monthly meeting of the society.

The Calling Committee consists of about twenty-five members of the League, who are given names of strangers and of new members in the congregation for the purpose of calling upon them in a friendly way, to express the cordial welcome and hospitality of the church, and to invite them to the League meetings, where there is an opportunity to become acquainted with the older members of the church and also with the pastor and his wife. The new names of women which may come into the possession of the pastors through pulpit receptions or by other means, are at once handed to the president of the League. Such names are entered by her in a "Name Book," and are registered alphabetically and also by streets. The book is simply a ledger, and a page or half a page is given each name. All calls made by the members of the visiting staff are reported in writing upon the following blanks: —

Name, ...
Address, ... *Date of Call,* ....
Remarks, ...
         Signed, ...
Madison Avenue Presbyterian Church.

The substance of these reports in turn is entered in the Name Book. Helpful information, such as previous church affiliations, the religious status of the several members of the family, and any suggestion for reaching them, is recorded. In this way the work is thorough and systematic. This is one way of being "wise as a serpent and harmless as a dove." Such information often lights a straight path to the hearts of the people. Only the members of the League and the pastors of the church have access to the Name Book.

The Calling Committee meets for half an hour preceding the regular monthly meeting of the League. Each member reads a report of her calls, and then hands the report in writing to the president of the society. To hear what the several members are doing is stimulating and encouraging to all, as well as otherwise helpful.

The second distinguishing feature of this League is the Monthly Meeting. It is this that gathers up the results of the previous invitations and calls by members of the League; it is the focal point of all the work of the society, — the society itself being only the means to the greater end of winning the people to Christ and bringing them into the membership of the church.

The monthly meeting is held in the church parlors on the first Saturday of each month. The best day for holding monthly meetings will, of course, be determined by local conditions. With some, Saturday is an unusually busy day. But with others, teachers and young women in the schools, Saturday is the only day in the week when they can be at leisure. The meeting is held from three to five o'clock, and consists of two parts. The first part may be called devotional and educational, and is also given to the business of the League, such as reports of committees, discussions, plans for work, and so forth. Sometimes a stranger is invited to give a short address upon some topic of the day of special interest to women. At the close of the first hour, a formal adjournment is made, and the second hour is spent wholly in a social way. The members of the Calling Committee take especial pains to introduce the ladies whom they have called upon and with whom a friendly intercourse has been begun, to the other members of the League, and to visitors. This gives opportunity for meeting a goodly number of the members of the church. A pleasant acquaintance is begun, and oftentimes relations are established between the families of the old and new members which grow into strongest friendships, and many families become regular attendants and members of the church. Some strangers who would hesitate to accept invitations to private homes, accept invitations to the League meetings and to this social hour. Here they can come and meet not merely one family of the church, but many. And here in the Father's house, where there is an atmosphere of cordiality and home welcome, even the poorer forget that there is such a thing as class distinction, and feel comfortable and at home under the gracious influence of that spirit which hath made us all one. During the social hour a cup of tea is served, the table being attended and the people waited upon by some of the newer members of the society. An effort is always made to enlist the co-operation of the new members as soon as possible. The Entertainment Committee provides a short programme in the way of music, vocal or instrumental, and sometimes readings and recitations are given. Variety is aimed for, and "everything is done to fill the hour with delightful social intercourse void of formality."

Invitations in writing are sent out a few days previous to the monthly meeting of the League. These invitations are mimeographed on postal cards, making the expense very slight. The mailing list is taken from the Name Book.

Although all the strangers do not come to the League meetings, some because they cannot, and others because they have not the disposition to come, still invitations are always mailed to them. Many families upon whom no apparent impression was made for months, — through the gentle persistency of the women, through their calls and invitations to the meetings, — have been finally brought not only into the society, but also into the active membership of the church.

Much depends in this work, as in all societies, on the president of the League. It demands a woman of clear, good judgment, who is sympathetic and spiritual. She, too, must be a leader, capable of keeping the members of the society at peace with one another, and a woman who can hear much and say little. Such a president will not only direct wisely, but will also inspire.

The League in the Madison Avenue Presbyterian Church has been copied in other places, and many people are being reached through it. It is an effective means of expressing the hospitality and the gracious welcome which the church, standing in Christ's stead, ought always to express.

2. Gatherings like the Mary and Martha League open the way to the larger social gatherings of the church. The church social may be one of the happiest and most helpful parts of church life. But sometimes they are formal and unfeeling and as destructive of goodly fellowship and influence as "monotony is destructive of art." Such socials are of no avail to heaven or earth. The wise soon learn to shun them, though the saint may endure them. But this need not and should not be so. The cause lies not so much in the unwillingness of people to be social as the fact that they

have so little in common, coming as the members of the ordinary church do from circles differing in interests and mutual tastes. Then, too, there is something formal about the church parlors or assembly rooms. The absence of the bright accessories of the home seems to produce a feeling of stiffness unknown in other social gatherings. But this can be overcome, at least in part, by *bringing in* the accessories. Let the room be aglow with pretty lamps and a flood of light. Break up the "straight rows" and arrange the furnishings with the pleasant orderly carelessness of the drawing-room. Above all, have a social committee that is *alive*, and whose one care and concern will be to promote the pleasure and acquaintance of others. Music early in the evening will do much in bringing the people together in sympathy and interest and starting the flow of conversation. There is no ritual for the church social. As Emerson says of manners, "Good sense and character make their own forms every moment," so the church social must "yield largely to the energy of the individual," and to the requirements of the occasion. The programme of the evening should be carefully prepared. The Entertainment Committee will do well occasionally to break up groups of people into new groups, and so extend the pleasantest company and make it easy for the timid. But do not leave all responsibility with the committee. Every one in the church should appreciate his duty to make it pleasant for others. Happy is the pastor who can bring this spirit to prevail with all his people! He will then realize the ideal social. Such an ideal will take time, patience, and persistence, but nothing short of it is worth working for.

The church social or reception may at times be given especially in the interest of new members. When persons are received into a church, it would seem the part of courtesy to do everything possible to make them acquainted with those who joined the church before them. To this end, a reception to new members may be held closely following the Sunday on which they were received into the church. But this reception must be more than such in name. It often happens that no one in such a reception is so little noticed as the so-called guests of honor. A good plan is to have the new members, in company with some of the officers of the church and the pastor and his wife, stand to receive the other members and friends of the church. Ushers may escort all comers to those receiving.

3. Another direct and pleasing way of expressing the welcome and interest of the church is the plan of the Shawmut Church of Boston. With rare tact and discernment certain members open their homes on every evening during the week except the night of the weekly prayer meeting or other public church gathering. A little leaflet is distributed at the church bearing on its titlepage, "Shawmut Church Evenings at Home." Then come the evenings and the names and addresses of those receiving. The leaflet concludes with a hearty invitation to any of the church and congregation, particularly strangers, to call at the homes thus opened on the evenings designated. The idea of thus offering Christian hospitality is so gracious, so wholly in accord with Gospel teaching, that no words of commendation need be added. Though no angel be entertained unawares, the heart of the stranger may be gladdened, and a Christlike interest shown in him in a very real way.

These several ways of personal contact not only promote acquaintance and enable us to help others by a friendly interest, but also afford opportunity for bringing to bear a Christlike personality, which is ever honored by the Spirit in the great work of the kingdom.

> "Only a kind word spoken,
> Only a kind look given,
> But they filled a life with beauty,
> And a soul was raised to heaven."[1]

[1] Anonymous.

CHAPTER XXVII.

THE CHILDREN OF THE CHURCH.

The parents are inflexible, but the children are malleable.
EDWARD JUDSON, D.D.

THE future of the Church and of the nation is with the children. Would we have that Church a great and growing power for extending the kingdom of God, that nation a righteous people, we must work to-day for the children, or to-morrow they will be the impressionless men and women. Rev. Stephen H. Tyng, D.D., says: "The devil would never ask anything more of a minister than to have him feel that his mission was chiefly to the grown-up members of the congregation, while some one else was to look after the children."[1]

With all our "ransomed powers" we are toiling for the redemption of the masses and the reclaiming of the degraded and fallen. This is well, and may merit the benediction, "Inasmuch as ye have done it;" but is there not danger of our forgetting that, as Dr. Judson says, "the key to the hard problem of evangelization lies in the puny hand of the little child"? Children as "an heritage of the Lord" are the precious charge of the Church, and they may justly lay claim to its fostering care. When we look at the children in this way and realize that every child whom no other church is caring for is *our* child, the feeling of responsibility broadens and deepens.

[1] Quoted in Publisher's Note to "Our Greatest Work," by G. R. Robbins.

THE CHILDREN OF THE CHURCH.

The importance of work for children cannot be overemphasized. The school-boys of Bourges, in the early French Revolution, bore a flag displaying in shining letters the words: "*Tremblez, Tyrans, nous grandirons!*" (Tremble, Tyrants, we shall grow up!) Oh that these words, "We shall grow up," would ever ring in our churches! — grow up and make tremble the enemy of our God, or grow up *with the enemy* and make us tremble. The Romanists are wont to say, "Give us the child until he is ten years old, and you may do what you *can* with him after that." Trebonius, the instructor of Martin Luther, always uncovered his head in the presence of any of his boys. He was accustomed to say, "Who can tell what man may yet rise up amid these youths? There may be among them those who shall be learned doctors, sages, — nay, princes of the empire." Even then there was before him the great leader of the Reformation, that " solitary monk that shook the world." The children must increasingly receive the attention, thought, and care of the Church.

There are several agencies in working for and with the children which have met with blessed results.

1. First and foremost among these agencies is the Sunday-school. Nothing has ever been devised to take its place. Old and yet ever new, full of fresh plans and methods, the best products of the best minds in the Church, coming on the one day of the week when school and home and work release their grasp, the Sunday-school has been " a power unto salvation." It is strange, but many people who never enter a church themselves are willing and glad that their children shall become members of the Sunday-school. Often the Sunday-school proves the open door to other members of the family, and the promise is fulfilled, " A little

child shall lead them." The teacher who comes to call upon the child of the house will be welcomed where the district visitor would be denied admittance. Much grows out of the Sunday-school. Once brought into contact with the children in the classes, the social opportunities increase. The picnics and other gatherings arranged for the pleasure of the children become fruitful opportunities of coming into closer touch with them along the lines of their daily living; and much kindly counsel may be given, which will be incorporated into their after lives. Care should be exercised to make the festivals of the church red-letter days in the calendar of the school. The glorious facts of the birth and resurrection of our Lord may thus be associated with all that is brightest in childish experiences. Children's Day with its flowers and music is perhaps the most attractive day in the year to the school. So bright are the little faces, so full of the spirit of the season in this blossom-time of the year, that no church will need to be urged to give them the encouragement of their presence. Rally Day should mean a rallying of the church around the Sunday-school, as well as the usual meaning in the vocabulary of the school. In the Wesley Chapel, Methodist Episcopal, of Columbus, O., they have their Rally Day exercises in the Sunday-school room in the morning, and in the evening of the same day a Harvest Home Praise Service in the auditorium. The church is decorated for this service with autumn boughs, fruits, and vegetables, while a shock of corn and a sheaf of wheat also find a place to mutely show forth the goodness of God. This Sunday-school also sets apart a week-day evening during Thanksgiving week for the bringing in of donations by the members of the school. These supplies are stored up and distributed as there is necessity for them. The superintendent of the school, Mr. J. E. Huff, writes: "For this service we have a special programme arranged, with good music, and, being held on a week night, have a little fun mixed with it. This is a great occasion with us. Our school is not made up of members of wealthy families, but you would be surprised to see the large amount of articles of every kind that are brought in. These donations have at times run up as high as $500 in value, in goods such as groceries, dry-goods, coal or orders for same, clothing (new and old), boots and shoes, etc., and some giving cash."

2. A second agency in promoting the spiritual development of the young is found in addresses to them on special occasions by the pastor and by sermons to children on Sunday. It is not every church that is blessed with a pastor who can do his part on Children's Day and other occasions so well as the children do theirs. It takes a man who remembers how he felt when a boy, and who knows the golden mean between his ordinary style of preaching and a relapse into foolish anecdotes, to preach to children. A man must be thoroughly in sympathy with children's lines of thought, not merely fond of children, — which is a very different thing, — to address them acceptably. The methods in use by the Rev. Henry Evertson Cobb, D.D., of the Collegiate Reformed Church of New York, are very simple and practical. The music of the preliminary exercises at every Sabbath morning service in his church is selected bearing in mind the presence of the children. The second hymn is also a children's hymn. The pastor then gives a five-minute sermon to the children, and the smallest ones leave the church before the regular sermon. In the Church of the Covenant, Chicago, Rev. W. S. Plumer Bryan, D.D., pastor, the plan has been tried of offering prizes to boys

and girls for written outlines of the pastor's sermons. The method is to divide the young people into four classes,— those under twelve, between twelve and fifteen, between fifteen and eighteen, and over eighteen. The outlines are written in books supplied for the purpose. They are numbered and no names appear, so that the judgment passed upon them is strictly impartial. No notes are taken and no assistance received. Dr. Bryan also preaches a bi-monthly sermon to children. The practice of the Presbyterian Church of Scotland — a plan which is being increasingly adopted by the churches of other denominations in Scotland — is to devote a Sabbath morning service once a month to the interest of children. The whole programme is prepared with a view to their edification; but, as a matter of fact, the service is greatly enjoyed by all. There is no doubt that in the reaction from the rigid methods of our forefathers, who insisted that the children should hear at least two *long* sermons on Sunday, we have gone too far in the opposite direction, and plans to encourage the attendance of children at church are worthy of especial attention.

3. There is another step in Christian nurture, the outcome of instruction in the Sunday-school and from the pulpit, which is leading children to form themselves into societies in which they shall grow in the Christian life. The Junior Society of Christian Endeavor, and such denominational societies as the Junior Epworth League and the Junior Baptist Union, are all the outgrowth of the idea that the sooner the child begins to express his gratitude to God, his desires to be good, and his ideas about the things he has been taught, the more likely he will be to make a strong active Christian. Much depends upon the organizer. I do not say the leader, as the leader proper is one of the children; but there

should always be some consecrated older Christian who has the Society in his charge. He may give a brief, simple talk on the topic, may lead in prayer or illustrate the subject with a chalk talk. His chief work with the Society should, however, be on the outside, and his presence in the meeting the unobtrusive yet friendly attitude which the pastor takes when in the Senior Society, — always ready to help when needed, yet never dominating. Kindred to these societies is the Growing Legion, which is a children's society of the Lincoln Park Baptist Church of Cincinnati, O. Their meetings are held on Tuesday afternoon from four to five o'clock. The exercises consist of singing, a five-minute address, ten minutes devoted to the catechism, followed by quotations from the Scripture by the boys and girls. A collection too is always taken. After singing, the children march from the chapel into the auditorium. As they pass through the door, each receives a small flag. They march to the music of the pipe organ around the church, double file and countermarch, waving flags and singing songs of an inspiring character. After marching for fifteen minutes, they halt and lowering their flags receive the benediction, then, marching to the side entrance of the church, are dismissed. This service is directly under the supervision of the pastor.[1]

The First Congregational Church of Michigan, Ind., holds a children's service of song once every month. The choir renders some selections, and there is an address by the minister, but the exercises of the evening are mainly given by the children, accompanied in the vocal performances with various musical instruments. The pastor, Rev. W. C. Gordon, writes that these song services have filled the church, have made a most cordial relation between pastor and children, have devel-

[1] See "Our Greatest Work," by Rev. George R. Robbins.

oped the musical taste of the children, have increased the attendance in the Sunday-school greatly, have opened up the homes of the non-church-members where there were children, and have increased the membership of the church. Of twenty-five who united with the church on profession of faith, in one month, several were primarily drawn in through the instrumentality of the children's service of song.

4. All these plans outlined above have been designed mainly for the benefit of the children themselves; but we must not forget, nor allow them to forget, that, while " grow in grace and in the knowledge of our Lord and Saviour Jesus Christ "[1] is an injunction laid upon them as well as upon their elders in the church, there is also a command given to all, " Go ye therefore and teach all nations."[2] There is no time in human life when stories of far-off countries and different conditions of life and surroundings are listened to with the same avidity as in childhood. The heart is tender too; and when the teacher points out the sad state of those who live in heathendom, little folks are not only interested but anxious to help. Thus, in the time of youth, the habit of systematic giving to, and interest in, missions may be established. Children are often formed into mission bands, in which they are instructed in the work being done in missionary fields. There are many happy ways of stimulating giving, such as birthday boxes, banks to be opened on a certain day, or jugs to be broken and their contents counted. But if an abiding interest in the people of the missionary lands has not been created, these things will in time be put away with other " childish things." These people are so far away, and so little real knowledge is possessed of them by the children, that it seems difficult to bring

[1] 2 Peter iii. 18.   [2] Matthew xxviii. 19.

the two into living touch. Map and blackboard exercises are all very well in their way, but to awaken enthusiasm for, and personal interest in, a country, a stamp album seems to have a special power. You hear boys and girls talking glibly of Brazilian stamps who would otherwise never think of Brazil. A novel and interesting way to bring foreign countries before the children is to purchase inexpensive stamp albums for them and set them to collecting. The United States stamps are easy to obtain, and as an encouragement some reward might be offered for the most complete and best mounted set. While these are being collected, a series of lessons may be taught on Home Missions; a map of the United States having been procured, the various schools and churches in which the church of the children's denomination are interested may be pointed out. The peculiar conditions of the people, as the negroes of the South or the Mexicans of the Southwest, might be set forth, and what we can and ought to do to help them, discussed. Then later, as the children are able to secure stamps, each country might come in as a lesson. In the case of the civilized countries, such as England, some facts might be given as to what they are doing in foreign fields, also what peculiar work they have to do at home. It should also be pointed out that what makes the essential difference between a civilized and an uncivilized country is the religion of Jesus Christ. In the foreign countries where the church of the denomination with which the mission band is connected is working, after dwelling on the condition and needs of the people, the missionary stations may be described and interest awakened in the missionaries, their children and the children they teach. In case the children cannot get a stamp of such a country, the teacher may procure one, and after the lesson give it to some member of the band as an encouragement for good work. It will be found that the missionaries will gladly help with cancelled stamps and with special points of interest to use in the work. It would be well to select from the children's stamps the country which will be the subject for the coming study, and let them learn as much as possible about it in the meantime. These and other geographical exercises will be of great value in awakening the interest of the children in those less fortunate than they. And an interest based on an intelligent comprehension of the needs and environment of the people will be an abiding one.

5. The band idea is a good one, and temperance workers have availed themselves of it in gathering the children into their work. The Woman's Christian Temperance Union [1] has under its supervision the Loyal Temperance Legion, which consists of bands of young temperance workers organized under the auspices of some local union. A work very similar to this is done by that juvenile temperance society known as the Band of Hope. In these societies careful instruction is given as to the evils of intemperance, and various attractive methods employed to win the boys and girls into temperance work.

[1] Mrs. Catharine Lente Stephenson, Corresponding Secretary, The Temple, Chicago, Ill.

CHAPTER XXVIII.

THE SUNDAY-SCHOOL.

The limits of this book permit only a brief mention of some of the methods of working of that tremendous agency for good, the Sunday-school. Many books have been written on this subject, among them none better than Rev. Dr. A. F. Schauffler's "Ways of Working." The book abounds in suggestions as to methods of work. Dr. Schauffler recommends object-lessons, the use of the blackboard, and commends especially a Superintendent's Cabinet, consisting of the teachers. The meetings of this Cabinet differ from ordinary teachers' meetings for the study of the lesson. They are for the purpose of discussing the best ways of working for the school, and if intelligently carried on will result in arousing a hearty spirit of co-operation with the superintendent among the teachers.

Another excellent work is "Sunday-School Ways of Working," compiled by Rev. Carlos Tracy Chester from the "Sunday-School Times," and published by that paper. The book is an epitome of the best methods of working in the most successful Sunday-schools of our country, and is invaluable to every pastor and Sunday-school worker, being packed full of practical suggestions.

1. The question of attendance is a very important one to the Sunday-school, both as to getting new scholars and retaining in regular attendance the old ones. To secure new scholars, the Brick Church of Rochester, N. Y., issues the following card to be used by Sunday-school scholars.

> **BRICK CHURCH SUNDAY-SCHOOL.**
>
> *To the Superintendent:*
>   *Below please find name and address of a person I know of not now attending Sunday-school who, I think, might be gotten into our School by your personal attention and effort.*
>
>   ....
>   ....
>
> *Please sign your own name and address.*
>
> **POSSIBLE NEW SCHOLAR.**
> *Name,* ....
> *Address,* ....
> *Remarks,* ....
> *Return, when filled out, to Rev. G. B. F. Hallock,*
>   *10 Livingston Park.*

The persons whose names are thus obtained are immediately visited by the superintendent, who when he has secured the promise of a child to attend the next Sunday, gives him a card to present at the door, as follows: —

> *Introducing*
> ....
> ....
>   TO THE
> **Reception Committee of the Brick Church Sunday-school.**
>   G. B. F. HALLOCK, *Assistant.*
>
>   The Sunday-school meets at 12 o'clock, noon.
>   A member of the Reception Committee will be in waiting at the door of the Sunday-school room to welcome you. Bring this Card with you.
>   Regular Church Services every Sunday morning at 10.30, and Evening at 7.30. All are cordially welcome.

THE SUNDAY-SCHOOL.

Some churches distribute printed invitations by means of teachers and scholars, while pastors of other churches issue a circular letter to members of the school, urging them to make personal effort to bring new scholars, and award a banner to the class bringing the largest number within a quarter.

With regard to retaining and encouraging regular attendance at the school, various plans have been tried. Some schools rely on punch marks made in a record card, presented each Sabbath at the door. In other schools attendance is encouraged by a roll of honor for punctuality, regularity, and acquaintance with the lesson. The Church of the Ascension, New York, has in its Sunday-school the following somewhat strict rule, — the object being, perhaps, to bring into exercise that peculiarity of the human race which makes it appreciative of that which requires effort to retain: "The name of any pupil who is absent *three successive Sundays without excuse* shall be removed from the Sunday-school roll, and notice sent to the parent. Such a name *may be reinstated twice* on application to the Secretary, but *three such removals shall exclude the pupil* from attendance at the school during the rest of the year." This school aims at great thoroughness in the matter of preparation of the lesson, and gives badges of scholarship at the end of each quarter to those whose proficiency and neatness are shown by the work done in the Quarterlies. Certificates are given to those who pass satisfactory examination.

2. Reports from the teachers may be used as an agency for gathering facts. First, as to classes themselves, when a schedule may be sent to each teacher to be filled out so as to indicate the spiritual condition of the class. The reports give the names of scholars

who are members of the church, those who are Christians but not members of the church, those who do not call themselves Christians, and those who will begin the Christian life at once.

Second, reports of teachers may be used to find facts to assist in reaching families whose children attend the Sunday-school while the relatives are non-attendants, as indicated by the blank below. This is in use in the Brick Church of Rochester, N. Y.

TO THE TEACHER.

Please give below the names and addresses of any Parents, Relatives, or Friends of your Scholars, who do not attend church regularly, or who attend the Brick Church but are not members nor renters of sittings.

Please be as explicit as possible in your statements, being sure to give at least, —

1. The Scholar's name and address.
2. The names and addresses of his or her Parents, Relatives, or Friends as above, with their relationship to Scholar.
3. Their general practice with regard to church attendance.

Any other facts which you consider important will be thankfully received.

Superintendent.

---

3. The Home Department of the Sunday-school may be made a very effective adjunct to the church. The object of this organization is to engage in Bible study those who cannot well be members of the regular Sunday-school, — the sick, the aged, busy mothers, and families who live so far from the church as to render it inconvenient or impossible to attend. The work and study is under the direction of a Home Department superintendent, assisted by visitors, who each

have charge of a class. They visit each member of this class, have friendly and spiritual conversation with him, and take him the lesson helps, receiving at the end of the quarter the report of each member, with whatever offering to the benevolent objects of the church such member may wish to give.

The advantages of this home work may be thus briefly summarized:—

1. It develops the study of the Bible.
2. It brings its students into relationship with other students of the Word.
3. It brings its students into relationship with the Church and Sunday-school.
4. It promotes Christian usefulness.
5. It increases benevolent contributions; one Home Department contributed in one year forty dollars, another one hundred and thirty, and another two hundred and thirty.
6. It increases attendance on the main school. One city school of eight hundred members reports that one hundred and thirty-nine were transferred in nineteen months from the Home Department, which numbered two hundred and seventy-five at the outset.
7. It brings new attendants to the church services. In one Sunday-school fifty persons were brought to church attendance in less than two years.

Finally: thousands of souls have been led to Christ and have united with the Church through the instrumentality of the Home Department.[1]

Mr. W. A. Duncan, Ph. D., who originated this movement, has published a very complete little pamphlet which sets forth the whole plan of its working, and which he cheerfully furnishes on application to him at Syracuse, N. Y.

4. TEACHERS' MEETINGS AND NORMAL CLASSES. The superintendent of a Sunday-school is sometimes re-

---

[1] Home Classes, by W. A. Duncan, Ph. D., pp. 59-64.

garded as entirely responsible for its well-being, while the fact is that upon the teachers as well as upon the superintendent depends the welfare of the school. It is therefore important that teachers should not only be consecrated men and women, but also should be trained for their work. Teachers' meetings are valuable, but sometimes difficulty is experienced in getting the teachers to attend. It seems impracticable in many congregations to hold such meetings on another night than the evening of the mid-week prayer-meeting. To hold them before that service seems early; to postpone them till afterward, quite too late. The Congregational and Presbyterian combined church of Storm Lake, Iowa, has a plan which admirably meets the difficulty. The teachers and officers meet at some one of the homes at six o'clock for tea, — a plain tea, restricted to four articles of food. At six-thirty, they commence the study of the Sunday-school lesson and continue it until time to go to prayer-meeting, where the Sunday-school lesson of the coming week is the subject of the service. The pastor, Rev. J. MacAllister, writes, "We have been greatly benefited by it."

But aside from the general study of the teachers' meeting some more specific training seems to be needed if our teachers are to reach the highest degree of efficiency. To meet this demand, normal classes have been carried on with the happiest results in many schools. The superintendent in a school blessed with such a training-class is at no loss where to find a substitute teacher who has made special preparation for teaching the lesson of the day. In some schools such a class meets for study at the time of the Sunday-school session; but in the Central Presbyterian Church of Rochester, N. Y., there is a teachers' supply

THE SUNDAY-SCHOOL.

and training class which meets once each month or oftener at call of teacher or class. The members of this class, which is limited to twenty-five, pledge themselves to study and prepare the lesson each week, and conscientiously to respond when called upon to teach a class.

Rev. E. P. Armstrong, in an article in the "Sunday-School Times" of September 5, 1895, entitled "The Sunday-School of the Future," gives us a very lofty ideal for a Normal class. He would have it include a course in mental and moral philosophy, pedagogics, child mind, and kindergarten, as well as a systematic study of the Bible. He would also have in the Sunday-school a department of archæology, giving instruction in antiquities of all descriptions, and a department of Old Testament Hebrew and New Testament Greek. Such a conception of the office of the Sunday-school in training pupils and teachers lifts it out of all narrowness and gives breadth to our view of its mission. While we may not be able to reach this high standard of preparation for its service, we may improve on the methods with which we have hitherto been content, and realizing our "high calling" may earnestly strive the better to prepare ourselves for its duties.

CHAPTER XXIX.

LECTURES TO BOYS ONLY.

"It is far better to be innocent than to be penitent;
To prevent the malady is better than to invent the remedy."

THE Bible places great emphasis on purity of life. In the Second Letter of Paul to the Church at Corinth he said, "Beloved, let us cleanse ourselves from all defilements of the flesh or spirit; perfecting holiness in the fear of God."[1] Dr. C. Irving Fisher, in speaking of physical purity in its social aspect, says, "There is no subject on which Scripture is more plain and outspoken, no subject in which science and Scripture more fully sustain one another."[2] Yet I doubt if we as a church realize the dangers surrounding our youth. It may not be regarded as altogether strange if we do not. We are not all scientists, and the penalty of sowing "wild oats" has not always been apparent to us. Surrounded, as the most of church people are, by the sweet and drawing influences of home, it is hard to realize that our children or the children about us may wander from the life of purity which the Bible enjoins. If there is danger, what would we not do to keep our boys and our girls pure! But those who have looked into the subject strongly assert that there is danger, and sustain their assertions by most startling facts. It is appreciation of the startling revelation which has been made by science in recent years that has given

---

[1] 2 Corinthians vii. 1. [2] Manuscript lecture.

rise to lectures to men only. But the objection to these lectures to men, as an eminent physician has said, is that the lectures are heard too late in life, given when men may mourn, but when they cannot undo, the past.

It is not strange that those who have given years of careful study to the subject of personal purity are urging that there are important truths regarding our bodies that even boys and girls ought to know. True, much is learned at some time or other of the human organism by the study of general anatomy and physiology, much that is of real value and essential to the maintenance of the highest state of health and vigor. But there are parts and functions of the body that are not mentioned or explained in these studies and cannot be in mixed classes of boys and girls. To the objection which some parents make to speaking to their children of the mysterious laws of their being, — that sooner or later the children will come into possession of this knowledge, — Professor B. G. Wilder says, '*For this reason sooner rather than later* should the children receive instruction.'[1]

Now, why should not the pastor take the boys of his church and of the community and see to it that they have what one has called "perfect, rational, godly information"? It may be urged that this instruction should be left to the parents, but it is doubtful whether they would give such instruction, and it is not always prudery that restrains them; some parents do not realize the importance of this teaching, and many, if they did realize the importance, would not have the tact or the facts for presenting the matter in the best way. It might be well when giving such a lecture to request the boys to bring a written permission from their par-

[1] What Young People Should Know, p. 166.

ents to attend. Dr. V. P. English tells of a school-teacher who discovered that many of his pupils were greatly injuring themselves by violating certain laws of the system, and he kindly tried to explain and to reclaim several of the boys. Says Dr. English: "A few appreciated his kindness, but the greater number did not, and many of their parents and friends became angry and treated the teacher in a shameful manner, supposing that he had done something very censurable."[1]

There are many reasons for instructing our children, at a very early age, regarding the nature of their being and the penalty of transgressing its laws. The first reason is to prepare the boy to meet the influence of the baneful information that comes to him outside of his own home. "We have got to recognize the fact that information of the most dangerous sort is waiting for the boy the moment he leaves his mother's side."[2] In the general discussion which followed a lecture delivered by Dr. C. Irving Fisher before the Congregational Union, New York City, a story was told by a clergyman of a minister's son who came to his father and repeated something he had heard and something that one of the boys had prompted him to do, and he told his father because he had been urged to come to him if he wanted anything explained. Through this revelation by the boy the father found out that the sons of some of the best people in his church — the very best families — were given to some of the most wicked sins. Volumes might be written showing how this temptation comes to boys whom we suspect of having no temptation. The trouble is that we think *our* boy cannot go wrong; the sooner we realize that every boy can go wrong and that every

[1] Plain Talk to Young Men, p. 16.
[2] Manuscript lecture by C. Irving Fisher, M.D.

boy is in danger, guard him as we will, the sooner we shall break over the prudery which sometimes controls us, show him that God has made all things pure, and then in a straightforward, manly way warn and instruct, and so help to a life of purity.

Another reason for thus instructing boys is that through ignorance they are often entrapped by those "who proclaim themselves by hand-bills, and in certain newspapers which find profit in a disreputable column."[1] The eyes of bright boys scan even the advertising column of the newspaper, and no hand-bill or poster escapes them. Their minds are inflamed, says Dr. Hall, by "vicious reading; from perusing books which are sent gratis and postpaid by cart-loads to all parts of the country every year, through the agency of the newspapers, with advertisements headed in this wise, — taking a city daily, at this present writing, — and which are copied, for large 'consideration,' by the country press (nor are all of our religious papers guiltless of this damning iniquity): 'To the Unmarried,' 'Marriage Guide,' 'Physiology,' 'The Benevolent Association,' 'Physiological Inquiries,' 'Young Man's Book,' 'Warning to Young Men,' 'Manhood,' 'Physical Debility,' with a variety of other headings. These publications have the same aim, object, and end : . . . by speciousness of argument and reasoning and statements, to mislead the mind, inflame the imagination, corrupt the heart, and eventually degrade the whole character. . . .

"It is an often remarked fact that, among the young gentlemen who attend a first course of medical lectures, there are many who imagine themselves the victims of each disease as it is presented by the lecturer.

---

[1] What Young People Should Know, by Professor B. G. Wilder, p. 135.

And any person not versed in medicine can scarcely read a book on any disease, without beginning to imagine that he has many of its symptoms; leaving us to suppose that imagination has something to do in causing or at least in aggravating some maladies. It is not surprising, then, that youths in their teens, or just entering manhood, in reading a treatise strongly depicting the ultimate effects of certain symptoms, alleged to be connected with certain conditions of the system, should run riot in their fears and throw themselves helplessly into the hands of those who seem to know so much on the subject, and by their own accounts have such remarkable success in their line. In every one of these books, without exception, certain symptoms are mentioned (not peculiar to any one disease, but common to a number, or may exist, and if let alone, in time disappear of themselves)."[1] Thus an uncounted number of young lives every year are wrecked, and, though unnoticed, this great evil has as many victims annually as has the saloon. We must believe regarding this matter what eminent Christian physicians tell us. As further evidence that this evil is widespread may be mentioned the large number of advertisements in the papers on such subjects as lost manhood, physical debility, and kindred subjects. If the quack advertisers did not meet with large results, we could be sure that they would not so advertise.

Another reason that may be urged for thus instructing our boys is that the knowledge of the consequences of certain evil-doing would restrain them from such transgression. We can easily teach them that there are laws or rules for the different members or organs of the human body which are called physical laws;

[1] Quoted by Professor B. G. Wilder in his "What Young People Should Know," pp. 136-138.

that the breaking of these laws causes pain and sickness.[1] We can further tell them that the breaking of certain laws entails greater suffering than the breaking of other laws. It is startling to hear it affirmed that "a larger share of sorrow, poverty, and vice depends upon the want of proper education in regard to the legitimate uses of the reproductive organs and to their illegitimate uses than upon the perversion or improper indulgence of any other human propensity."[2]

It is not necessary here to mention other reasons which might be given for teaching our youth to avoid that which is wrong, and so help them to grow up with vigorous bodies into true manhood.

When the lectures are given to boys only, it may be well to speak of the White Cross Society or the Silver Cross Society; the object of both these societies being prevention rather than reform. The White Cross Society[3] is a movement distinguished in being a work by young men; the following is the White Cross Pledge:—

I, ..., promise by the help of God:

I. To treat all women with respect, and endeavor to protect them from wrong and degradation.

II. To endeavor to put down all indecent language and coarse jests.

III. To maintain the laws of purity as equally binding upon men and women.

IV. To endeavor to spread these principles among my companions, and to try and help my younger brothers.

V. To use every possible means to fulfil the commandment "Keep thyself pure."

---

[1] True Manhood, by E. R. Shepherd, p. 69.
[2] Quoted in Professor B. G. Wilder's "What Young People Should Know," p. 161.
[3] Mr. Willoughby R. Smith, General Secretary, 224 Waverley Place, New York.

The Silver Cross Society[1] was organized in 1886 by the Rev. B. F. De Costa, D.D., of New York City, one of the first leaders of the White Cross Movement in this country. The "Silver Cross" was organized to meet the growing need of such a society for boys. Its members are known as "Knights of the Silver Cross;" the following is the pledge: —

I, ..., promise by the help of God:
I. To treat all women with courtesy and respect, and to be especially kind to all persons who are poorer or weaker or younger than myself.
II. To be modest in word and deed, and to discourage profane and impure language, never doing or saying anything I should be unwilling to have known by my father or mother.
III. To avoid all conversation, reading, pictures, and amusements which may put impure thoughts into my mind.
IV. To guard the purity of others, especially of companions and friends, and avoid speaking or thinking evil.
V. To keep my body in temperance, soberness, and chastity.

By using these pledges at the time of the lecture to boys and young men, which lecture ought to be given as often as once a year, also by circulating these pledge cards through the Sunday-school classes and church societies, as may be practicable, much can be done, I believe, to help our young men and to cultivate that purity of heart without which no man can see God.

[1] Rev. B. F. De Costa, D.D., President, 224 Waverley Place, New York City.

CHAPTER XXX.

THE BOYS' CLUB.

Two little boys whose appearance plainly showed that they were brothers approached the Superintendent of a Boys' Club in New York City, and applied for membership. "Are you brothers?" kindly asked the superintendent. "No, Sir!" replied one of the boys; "we's only twins." This anecdote is at least illustrative of the fascinating interest of work for boys. Away down under the ignorance, mischief, or disobedience of every boy, there is a heart. But as time goes on, that heart may be hardened. At seventeen the young man may be hard to reach, at thirty almost impossible to get hold of, and at fifty steeped in iniquity or bound fast with the chains of unbelief. But while he is young we may reach him; and his boyish delight in games and pictures and his thirst to know about new things may be turned to good account in leading him up to better things.

There are boys in every community who need some outlet for the superabounding energy of youth-time. Other boys are untrained, wild, and ready for any kind of mischief that can vex the souls of their quieter neighbors. There are churches also in every community, and consecrated money, and those who are anxious to do the Lord's work. These two groups, the need and the supply, ought to be brought together and result in some permanent work being undertaken for the lads. It is within the power of almost any church to establish a boys' club. It may be held in the Sunday-school room or church parlors, or better still in some room especially devoted to that purpose. It should be well equipped with games, with periodicals and illustrated papers. Cabinets containing specimens of various kinds may be provided, and the boys encouraged to make additions to them. Tables to accommodate two, or at most four, should be arranged for reading, and the books and magazines put on reading-racks. Games that are at the same time instructive and entertaining are most desirable, and should be used at tables seating not more than four boys. A rule in force in many clubs provides that every boy must be occupied with a book or game, or he is not allowed to remain in the room. Men or women may come in and play on the piano for the boys during the evening, without interrupting them at their reading or games. Or on another night they may be required to lay aside all employment and listen to a talk on some instructive subject, such as Electricity, Temperance, or How the President is elected, or the description of some beautiful part of the world, or the display of some works of art. The very best is none too good for the coming man. Besides these evenings, there should be at least one "quiet evening" in the week, when the boys have nothing but their books and games.

On every evening there should be short religious exercises of some kind, a short passage of Scripture and a short prayer, or the Lord's Prayer. A good time for this is about one half hour before the closing of the club. I have been surprised that some clubs never have such religious exercises. A great opportunity for good is thus lost. If it is a Catholic community, the Gospel may be *sung* into their hearts, instead of being read. But by all means let there be the positive influence of worship upon the boys.

During suitable seasons, outings may be arranged for the club, picnics and excursions by boat or, if in the country, by wagon. These will require considerable tact and executive ability to manage successfully, but, if well carried out, they will become fruitful in opportunities of getting close to the boys' hearts.

Some clubs have gymnasiums, which are simple or elaborate, as circumstances permit. And almost all clubs have the Penny Provident Fund. Again, there are classes in carpentry, bracket-carving, type-setting, drawing, stenography, and similar helpful studies. A small charge, say two cents an evening, is sometimes made for these. And some churches charge a penny an evening for the privileges of the club.

One person should be in charge of the club, but different people may be pledged to come in on certain evenings and assist with the management. But few rules are needed for governing a club. One thing that must be insisted on is cleanliness; and to this end there should be facilities for washing dirty hands and faces. In cities, the door-keeper quietly notices the boys as they come in, and, when necessary, requires that they qualify for entrance by use of soap and water; the return to homes of squalor of such boys with clean hands and faces has a leavening influence. Orderly behavior and abstinence from tobacco and rough language will naturally be required. No boy is permitted to go home without permission from the superintendent before 8 or 8.30 P. M. To send a boy from the room is usually found the severest and most reformatory measure for breaking rules. On three such dismissals, the boy is suspended from the club for as many weeks as, in the judgment of the superintendent, may seem best. The following membership card, in use in many clubs, is presented by the holder each evening, and is punched by the doorkeeper on entrance: —

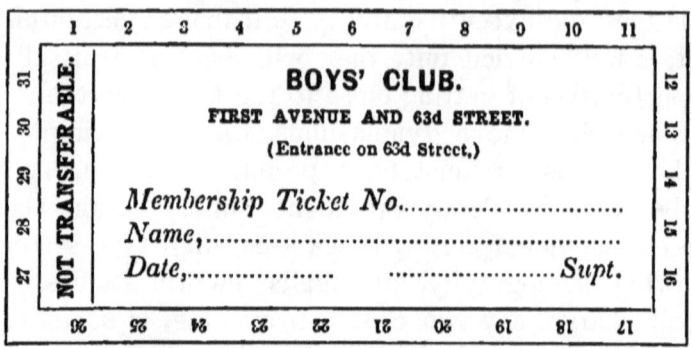

It may be remarked in passing that there have been many signal failures in conducting boys' clubs. Other clubs have met with marked success. And the above rules and the above arrangement of tables, literature, and games is the plan in operation in the successful ones.

The expense of these clubs is small. Different individuals will be found willing to pay for different juvenile papers, some publishers will contribute papers, and for ten dollars a quantity of good games can be procured. Further entertainment can be provided for the boys in inexpensive ways.

Out of the contact with the lads in the club-room, many opportunities to serve them will naturally arise. The superintendent will visit them and will have others visit them in their homes, will be attentive when they are sick, sending flowers and delicacies when possible, and will assist them to find employment when needed.

THE BOYS' CLUB.

There are clubs in some churches that have a military form. Among these are the Battalion Club of St. George's Church, New York; the Temple Guards, an organization for older boys; and Temple Cadets for younger ones in Grace Baptist Temple, Philadelphia. Then there is a club which other churches have organized, called the Knights of King Arthur.[1] It is modelled on the Boys' Brigade without its military features.

There are also clubs for temperance work, among them the Knights of Temperance,[2] and Young Crusaders,[2] which have been extensively organized in the Episcopal Church.

The club may be made a power for good among the boys of any community. Its attractions will keep them off the streets at night, the association with Christian men and women will elevate their ideals, and through the kindness of the church people they will be drawn into the Sunday-school and ultimately into the Kingdom.

There is another kind of boys' club which may be formed among boys of any class. They are called "Ten Times One," "Lend-a-hand," or "Harry Wadsworth" clubs.[3] Their work is on the plan of the King's Daughters and Sons, and they wear the same badge and have the same motto. These clubs usually consist of ten members. The first one was formed among the bootblacks of New York, and they took it for their work to take home the drunken men that

---

[1] Rev. Wm. B. Forbush, Ph. D., General Secretary, Yarmouth, N. S.

[2] For information, cards of membership, etc., address Church Temperance Society, 281 Fourth Avenue, New York.

[3] Mrs. Bernard Whitman, Secretary, 3 Hamilton Place, Boston, Mass.

they found in the streets, and to carry water to the poor washerwomen who lived in the highest stories of the tenement houses. Of these original ten, seven have been traced and found to be holding honorable places in life. A Lynn, Mass., club reads the newspapers and goes where they read that people have been injured to see what they can do to help. A Maine club makes and collects toys to give to poor children at Christmas. Another devotes itself to bringing in children into the Sunday-school of the church with which the boys are connected. Any line of work is open to clubs of this character, and no service is too small to be undertaken by these lads working "In His Name." These clubs are worthily commended to us in their mottoes: —

> "Look up and not down,
> Look forward and not back,
> Look out and not in,
> Lend a hand."

And,

"Now abide faith, hope, and love, and the greatest of these is love."

CHAPTER XXXI.

THE BOYS' BRIGADE.

THE Boys' Brigade was organized in Glasgow, Scotland, by William A. Smith of the First Lanark Rifles. Mr. Smith, like all Sunday-school workers, found how exceedingly difficult it is to keep boys in the Sunday-school after the age of twelve or thirteen. The Boys' Brigade was his solution of the problem. The first company was organized in this country in August, 1889, in the Westminster Presbyterian Church, San Francisco, Cal. Since then the number of companies has constantly increased. The aim of the Boys' Brigade is briefly outlined in its motto, " the advancement of Christ's kingdom among boys, and the promotion of habits of reverence, discipline, self-respect, and all that tends toward a true Christian manliness." Its practical success depends upon the keeping of the pledge, which reads as follows: —

"I solemnly promise, that while I am a member of the Boys' Brigade, I will abstain from the use of all intoxicating liquors, and tobacco, and the use of profane and vulgar language. I also promise that I will faithfully obey all the company rules and regulations, and will always strive for the best interests of the company. I also promise to serve honorably in the company in which I enlist, until transferred to another company, or honorably discharged by the company officers."

The methods in common use are: first, the military drill according to the infantry drill regulations of the

United States Army; second, the Bible drill; third, the summer camp. To these have been added, in many companies, the missionary meeting, prayer meeting, and reading club. Also in connection with almost all, there are clubs for football, baseball, gymnasium work, etc. Whatever will tend to make the boys' lives brighter, healthier, happier, and better may appropriately be incorporated into the Brigade. When the boys are in camp, the military discipline is still in force. The reveille, which calls to early rising, the roll-call, which insures the presence of all, the drill, and the relaxation of the day, give a brief outline of camp life. The presence of the officers and the strict military discipline as to bounds gives confidence to anxious mothers, and the enjoyment that the boys get out of these annual outings no pen can describe. Even guard duty becomes a proud privilege. Ambulance drill is one of the departments of practical usefulness. Instruction as to laws of health, care of the injured, and other important facts are given by physicians and surgeons who are to be found in every community, willing to give this help without charge. Military bands have also proved a very attractive feature of the Boys' Brigade. Boys of musical taste often find in the Brigade for the first time the opportunity to develop their talents. Every company must be connected with some religious organization, and every member of the Brigade must be a member of the Sunday-school. The commissioned officers of a company must be approved by the church with which the company is connected.

This movement has three headquarters in the United States: Brigade Headquarters for the United States, 23 Nevada Block, San Francisco, Cal.; Central Division Headquarters, 399 Thirty-third Street, Chicago, Ill.; and Eastern Division Headquarters, 38 Burroughs Street, Boston, Mass. Every company is enrolled at one of these headquarters, and may obtain supplies there. The age limit varies, seldom being younger than twelve, and varying between that and eighteen and twenty-one. The officers are always chosen for sterling piety. Upon them depends not only the discipline and military success of the Brigade, but its spiritual life. The officer is "guide, philosopher, and friend" to the boys of his company. To him they turn for counsel; to him they bring their troubles. He comforts them in sorrow, finds work for them when needed, and stands by them in all places where they need a friend. Standing before them on drill night, he gives them a five or ten minutes' talk on some simple religious subject. The drill is followed by a short prayer. Standing Order No. 1 usually directs that the company shall report at Sunday-school every Sunday until further notice. Sometimes the company has its own special Bible class. Always the boys are made to feel that the motto of their organization, "Advancement of Christ's kingdom among boys," is the great object of their organization and is to be lived up to with military exactness.

In regard to the uniform, Professor Henry Drummond thinks we are shockingly extravagant in this country, with our jaunty and complete uniforms. He tells us that in Scotland the only uniform needed or used is a twenty-five-cent cap and a fifty-cent belt. But when we remember how dear to the boys are the stripes, the epaulettes, and shining buttons, and that oftentimes the wealthy and generous, perhaps childless, members of the church gladly furnish the means to afford our boys this harmless gratification, we can under such circumstances afford to be liberal. However, where such help in purchasing the uniforms is not forthcoming, and where the cost of equipment stands in the way of any boy's becoming a member of the Brigade, let the uniform go. We, as well as the good people of Scotland, can "make a boy for seventy-five cents." Mr. Drummond tells us that the rifle in use in Scotland costs one dollar. In this country, where the model gun with which it is impossible to fire a shot is used, the cost is more. The expenses of the Brigade are met in some cases by a twenty-five-cent membership fee on the part of the boys and five cents a month thereafter. In other churches, the older people assist the Brigade by becoming honorary, annual, or life members.

And now what is the benefit to the boy, that so much time and patience, money and thought, are to be lavished on this organization? Let us consider for a moment what are the virtues that we wish to inculcate in the boys about our own firesides. Are they not punctuality, neatness, courtesy, obedience, and reverence, as well as spirituality? The boy who comes a moment late to drill, finds the door locked; the one who appears with dirty face and hands is dismissed to wash them, — and these things are not done by any arbitrary dictum, it is military rule, and as such is submitted to, for the most part, with a good grace. Is not this of prime importance to the wild street urchin who, not many days hence, will hold the ballot in his hand? Do we not know that respect for constituted authority forms the basis for good citizenship? Obedience to the officer, to the rule of the company, — that is also the rule from headquarters, — begets obedience to the law of the land, and, may we not hope, to the wise commands of the great Law-giver? Then, courtesy, to touch his hat, would be to the street boy the greatest exhibition of dandyism; to salute his superior officer, on the other hand, with the rules of the Brigade to justify such action, is quite the proper thing to do. From courtesy to reverence, the step seems short; and yet what heart would not be touched at the sight of heads, black, brown, and yellow, bent reverently, as with cap in hand the boys repeat the Lord's Prayer at the close of the drill? And worship and religious exercises, let it be remembered, have part in all their meetings. What opportunity is here for spiritual influence, for the developing and nurturing of manly Christian character!

On the physical side, the arguments are too well known in favor of the drill as a means of expanding chests and straightening backs, to call for more than a passing word. The great army of parents who choose a military school for their growing boys bears sufficient testimony to the benefit they expect their sons to derive from the drill and the discipline. Through the attractiveness of the Brigade many evenings which possibly would otherwise be spent on the street or in idle and demoralizing talk, are occupied in helpful and ennobling exercise and study.

On the other hand, it is sometimes charged that the Boys' Brigade tends to spread the military spirit, which is contrary to the genius of Christianity, or even to the advancing spirit of civilization. "Why," it is asked, "when the Church is constantly urging the advantages of arbitration over the sword, should she train up a body of young warriors within her gates?" In this connection we cannot do better than to quote the words of Professor Henry Drummond: "Contrary to a somewhat natural impression, the Boys' Brigade does not teach 'the art of war,' nor does it foster or encourage the war spirit. It simply employs military organization, drill, and discipline, as the most stimulating and interesting means of securing the attention of a volatile class, and of promoting self-respect, chivalry, courtesy, *esprit de corps*, and a host of other kindred virtues. To these more personal results, the military organization is but an aid. . . . As to the retort that the end can never justify such means, it is simply to be said that the 'means' are not what they are supposed. To teach drill is not to teach the 'art of war,' nor is the drill spirit a war spirit. Firemen are drilled, policemen are drilled; and though it is true that the cap and belt of the boys are regalia of another order, it may be doubted whether drill is any more to them than to these other sons of peace."[1]

So Mr. Drummond disposes of the arguments against the Boys' Brigade in a few sentences; the things, on the other hand, to be said in its favor would fill a book. The boys for Christ, the boys of all nationalities, the rich and the poor, is the aim and end of the organization. It is a grand way to encourage the lads. May they be encouraged till the military spirit in Christian duty prevails with old and young!

[1] Christianity Practically Applied, p. 248.

CHAPTER XXXII.

INDUSTRIAL CLASSES.

We have come in recent years into a larger appreciation of the value of industrial training, — thanks to the introduction of the Sloyd System, the Armour and Jacob Tome Institutes, and other notable industrial institutions. The advantages of manual training are more than at first sight appear. Carpentering, for example, in addition to its practical value, supplies a healthful training, without becoming a mere trade; trains to general dexterity and promotes physical development; disciplines the faculties of the mind; cultivates the perception of form and order; teaches neatness; trains the power of comparison; aids concentration of thought; awakens respect for manual labor; inculcates love for the true and a taste for the beautiful. What a wealth of blessings for the Church to bring within reach of her boys! With this mental and physical equipment may easily come the higher gift of spiritual training, and the lessons of the New Testament will gain vividness as the boys realize that He who spoke the golden words once labored like themselves amid the chips and shavings of the carpenter's bench. There is another thing which is very suggestive in the consideration of industrial training in its relation to the Church: two-thirds of the convicts in the penitentiaries of the United States are young men under thirty-five years of age, and over one-half of these young men never learned a trade.

MODERN METHODS IN CHURCH WORK.

All that is said of the advantages of carpentering applies in most respects to other forms of industrial training, the kitchen-garden, cooking, sewing, bracket-making, wood-carving, wood-engraving, and so forth. It is not possible for a church to go fully into manual training, but something may be done with classes in carpentry and wood-carving for the boys, and kitchen-garden, cooking, and sewing for the girls.

I. CARPENTERING-CLASSES. In organizing carpentering-classes, it may be possible to find some mechanic in the church who will gladly give his time on certain evenings to teach the boys and at the same time exert a Christian influence over them. If no such person is available, then the salary of a teacher may be raised by personal contributions and the small admission fee to classes of fifteen cents per month, — which is the charge in many schools. In most cases it will be impossible to give the boys more than a rudimentary knowledge of the trade; but if they are able to do little jobs of repairing at home, it will prove a benefit to them.

Mr. E. Scotter makes the following pertinent suggestions for teaching carpentry: first, in all cases the why and wherefore of the object must be fully explained, and drawings made by the boy himself; secondly, he must be shown how beautifully the principles of mechanics enter into the work and the tools; thirdly, he must have few tools and rough pieces of board to work with, and must be allowed to finish his own work and taught from the first to utilize waste. Mr. Scotter says: "One aim, at least, of all true education is to forestall and provide against the difficulties of common life. Surrounding the boy with many appliances which he will never be able to obtain when he leaves the school work-shop is decidedly a worse policy than allowing him to experience the common difficulties of life when and where he will be best instructed in battling with them."[1] The foregoing is encouragement for the church which is unable to provide the expensive appliances of the regular training schools, to believe that with few tools and rude materials she may be able to teach the boy lessons of accuracy and skill which will serve him well in the struggle of life.

The Sloyd System of manual training may be taken up by the church. This differs from ordinary carpentry work in that its primary object is not to teach the child a trade, but to educate him. The tools used comprise all the essential ones of carpentry, but in Sloyd the knife is always used instead of the chisel. One reason why Sloyd could be better carried out in a church than other training is that in carpentering there are many things which, if done at all, must be done by a turning-lathe, while the Sloyd provides for hand-work in every case. The pupils in Sloyd who are about ten or eleven years of age do their work by copying a series of models, and absolute accuracy is aimed at. The work is not to be painted or polished; when completed, it may be taken home, but is not to be sold.

II. THE KITCHEN-GARDEN. The kitchen-garden, which is usually taken up before cooking-lessons, is very comprehensive, as it takes in all of the operations of housework, exclusive of cooking. The materials for an outfit for twenty-four girls, including kindergarten tables, chairs, dishes, and household implements, cost only one hundred dollars. The work is accompanied by music, and a piano is a very desirable adjunct to the lessons. Each child is provided with a miniature outfit of utensils for performing the work of the day, and individually does the task assigned

[1] Westminster Review, October, 1892.

to the class. Besides the songs which in general outline what is to be done, there are a series of questions, the answers to which are given in concert by the class. In teaching table-setting, each child has a small oval table in front of her on the large table, and she is taught how to lay the covers carefully and methodically, and dispose of the table appliances. In dish-washing the whole operation is performed by each child and practical instructions given at every step. In washing and ironing, everything, even the care of the tubs and flatirons, is systematically taught; while in caring for a room, such points as the careful treatment of bric-a-brac are not overlooked. In addition, the duties of a parlor maid, including answering the doorbell, are taught, and, incidentally, the proper way to make and receive a call. Punctuality and neatness are inculcated, and the importance of system and attention to details is urged. It is a valuable drill to those who otherwise would have little but hap-hazard ways of doing things, and is a needed instruction for girls of all classes. Girls of every rank in life need to be brought together on a common plane of respect for household service. The child who takes part in the pleasant exercises of the kitchen-garden can never feel that contempt for household tasks that too often most unjustly condemns an honorable vocation.

> "A servant with this clause
> Makes drudgery divine;
> Who sweeps a room as for Thy laws
> Makes that and th' action fine."

Miss Emily Huntington, the inventor of the kitchen-garden, whose work entitled "The Kitchen-Garden" gives full instructions for teaching it, makes the following suggestions in taking up this work: "A room in a sunny situation, which is given up especially to the

INDUSTRIAL CLASSES.

kitchen-garden, is, of course, to be preferred. It should have a bright paper on the walls, and be decorated with the charts, brooms, and tins, as well as furnished with kindergarten tables and chairs. A large closet to keep the material in should open out from it. Such a room should be in constant use, being occupied by different sets of children. It is not, however, a necessity. A class can be taught in any room where there is enough space to have two tables and chairs or benches for twenty-four children. Or, if the room is not large enough for this, there should be a smaller class and one table. . . . One teacher acts as the leader; she should have two or three assistants who will be at the piano and oversee the tables. The classes meet for two or three hours weekly. An interesting plan would be for fifteen or twenty young ladies each to buy a kindergarten table of her own accommodating six scholars, provide herself with her own outfit, and be responsible for the advancement of her own six pupils. They could meet in a large hall, open the exercises with a song in which the entire school would join, and then separate into classes, much as is done in Sunday-school. The lesson would of course be uniform."

In conducting kitchen-garden classes, as well as every other kind of educational work under the charge of the church, the opening exercises should be of a religious character. To fail in this regard is to lose sight of the end for which the church is laboring in all this work for the uplift of mankind.

III. COOKING-CLASSES.

> We may live without friends; we may live without books;
> But civilized man cannot live without cooks.
>   .   .   .   .
> He may live without love, — what is passion but pining?
> But where is the man that can live without dining?
> *Lucile.*

The poor man is the one who suffers most often from an illy prepared or meagre meal. Rising from his unsatisfactory repast of sodden potatoes, sour bread, and tepid coffee, the working-man feels an aching void that can find satisfaction only in the saloon. "Intemperance," says Professor John R. Commons, "is the excessive use of some anæsthetic, either alcohol, opium, chloral, ether, or chlorodyne. . . . An unbalanced nervous system, having its origin in many different causes, gives rise to the most intense feelings of unrest, irritability, and a peculiar 'nagging' sensation, as though the whole body were in a state of terrible, unceasing agitation. These feelings, accompanied by the memory derived from previous experience on the part of the sufferer, that alcohol or some other anæsthetic will quiet the nerves, creates the irresistible craving for that anæsthetic. It is a morbid appetite, but it is overwhelming, and is far more inexorable than the simple appetite of taste for some palatable drink."[1] It has been claimed that the French, by reason of their consumption of light wines, have their natural appetite for "something to drink" gratified, and are therefore a sober people; but some one has stated a better reason for this temperance, saying, "The French are a sober people, not because they drink wine, but because they are good cooks." It is the man whose nervous system is satisfied with sufficient and nourishing food who does not feel the craving need which drives many a one to the dramshop. On the other hand, to again quote from Professor Commons: "The salted meats and the adulterated groceries of the poor, together with the ignorance of cooking, are probably a co-operating cause for more than half our intemperance. Children

[1] Christianity Practically Applied, p. 227.

INDUSTRIAL CLASSES.

are brought up without wholesome or sufficient food, their bodies are starved and puny; and when they grow older and are compelled to work, their strength cannot withstand the nervous strain. Intoxicating drink is their inevitable refuge. I know of no temperance reform more urgently needed than cooking-schools."[1]

Efforts have been made in the various cities to supply the working-man with meals at a moderate price, and this, doubtless, works much benefit to the unmarried man. But how about the married men, their wives and their children? Will the husband and father go and enjoy his meal in solitary comfort? Happily, the ties of family are too strong for such a course. The remedy clearly lies in educating the wife and mother so that *all* may enjoy the comfort of good cooking.

Aside from the evil of bad cooking as a promoter of intemperance, it is also a source of great waste. Edward Atkinson estimates that the net loss from bad cooking and waste is $1,000,000,000 per year. Through bad cooking the working-man's hard-earned money goes but a little way; the family is deprived of comforts; the food is scant, and this little, through ignorance and waste, falls far short of the demands of labor and of health.

Granting the deplorable need of better cooking among the working-classes, how shall the remedy be applied? One remedy is to teach poor mothers, whose families are the victims of their waste and ignorance, how to do better, — how to save and how to cook. Cooking-classes for mothers are now conducted by many churches. The women are taught how to cook food and how to prepare the best possible meal at the

[1] Christianity Practically Applied, p. 230.

least cost. But this teaching of mothers is at best only temporary relief. The real solution of the problem is, to use a time-worn formula, "to begin with the children." No worthier field for elevating the masses is before the church.

Work may be self-supporting if properly managed. To this end, a thoroughly competent teacher must be engaged, so that private classes may be obtained to secure revenue requisite to cover the expenses, inclusive of the free classes. The teacher, therefore, must be qualified to teach, not only simple cooking to the children, but also chafing-dish receipts and fancy cooking, which many of the patrons may wish to learn. In the private classes a charge will be made also for all materials used. The prices will be much greater for single lessons than when taken as a course in a class.

In teaching cooking to children, it is not necessary, as some would have us believe, that each child should have her separate outfit of table and utensils, so that the same operation may be performed by all at the same time. This is very pretty in theory, but involves great expense. All that is necessary is a long table, several moulding-boards, plenty of the ordinary utensils for the preparation of various articles of food, and a good-sized range. In teaching the children, great stress must be laid on cleanliness. In some classes both pupils and teachers wear caps and aprons. These are usually furnished by the school. All ornaments, especially rings, are usually discarded during the class. "Care must also be taken," writes an experienced worker, "to adapt the instruction to the various offices which the class expect to fill in life. Many of them may wish to use their knowledge in domestic service; others will only make use of it in their homes."

INDUSTRIAL CLASSES.

"The Cooking-Garden or Systematized Course of Cooking-Lessons," prepared by Miss Emily Huntington, founder of the Wilson Industrial School in New York, will furnish a perfect guide to those who wish to conduct a cooking-school without engaging a skilled teacher. It contains the music for the songs used, materials for the lectures, lists of articles required, estimate of cost of materials used in each lesson, and explicit directions how to teach it, even reducing the instruction to the form of question and answer. The lesson opens with a march, the children to be, if possible, accompanied by the piano, or they may sing as they march. They then are seated and sing a song suited to the lesson. This is followed by a short talk or lecture on the subject to be taught, after which a few questions are asked. Then the bill of fare is read, and the cooking begins. Three girls are assigned to each receipt. The teacher assists and directs the children, stopping all work and calling attention to special points as the lesson progresses, until the food is prepared. Then the class is seated and the food is eaten. After that some more questions are asked, and the class sing another song and march out of the room. The questions following the lecture are designed to find out how much the children have retained of the matter presented and to emphasize special points; the questions after the cooking, to test the accuracy of the pupils' knowledge of the way things have been done. Both series of questions are conducted with the class seated and giving their whole attention to the teacher. By the use of the plan outlined by Miss Huntington, she tells us, "little cooking-centres can be formed at comparatively small expense. In a quiet way, a dozen girls can be gathered around a cooking-stove, and learn what will make their lives more valuable in any home, whatever capacity they may fill, whether as wife, mother, sister, or friend."

IV. SEWING-CLASSES. What a blessing it would be to the poor if they only took good care of the little they have! How much more comfortable and economical they could be in dress if they exercised the care in keeping their clothes in repair that is taken by people in moderate circumstances! The causes of this lack of thrift on the part of the poor are three, — carelessness, lack of time, and, chiefly, ignorance. It is the office of the sewing-school to raise up a class of women among the poor who shall know how to mend and fashion their own garments, and also to give skill in the use of that slender but effective weapon, — the needle, — which has in so many cases been the only one at hand to drive the wolf from the door. And yet it must not be inferred that the sewing-school is alone for the poor. Sewing is something that every young woman should know, and the sewing-school has valuable lessons and provides happy and helpful hours for children of all classes.

The requisites for a sewing-class are more simple than for almost any other work for children that can be taken up, since the materials used are much less expensive than for almost any other industrial work. It is customary to have a Directress who conducts the general exercises of the school, presides at the meetings of the teachers, and decides on the merits of completed work. Children of all ages are admitted to the school, a primary class being conducted for the "little folks." Each lesson is about an hour and a half long, with an intermission of five minutes. The school is opened and closed with religious exercises, songs, scriptural verses, the Lord's Prayer, etc. Sometimes at the close of the class, among poorer children, a piece

INDUSTRIAL CLASSES.

of cake is given. This is not given as a reward for their attendance, but to bring a bit of brightness into their lives and give them a sense of the teacher's care for them.

The following outline of the plan pursued in sewing-societies is largely taken from "Handbook for Sewing-School Teachers,"[1] in use in the Emmanuel Chapel Industrial School and several other schools in New York.

According to this plan, there is a series or grades of work, and the children are promoted regularly from grade to grade. A box marked with her name is assigned to each pupil, and any piece of completed work is put into this box, and the whole given to her when she has finished the course. This does not preclude the child from occasionally taking home work of unusual excellence to show to her parents. Such pieces are then returned by the child, and placed in her box with other finished work. In teaching the children to sew, the teacher begins with the most elementary principles: teaching how to thread a needle, wear a thimble, and tie a knot. From these foundation precepts, the work proceeds regularly and systematically, from outlining a pattern to making a dress, and the children are carefully trained in every kind of sewing. Some schools have a supplementary class in embroidery and cutting and fitting.

Having completed the graded course of instruction, the girl is mistress of her needle, so far as the ordinary needs of life are concerned. Making the best of everything has been inculcated throughout the course, and the most thorough methods of doing work constantly studied. If she puts these precepts into practice in her after life, she will save herself many dollars. But of

[1] Published by Thomas Whittaker, New York.

far greater value to her than this, has been the teaching of the sewing-class. Her hand and her eye have been trained together; lessons of neatness and thrift have been taught her; patience and sweetness of temper have been the necessary adjuncts of her work; courtesy, and the spirit of accommodation have presided over her task. Under the Christian influence that has been the ruling spirit of the sewing-class, it will be strange if her life has not opened to the reception of that love which has done so much for her in the name of Him who was so familiar with the humble details of the homeliest life that He used the lesson of the "patch" in teaching the simple folk around Him.

Sewing-classes, as also classes in Carpentering, Kitchen-Garden, and Cooking, are in successful operation in a large number of churches, including almost all denominations and many of the most prominent churches of our various cities.

DAY NURSERIES AND KINDERGARTENS.

CHAPTER XXXIII.

DAY NURSERIES AND KINDERGARTENS.

To the poor mother who is necessarily absent from home all day to earn food for her family, the Day Nursery offers most practical help. The nursery is open from 7 A. M. to 7 P. M., and a charge of five cents per day is made for the care and boarding of the child. When the little ones are brought in, a bath is given, if necessary; but the parents are encouraged to bring the babies clean, it being no part of the nursery idea to relieve the mother of the proper responsibility of her child. The children are then dressed in clean clothes, and made comfortable for the day.

The years, in most nurseries, during which a child may be brought to the nursery are from the first to the ninth, but no child is admitted for the first time after eight years. As soon as the little one is old enough, he is put into the kindergarten, which is usually under the same roof as the day nursery. From there he is sent in due time to the public school. Up to nine years he may, however, outside of school hours, spend the time of his mother's absence at the nursery, returning thither at noon for lunch. The extension of the privileges of the day nursery to those young children who are old enough to go to school has been forced upon these institutions by the conditions of tenement life. The mother going away to work in the early morning, with no one to leave in charge of her children, and not daring to lock them in her rooms nor to leave the door unlocked, is confronted with a hard problem. In the afternoon the case is still worse. The children may return to a cold, cheerless home, and where there are no loving arms to welcome them, but the child is rare who will long remain there; the attractions of the street are too great, and here the children go, — where sights and sounds occupy them, and where the evil lessons in one hour are more numerous than the good ones their teacher has been able to crowd into all the school hours. But the accommodations of the day nursery are limited. The influence of these older children is not good over the little ones at the hour of the day when the best of babies is feeling the need of gentle treatment. School children, therefore, cannot be admitted in great numbers. Thus we see the streets crowded hour after hour with the children of the poor, amid evil surroundings. A much needed institution in the larger cities is a place where school children can be cared for during the hours outside of school, where the innocent recreations of home life will replace the coarse contact of the street.

The day-nursery idea has been happily turned to account in another way. Many a tired mother has longed with soul hunger to respond to the call of the church bells on Sabbath mornings, but could not, for there was no one to leave in care of her darling child. Without one thought of sacrifice the mother has gone on singing her lullabies, forgetting that they might have been sweeter and stronger for worship in the house of God. It is here that the day nursery is again of real help. Many churches have fitted up a room in the church where little children may be cared for by an attendant during the morning service, while

DAY NURSERIES AND KINDERGARTENS.

their parents are at worship. The Simson Memorial Methodist Episcopal Tabernacle, Los Angeles, Cal., combines kindergarten features with its nursery work, and reports a large attendance each Sabbath morning.

2. THE KINDERGARTEN. The kindergarten is another way of caring for children, and is of great service as an educator. Between the time of the physical care of the baby in the day nursery and the time when the public school takes him, there is a gap of several years when the care of the child is a great responsibility. The capacity of a child between the ages of three and seven for getting into mischief is one of his strong points. Then, too, he is quite old enough to take on impressions of evil, to form habits that will become a part of the furnishing of his moral nature, and with each passing year the tendency to wrong-doing, which is his birthright, will gain a stronger hold on him. It is here that the kindergarten takes him into its wise, loving, systematic embrace, and changes the current of his life. In some cities there are free kindergartens, supported by private and public benefactions. But where there are not adequate accommodations for the care of children of this age, it is quite in the province of the church to establish and undertake the support of a kindergarten, which, in connection with the day nursery, will make a safe shelter where the toiling mother may leave her children, and where other children of the church may be early trained by the church. The kindergarten children bring a penny a day, which assists in buying the materials; but the kindergarten must in the main be supported. Does this seem a good deal to undertake? Remember you are getting almost entire possession of the child's life at the time when it is innocent of evil, and when the spirit of good

temper, self-control, and unselfishness may be made a part of his daily growth. Rev. Percy S. Grant, rector of the Church of the Ascension, New York, in an address before the Free Kindergarten Association, in giving an account of the opening of the kindergarten of Fall River, Mass., said: "As they came to the school-room in those first days, they were dirty, shy, sullen, and disobedient, — indeed, the most obstinate bit of material to mould into intelligence and beauty. The school opened late in the fall; in about six or eight weeks came Christmas, and no Christmas pantomime ever beheld so remarkable a transformation, for when the same children gathered in a circle with their teachers around the wonderful tree, there was cleanliness, there were brightness and alertness, there was quick and Argus-eyed observation, there were sweet manners; and indeed, it seemed to me that there had been developed in those children all that we imagine should grace the early years of human life."

The kindergarten takes hold of the imitative faculty in the child, and in giving him images of beauty and order to copy, replaces those which would otherwise occupy him. Thus we have the spectacle of little children "playing kindergarten" on the street, singing the songs they have been taught or going over the experiences of the day in the home. A perfect example of "the expulsive power of a new affection." Then, too, the spirit of the kindergarten is religious. All the lessons point through nature "up to Nature's God," and, as Mr. Grant so aptly says, "from the beauty in life leads the child to the wonder and worship of beauty's Source." The songs are filled with reference to God and his love, and lips that never lisp the evening prayer at home now raise the kindergarten prayer and thank the dear Lord —

DAY NURSERIES AND KINDERGARTENS.

> "For rest and food and loving care,
> And all that makes the world so fair."

In the Kindergartners' Report of the City of New York, we find the story of a teacher who, one day walking on the street, came up behind one of the little girls and heard her singing softly to herself, —

> "Love him, love him, all ye little children, God is love."

Out of the kindergarten grows the Mothers' Meeting, where the toilworn woman learns to see a sacredness in motherhood that she never felt before, and where perplexing problems may be thought out and interest in the children's work cultivated.

From the day kindergarten to the Sunday class is but a step, and many of the methods found helpful in the day class will be found effective there. The Sunday-school lesson abounds in opportunity to use the precepts of Froebel. Along no other path may the little feet be so naturally led into the green pastures and beside the still waters of the kingdom of God.

CHAPTER XXXIV.

TEMPERANCE WORK.

THERE are many knotty things about the temperance question, and problems that puzzle and sometimes antagonize the stanchest friends of temperance. But on this much there is agreement: that intemperance is a gigantic evil that the Church is called upon to put down! It is to be said, however, that there is sometimes a tendency to shirk the responsibility and leave the burden to other organizations outside the Church: the Woman's Christian Temperance Union, the Christian Men's Union, the Good Templars, and, for the children, the Band of Hope and the Loyal Temperance Legion. These are worthy organizations and do a noble work; but it would still seem the province of the Church to teach its childhood and youth the lesson of temperance, as well as every other grace in the beautiful chain beginning with faith and ending with love.

Temperance work may be classified as follows: Educational, Preventive, and Rescue.

1. EDUCATIONAL. The Brick Church of Rochester, N. Y., has a Temperance Society which consists of four sections. Section I. includes all men and boys over sixteen, Section II. all women and girls over sixteen, Section III. all boys under sixteen, Section IV. all girls under sixteen. The principles of the Society are summed up as follows: —

"I. We declare for total abstinence from alcoholic liquors, as beverages, for Christ's sake and for others' sake.

"II. We declare for uncompromising hostility to the saloon."

There is no pledge, but every member considers himself bound to stand by the principles of the Society, so long as he remains in it. This Society uses the badge of the Christian Men's Union, a blue button with a red cross stamped on it.

Some churches have temperance societies for the young, with meetings of a literary character held on a week-day night. The programme for the evening consists of music, short talks, essays, and declamations, — all bearing upon the subject of temperance. This work among the young, with scientific temperance instruction, lessons in cooking, and work resulting in the improvement of the sanitary condition of the poor, all conserve the great cause of temperance.

2. PREVENTION. But with the fatal tendency to drink that so many men inherit, and with the frightful opportunity that the saloon gives for gratifying that tendency, what can the church do to furnish a counter-attraction to the saloon? In the first place, the church should study the territory under its care, and appreciate the fact that the men within its bounds who have learned to depend on the saloon for their entertainment as well as the gratification of their appetites must be won to higher pleasures and removed from the scene of temptation. To this end, pure and first-class amusement may be provided, with music, which, bright and attractive in character, shall take the place of the low songs of the groggery. Dr. John L. Scudder, Pastor of the Congregational Tabernacle, Jersey City, N. J., relates the following experience, which shows how clearly he understands the value of amusement:

"When I was in Minneapolis, two women from the Woman's Christian Temperance Union came to me and said, 'Don't you think it would be a good thing to start a prayer meeting over there in Central Avenue?' 'No, sisters,' I said; 'that is not the thing for you to do. Start an amusement hall, and charge one-half what the saloon does.' They went out of my house as if they thought I was with the devil. Three years ago Frances Willard wrote me a letter, saying, 'I have studied that work; I believe in it. We all believe in it. We are going to make it a department of the Christian Temperance work.'"[1] Everything that will provide amusement of a proper kind for the workingman, and appeal to his higher being, is a means of counteraction, and is helpful in weaning him from the saloon. Professor John R. Commons well says: "To merely tell a man to quit drinking is mockery. Tell him to quit, and then build up his character so that he can have pleasure in better things."[2]

But the entertainment provided by the saloon, we know, is not the only or the chief attraction that draws men there, and to find a substitute for the dram is something that will tax thought and heart to the utmost. Coffee-houses where a cup of good coffee and a sandwich may be had at a nominal cost will prove a formidable rival to the free lunch of the saloon, which draws in more people than most of us realize. Many men, too, on a hot summer's day go into the saloon for a cool drink of beer. And why should they not? What else are they to do? Let us put up our drinking-fountains and give them a chance to get a glass of cold water! A butcher in a Western city was remon-

[1] Proceedings of the Open and Institutional Church League, New York, 1894, p. 21.
[2] Christianity Practically Applied, p. 234.

TEMPERANCE WORK.

strated with by a neighboring saloon-keeper because the former had in his market a large tank filled with ice-water, accessible to the public. The saloon-keeper urged its removal on the ground that it interfered with his business. On the outer wall of Calvary Church in New York is a drinking-fountain. Over it is inscribed the following: " Praise God, from whom all blessings flow." Is not this suggestive of a grand work for the Church to do, to the praise of God?

The Church Temperance Society of New York, an organization in the Episcopal Church, has a number of night lunch-wagons, which travel over the ground occupied by the saloon. These offer to the wayfaring man a substitute for saloon refreshments of which many avail themselves. This Society also contemplates erecting temporary summer pavilions called " kiosks " on the principal bicycle roads of New York City, where refreshments and cool drinks will be within convenient reach of cyclers. This is a wise movement. If our cause is to succeed, we must remember the principle of displacement. " Refreshment for man and beast," the old signs used to read ; and right here the saloon-keeper lays a trap for the farmer and the teamster. Almost every public watering-trough in the vicinity of our towns and cities will be found in front of a saloon. It is easy to step inside when the team is watered. The rumseller knows this; that's what the trough is for! Why not combine the drinking-fountain with the watering-trough, to greet the dusty, thirsty traveller? So shall " the cup of cold water " be many times multiplied.

The Church must always be found on the side of temperance legislation. There are differing views as to the expediency of this or that measure, designed to promote temperance or to mitigate the evils of intemperance; but the constant aim of the Church must be to arouse the social conscience, and to do all possible that will argue to the general conviction. With an enlightened public conscience, and the Church with her far-reaching influence in this great movement, the question of ways and means will take care of itself, and the host pledged to temperance reforms will move on to victory.

3. RESCUE. So far we have considered the work of the Church in temperance with reference to work with those who have not been drawn into the drink habit and those who are not yet so much enslaved by drink that they may not be won from it by the substitution of better things. We must not, however, forget that there is a large class for whom pure amusements have no attraction, and who would pass by the drinking-fountains, were they as numerous as the saloons. Here lies the work of rescue. The Church must take her way down where the saloon has taken fast hold of men, must find the sinner where sin enchains and help him to unloose the fetters. Rescue work is personal. He who would touch a man, abandoned, hardened, and scoffing must go to him individually with the Word of Life. Such was the plan of Jerry McAuley in the Water Street Mission, New York; and such is the work so successfully carried on in St. Bartholomew's Mission, of which Colonel Henry H. Hadley is superintendent, in the same city. At the latter mission a training-class has been opened for teaching the best methods of reaching lost men. The students in training become, for the three months of their course, residents in the slums of the city, and in addition to receiving instruction as to the best ways of teaching of the All-Sufficient Saviour, they become during their whole course actual workers in such a field as they

TEMPERANCE WORK.

expect to occupy. The benefit is incalculable. Each student (and many of them are ministers of the gospel) carries with him to his distant home a heart burning with new zeal, and yearning to put into practice in his own community the methods of rescue he has learned. It may not be possible for every church to carry on the rescue work to the extent that is practised in St. Bartholomew's, but all may do some work of this kind. We have had quite enough of this looking at drunkards, shaking the head, and saying "Poor fellow, the devil has him." The thing to do is, by the grace of God, to take him away from the devil! We are to seek the lost, — not merely the *respectable* lost, but the *lost*, — all! The blood-stains of many a poor drunkard are upon the souls of Christians.

A successful plan in rescue work, where means are limited, is to rent a room in that part of town where the saloons are thickest. A little organ, a few chairs, a table, stove, and lights make up the outfit. Much depends on the leader. He should be a man filled with the Spirit, and able to see the suffering Saviour in the sinning ones around him. With these equipments the mission may be opened. It will depend on the sympathy of the church and community for material support and co-operation, in lending a helping hand to those who are trying to stand, in finding employment for those who are trying to regain their self-respect, in surrounding the mission with the heavenly environment of their prayers, and in helping in the work by their personal interest and presence.

Many men will come to the mission to be in a warm place or for other selfish reasons; but once there, workers with the love of God for lost souls will find a way to give them the warmth of a kindly greeting, to break to them the bread of life, and help them to "bear a song away." In some missions the plan of having a lodging-house with a wood-yard attached, where the men may earn a lodging and breakfast, has been successfully carried out. It is certainly very desirable to have some place to which those who express a desire to lead a better life and who have no home may be sent, otherwise the saloon may offer to them the only open door. The question of the "loaves and fishes" is an important one, and the rescue-worker will probably be many times imposed upon, but through it all will have the comfort of knowing that the Master counted the man who was "in prison" with the one who was "hungry," and ministering to both was commended of Him.

In smaller places co-operative missions have been opened by the union of Christian people of several churches. This brings the rescue mission into touch with the whole community. A Sunday breakfast is sometimes an institution of such a union, and is provided for by each church in succession, or furnished in common. And occasionally the young people of each church take charge of the evening gospel meeting. Their glad songs prove an inspiration to the service, and at the after meeting they greatly assist in personal work with inquirers.

The growth of spiritual life which a church having the rescue spirit will experience cannot be computed. A writer in the "Christian Treasury" well says: "As we view the whole question, we cannot help seeing how every effort that has to do with the uplift and redemption of the human race in the age in which we live must in some way centre around temperance. It must be reckoned as part and parcel of every effective philanthropic and gospel endeavor, for it is the demon of intemperance that meets us at every turn, and thwarts our best efforts just at the point when they seem about to be crowned with success. Therefore any one who would bring men and women to Christ must first reckon with the foe that keeps so many from the foot of the cross. . . . Is not our response to the cry of the needy the test of our love to God? St. John says, 'He who loves not his brother whom he hath seen, how can he love God, whom he hath not seen?' and in the same Epistle announces the true altruistic message of the Gospel: 'Hereby perceive we the love of God, because he laid down his life for us, and we *ought* to lay down our lives for the brethren.'"[1]

[1] Women and Temperance, by J. G. W., Christian Treasury, January, 1895, p. 7.

CHAPTER XXXV.

HEALING.

> A poor man served by thee shall make thee rich ;
> A sick man helped by thee shall make thee strong ;
> Thou shalt be served thyself by every sense
> Of service which thou renderest.
>
> MRS. BROWNING.

To heal the sick is the bounden duty of the Church,— just as much its duty and work as to minister to the soul. And the church which ministers only in "things spiritual" is as far short of the Christ ideal as he who confines himself to the "religion of humanity." In ministering to the sick and dying, we have the blessed example of Him who went about "healing all manner of diseases," and His own divine command to "heal the sick."[1]

The Church is awakening more and more to the necessity of foreign missionaries possessing some knowledge of medicine and surgery. In no other way can the ignorant man of every race be so quickly reached as by the healing of his body. God, who made "of one blood all the nations of the earth," has ordained that when a man of any color is sick and suffering, his heart becomes tender and impressionable; and happy is he who is able on the one hand to relieve physical suffering and on the other to minister in things spiritual. Accustomed all his life to the brutal treatment, the cutting and scarifying of the native doctors, — the simple remedies, the cleanliness of the

[1] Matthew x. 8.

HEALING.

bandages, and the cooling nature of the applications seem to the poor heathen little short of miraculous, and so he who brings the bodily relief has made an opening for the other and greater healing. In like pitiful state are the ignorant poor of our cities. They know more of the nature and possibilities of medicine, yet the lack of time and money to secure " the ounce of prevention," the horror many of them have of the hospital, together with the want of proper care in the crowded quarters in which they live, render their extremity the Christian's opportunity. To this end Christian people have established Dispensaries, Flower and Fruit Missions, the Order of Deaconesses, and deaconesses and private workers are sent out by individual churches for the purpose of visiting and relieving the sick.

The methods in use in the dispensaries are very simple and effective. The dispensary is announced to be open on certain days at certain hours. The patients gather, and the students and physicians in attendance hold a gospel service with them for fifteen minutes. They are then seen individually in an inner room in regard to their bodily and spiritual ailments. Meanwhile personal workers in the outer room further learn of the spiritual needs of those who come for treatment, and help them as they can. In some respects these Medical Missions have the advantage of other efforts of the same nature, since a man seeking aid for his body from those whose known object is the health of *both* body and soul, has taken one voluntary step in the direction of seeking such help, thereby placing himself in a receptive state.

St. Bartholomew's Church, New York, in addition to a free dispensary, has a medical clinic, a surgical clinic, and a night clinic for the eye, ear, nose, and throat.

MODERN METHODS IN CHURCH WORK.

Grace Church, New York, has two physicians and a trained nurse employed by its St. Luke's Association; maintains a diet kitchen for the sick, and Grace Hospital in three departments for men, women, and children. Grace Baptist Church, Philadelphia, has founded the Samaritan Hospital, which accommodates twenty-four patients, and has in connection with it a training-school for nurses. Religious services are held in this hospital every Sunday afternoon.

While all churches may not be able to maintain a hospital or dispensary, great good can be done in going with fruit, flowers, and delicacies for the sick among the sufferers in the hospitals and in private homes. We are long familiar with sick-committees in our churches, whose special duty is to show the interest and remembrance of the church of its members in some real way in times of sickness. This same interest should be shown in the godless and non-church-goers of the community, though they are perfect strangers. Such Christlike interest has direct approach to the heart, and prepares the way for the sweet message of the Saviour's love. A woman of education, culture, and wealth was slowly dying of cancer. She had been a sceptic and unbeliever all her life, — believed her sickness unjust, and had seldom attended church. A minister was called in by friends of the family, but words and prayers seemed of no avail. Flowers were sent by the Christian Endeavor Society of the church with a kindly and sympathetic note. The fact that *strangers* took such a *personal* interest melted the heart. Doubt gave way to faith, and she died trusting in redeeming love, and praising God for the unknown friends whose kindness led to peace and salvation.

There is another way of working with and for the sick. A circle of deaconesses is now an established part of the work of many churches. It must suffice here to outline briefly the different ways in which the work of deaconesses is carried on, whether by the order which bears that name, the salaried deaconess of the individual church, or the woman who in a private capacity ministers to the necessities of the sick and poor. The Order of Deaconesses, which was first organized under the auspices of the Methodist Episcopal Church, but which claims to be undenominational, is a body of women trained as nurses and Christian workers. In most cases they live in a common home called a Deaconess House. They wear a plain uniform, designed as a protection in their work which may take them to the worst parts of the city. They receive no salary, but provision is made for their maintenance in sickness or old age. They take no vows, and may leave the order at any time.

The deaconess or pastor's woman assistant and the woman who voluntarily goes among the sick and needy perform the same offices as those mentioned above. The field that this body of workers occupies is so great that we at once realize how inadequate is any attempt to enter upon a detailed description of it. After all, it is not in the dispensary nor in the hospital, but in the home, however humble and degraded, that the wounded ones of earth are found. They do not seek you, they may not always welcome you, but *they are there*, and the duty of the church is to search them out. The Lord said, "I was sick and ye VISITED me."[1]

Aside from the dread of the hospital, to which I have referred, it is impossible in many cases for the patient to be removed. When the mother falls ill, she can still direct the affairs of the household from her bed of pain. But when the children are small, cares

[1] Matthew xxv. 36.

are many, and the means are limited, then is the opportune moment for some Christian hand. The Order of Deaconesses has, as a part of its equipment, clean sheets, pillow cases, and towels, plainly marked with the name of the Order, to be returned, washed, and re-used. The mother once made comfortable with a fresh, clean bed and the proper nourishment or medicine, the nurse turns her attention to the family. The little ones are washed and fed, the fire is replenished, the room swept, and preparation made for the supper of the father when he shall return to the home which he perforce left a scene of discomfort in the morning.

Besides the nursing of the sick, which these women regard as the most important of their work, opening as it does so many avenues to the heart, and affording in many cases the last opportunity to speak the word in season to those who are "appointed to die," the deaconesses have other lines of work. In some cities there are children's meetings held every day in the week, and mothers' meetings held at the house of one or other of the mothers in a given district. Here the mothers gather with their younger children, and sew while the worker gives a little talk on some subject of practical interest which is followed by a Bible lesson. Sewing-societies for the girls, and penny saving-banks for the boys are also provided. In some of the Deaconess Houses in Germany they have opened schools for servants and working-girls. The deaconesses in that country are also to be found working in day nurseries, asylums, hospitals, and orphanages; but in this country their principal office is that of nursing the sick and passing from house to house giving the gospel of ministration, the sympathetic word, the help to find work and assistance that yet does not pauperize. Kindred to this latter side of their work is that done by the

HEALING.

King's Daughters and Sons. In New York the Board of Health sends ten or twelve physicians into the tenement districts to relieve the sick poor during July and August. They are trying to do the work of a hundred men, and can pay but one visit to each case. The King's Daughters and Sons provide these doctors with packages of postal cards on which the Tenement House Committee's address is printed. Using these cards, the physicians report the needy cases, briefly designating the kind of help needed. The nurses of the Order are at once sent, and, attending to the pressing needs, report the case to the Charity Organization Society for investigation.

Diet kitchens have their place in the ministration to the poor, in furnishing the sick with milk, beef tea, jellies, fruit, and other delicacies, and in many cases with ice.

We have been speaking of the ministry to the sick and helpless along the line of trained workers or organized effort, but let not any feel debarred from the privilege of sharing in this blessed work of the Master. There are many who, unable to devote themselves exclusively to this service, or even to make definite promises for a given portion of the time, yet have their place.

It is well for the pastor to arrange with physician attendants of his church, and with physicians of the community, to acquaint him with any case where the church can be of possible service. The members of the church at large should be encouraged to do for the sick. There are great swellings of human kindness in every breast. The people will gladly respond, and the service will bring its own reward, and the gracious benediction, "Inasmuch as ye have done it unto the least of these my brethren, ye have done it unto me."[1]

[1] Matthew xxv. 40.

CHAPTER XXXVI.

RELIEF WORK.

To pity distress is but human; to relieve it is godlike.
HORACE MANN.

THERE is no work more binding on the Church than that of bringing relief to sufferers, — giving meat to the hungry, drink to the thirsty, caring for the stranger, clothing the naked, visiting the sick and those in prison; but we must also remember, as Paul commanded the Thessalonians, "that if any would not work, neither should he eat."[1] In other words, we must discriminate between the needy and the impostor. To assist the latter is as great a sin as not to assist the former; and to aid the truly deserving without humiliating or pauperizing, requires great wisdom and care. Professor Richard T. Ely sums up the matter in the following admirable manner: "The test of all true help is this: Does it help people to help themselves? Does it put them on their feet? With respect to education, the answer is in the affirmative; with respect to gifts of food and clothing, it is the exception when it is not in the negative. . . . The danger in gifts and clothing is that people will cease to try to exert themselves, and will become miserable dependants on the bounty of others, losing their self-respect and manhood. . . . All help should include effort on the part of those aided. The sooner charity becomes needless

[1] 2 Thessalonians iii. 10.

and self-help sufficient in each case, the more successful the charity."[1]

1. The Church, through that tender-heartedness which is one of her chief graces, often errs in the direction of almsgiving. A substitute for this may be found in establishing some sort of industry for giving applicants a chance to show their willingness to work and opportunity to earn sufficient means to tide them over until better arrangements can be made. Such a place should always leave open hours for seeking more remunerative employment. Grace Episcopal Church, New York, has a parish laundry, in which all the work is done by hand. They charge the highest regular rates for doing the work and pay liberal wages, as it is no part of the plan to underbid other laundries or to underpay labor. They employ about thirty women, and the work offered them has far exceeded the capacity of the laundry. Calvary Episcopal Church, New York, has a wood-yard. This gives temporary employment to men, and they are paid in tickets at a restaurant which is also maintained by this church. St. Bartholomew's Episcopal Church, New York, has a tailor-shop where temporary work is given to deserving women.

2. Another worthy form of relief work is the Employment Bureau. Many churches have such associations; and it is possible for every church in itself to be an employment bureau, whether there is within it an organization definitely known as such or not. Why should not the business men and housekeepers take pleasure in employing, whenever possible, those within their own borders who need and desire work? Some one person in the church may be designated with whom may be left the addresses of those wanting

[1] Social Aspects of Christianity, pp. 105, 108.

employment, and the kind of work they are prepared to do; and those engaging help should deem it a part of their brotherly duty to keep themselves well informed as to names on the list. This is often as great a convenience to church-members as it is a real benefit to the unemployed.

3. A third form of relief work worthy of attention is that of a boarding-place where comfortable accommodations at reasonable prices and with Christian surroundings may be secured by persons away from home. St. Bartholomew's Episcopal Church, New York, has a lodging-house for men under the management of the Brotherhood of St. Andrew, where only one dollar a week is charged, and men are permitted to remain at this rate while looking for employment. The Judson Memorial Baptist Church, New York, maintains a boarding-house which is self-supporting. The rates charged, while reasonable, not only cover the running expenses, but also pay a surplus into the revenues of the church. The Central Christian Church of Kansas City, Kan., maintains Goodwill Home for "sheltering, feeding, and saving the worthy poor." In Los Angeles, Cal., is the Flower Festival Boarding-House, a home for business women under the care of a board of Christian women of that city. The rates charged vary according to the salary received by the women. At times, in especially unfortunate circumstances, a woman may be received temporarily without charge, but it is essentially a home for self-respecting women, and care is taken that there shall be nothing of the charitable institution about its working. The home is self-supporting.

4. There are various methods of giving material aid, such as food, clothing, bedding, and fuel. Extreme circumstances may demand our giving them out-

RELIEF WORK.

right. But usually the wise and only harmless way is to encourage the people to provide for themselves. The Bethany Presbyterian Church of Philadelphia has established a coal club, into the treasury of which the members pay a certain amount weekly during the year. The coal is bought at wholesale, and the members have the benefit of the reduced price during the winter.

Besides these well-known causes for relief, there are other and extraordinary cases, such as the need for legal or medical advice. While provision is made for the latter in free dispensaries and hospitals, but few have undertaken to meet the demands of the former, — to right the wrongs of the oppressed. The People's Mission of New York has the services of competent attorneys engaged, and free legal advice is given, and "numerous cases have been litigated for persons unable to defend their just rights." [1] St. George's Episcopal Church, New York, also has a legal bureau, and the relief work of the church is represented by the following bureaus: the Legal, Medical, Employment, Visitation, and Sanitation bureaus; "all of which," says their report, "is done, and done only, in the name of Jesus Christ." In that name, indeed, are found the incentive and reward of all this work.

[1] Second Convention of Christian Workers, New York, 1887: Report of Rev. C. C. Goff.

CHAPTER XXXVII.

BENEFICIARY AND LOAN ASSOCIATIONS, AND THE PENNY PROVIDENT FUND.

In view of the vicissitudes of life, no one doubts the importance of the insurance of weekly benefit in event of sickness or accident, and of funeral fund at death, but some have questioned the advisability of such work being conducted by the church. But beneficiary associations are not in the church without strong reasons for their existence. The hundreds of insurance companies, lodges, and associations, with their hundreds of thousands of members, bespeak the desire of men to provide for themselves and families in times of sickness and death.

1. The City of Brotherly Love was the first to suggest that the brotherhood of the church should have a beneficiary association, — not one in which there are large salaried officers, expensive offices, and not an association in which one class of people is enriched out of the losses of another, but an association where regular dues are paid, sick benefits are given, and at death a fixed sum is paid to relatives or friends.

The members of the Beneficiary Association pay a Proposition fee of one dollar, and monthly dues of fifty cents. Members of the society who are not more than one month in arrears are entitled, when sick or unable to follow their usual vocation, to five dollars per week for a period of not more than ten weeks in

BENEFICIARY ASSOCIATIONS.

any one year. On the death of a member in good standing, a funeral benefit of seventy-five dollars is given to the widow or legal representative. In event that the funds in the treasury are not sufficient to pay the death claim of any member, the President makes a *pro rata* assessment upon all the members in order to make up the deficiency. The society as an organization is dissolved every twelve months, when the funds of the society are equally divided among its members, according to their payment therein. Officers are then elected, and the Association enters upon a new year with a fresh set of books.

In speaking of the working of the Beneficiary Association of Grace Baptist Church, Philadelphia, the pastor, Rev. Russell H. Conwell, D.D., says: "We have found it to work excellently, but everything depends upon the men who manage it. . . . It must be carried along on thorough business principles, and conducted with the same care you would an insurance company, having an honest man to attend to it. We find the Beneficiary Society will relieve our church of a great deal of its charity expenses. The members will receive as a matter of right what might otherwise be demanded as charity only."[1]

Rev. J. Wilbur Chapman, D.D., pastor of Bethany Presbyterian Church, Philadelphia, writes: "We have many benevolent orders, the dues of which entitle the members to a benefit in case of sickness and a good sum in case of death. These societies have been very helpful to us, and we commend them heartily."

"With regard to the Association in our Hollond Memorial Church," writes the Rev. J. R. Miller, D.D., of Philadelphia, "I can speak only in the strongest

[1] Report of the Seventh Convention of Christian Workers, Boston, 1892, p. 101.

terms of commendation. Our Association is only in its second year, but already the help that has been given in many individual cases has proved a great blessing to the beneficiaries. Among people like those who compose our church there is great benefit in this banding together for mutual aid."

The Rev. Melville K. Bailey, associate minister at Grace Church, New York, in speaking of Grace Chapel Men's Club, says: " This is a fraternal mutual benefit society. It has one chapter only, that connected with Grace Chapel. Its members pay an initiation fee of two dollars, and monthly dues of thirty-five cents. In case of illness, a member is entitled to draw three dollars a week for a limited time. In case of death, one dollar is paid to the family by each surviving member of the Club. This Club has two especial advantages: 1. Every member pays a reasonable sum for its benefits; 2. Its resources are not restricted to receipts from dues, but the treasury receives voluntary contributions, in accordance with the spirit of Christian charity which acts in the church. The Club has an increasing membership."

In addition to the real relief given by these beneficial associations, there is a further good in that they school the people to provide for themselves rather than rely on friends and charity in times of misfortune. The associations also are trustworthy, and save the unsuspecting though well-intending people from being imposed on by unreliable and exorbitant insurance companies.

2. Kindred to these associations for the purpose of relieving the poor in times of special demand for financial help, are Loan Associations. While the patrons of the pawnshops and money " sharks " are many of them of the improvident or dissipated classes, there are in

LOAN ASSOCIATIONS.

every town a class who, solely through stress of circumstances, are brought into financial straits. To them sickness, lack of work, or failure of resources leaves no resort but the pawn-shop, where the exorbitant usury of thirty-six per cent renders the redemption of the pledge almost impossible. And there is always forfeiture of goods in event that payment of principal and interest are not prompt. In some cases the borrowers of money have been compelled to pay from sixty to a hundred per cent on money. To these, the worthy poor, loan associations offer a much-needed relief.

In St. Bartholomew's Church, New York, there is a Loan Association. The Rev. David H. Greer, D.D., rector of the parish, says that during the past two years they have loaned over a hundred thousand dollars, about seventy thousand of which has come due and been paid. The remaining thirty thousand is outstanding, and is being paid as fast as it falls due. This Association is incorporated under the laws of the State of New York, and has a capital of fifty thousand dollars. The Association charges but twelve per cent, which just about covers expenses, and does not press the payment of loans, but deals with its clients with Christian leniency. The results have shown that the loss to the Association is very small, while the benefits that have accrued to the clients, in renewed courage, improved conditions, and relief from distress, cannot be calculated.

The Provident Loan Society of New York[1] is an organization opened in that city in May, 1894, for the purpose of loaning money upon the pledge of personal property. It arose from the financial stress of the times. It is incorporated, and has as trustees some of the most substantial men of the city. Already it has

[1] Address, 281 Fourth Avenue, New York.

given evidence of the wisdom of its inception. It carries on its business very much after the manner of the Society in St. Bartholomew's Church. Although few churches can alone carry on so large an undertaking, there is encouragement to Christian people to enlist the interest of the substantial men of their community in a union enterprise of this kind.

But there is another side to this subject. In many of the cases where the time of distress seems unavoidable, it is not really so. In days when all goes well and the wages of the bread-winner come regularly in, there is a tendency to spend every spare penny in luxuries and amusements. Oftentimes it is a feast one day and a fast for *several* days. These people know little about planning and nothing about saving. Their training, Dr. Oliver Wendell Holmes would have said, should have commenced a hundred years before they were born. They have no encouragement to save. Their savings would be so small that no bank — not even a savings-bank — would receive them. The chance therefore to lay up for a rainy day is allowed to pass and the rainy day finds them unprotected. Our larger hope in this matter is in the training of children.

3. It is to educate the children in the principles of thrift and saving that the Penny Provident Fund was instituted. Incidentally, also, it teaches the parents the same lesson, through the unconscious influence of childhood; and many avail themselves of the privileges of the Fund, which is a simplified system for receiving and depositing for safe-keeping any amount from one cent upward.

The Penny Provident Fund was organized by the Charities Association of New York City in 1888. It found place for itself in the want of savings-banks which would invite deposits of small sums of less than

THE PENNY PROVIDENT FUND.

one dollar. The Fund is for all, old and young, but the largest number of depositors, probably, is among children from eight to sixteen years of age. There is now a large number of depositors, representing a deposit of many thousands of dollars, and it is believed that little of this money would have been saved but for the encouragement given by this society. The practical working of the system is very simple. Deposits from one penny upward are received, and receipted for by stamps affixed to little squares on a card arranged for this purpose. By presenting the card for cancellation, deposits may be withdrawn at any time, provided that no sum less than the whole amount deposited be withdrawn. No interest is paid to depositors. When the sum of five dollars has been saved, the depositor is advised and assisted to transfer the account to a savings-bank where interest can be earned. The American Bank Note Company makes the stamps in bright colors in denominations of one, three, five, twenty-five, and fifty cents, and one dollar. These stamps may be obtained on application to Miss Marian Messemer, Secretary, at the Central Office, Fourth Avenue and 22d Street, New York. There is no charge for material, — stamp cards, signature cards, envelopes for pass-books etc., — except the cost of transmitting. The stamps may be obtained to any amount desired. A station should invest in as many stamps as can wisely be kept on hand for the business of the stamp station. These stamps can always be redeemed at the Central Office, whether used or not; so no money can be lost. To illustrate: the stamp-station pays, say, $10 for that amount of stamps in seven different denominations; it receives, say, $5 a week in deposits by the sale of these stamps. It uses the amount so received to replace the stamps sold, so that it can continue to do business indefinitely on the $10 originally paid in, and can always obtain that money back by a return of the stamps or the cancelled stamps. The amount of money, new stamps, and cancelled stamps at a station always must equal the amount of capital at the Central Office, so that there is no opportunity for dishonesty. There is no bookkeeping, as every deposit and withdrawal is evidenced by a stamp. No one need to hesitate to open a station of the Penny Provident Fund, as, if found impracticable, it may be discontinued and money refunded.

Interest in this saving-system is rapidly increasing in churches, schools, children's societies, boys' clubs, and other associations. In some instances stations have been successfully opened in stores. "In all communities the larger part of the want and suffering is the direct result of a waste of small sums in unnecessary expenditures and the failure to provide, by laying up such sums, against possible loss of work or against an illness. This primary banking-business is educational in its tendency as well as remedial."[1] There is every reason why interest in the Fund should increase. It is a meritorious institution, and deserves support, as do all measures which encourage providence and thrift.

[1] Leaflet of the Penny Provident Fund Society.

CHAPTER XXXVIII.

THE PLURAL PASTORATE.

The idea of the plural pastorate carries us back to the time when Jesus sent out the Seventy, "two by two," and when "the Holy Ghost said, Separate me Barnabas and Saul, for the work whereunto I have called them."[1]

The mediæval idea, which has even yet a paralyzing effect upon the Church, that the minister's work is only to preach on the Sabbath, conduct a midweek service, marry the betrothed, and bury the dead, is giving way to the true and larger conception of ministering to the whole man, and working for the redemption of the whole world. Churches which have accepted this larger mission have for the most part yielded to the necessity of two and more pastors. It is sheer folly for *one* man to attempt to faithfully minister to a congregation of four or five hundred people, and direct them in efforts to disciple others and to bring the world under the dominion of Christ; and nothing short of this is required of the true minister of Jesus Christ. Granting then the necessity of the plural pastorate, what should be the relationship between these fellow laborers?

New York City has recently witnessed an illustrious failure of the co-pastorate. Some other cities have had like unfortunate experiences. Reasons are patent

---

[1] Acts xiii. 2.

enough why a co-pastorate is not likely to be the happiest possible arrangement.

Churches with successful plural pastorates have a recognized head and leader. In a few towns the second pastor is known as the Assistant. But generally the second minister is known as Associate Pastor, — a better term than "Assistant," which is more suggestive of a clerk than of a minister.

Some churches, like the Bethany Presbyterian Church of Philadelphia and others, make it a principle to have an older man as the associate pastor, — a man who because of his years prefers not to preach regularly, and who by reason of his experience and age at once commands the confiding trust of the people, and is otherwise qualified for the varied demands of a large parish.

The plan of St. George's Episcopal Church, New York, is to have only young men assistants. They are received from the seminary at graduation, and remain in the work two or three years or until receiving a call elsewhere. Grace Church, New York, has dormitory accommodations in Clergy House for six or more young men, who are received on seminary graduation and given two years' practical experience in the large work of Clergy House. Such practical experience, combined with thorough collegiate and theological training, is a grand preparation for the personal responsibility of a parish. Most churches having the plural pastorate have a younger man for the associate pastor. With difference of age added to difference of rank, there are recognized conditions which preclude such unpleasant comparisons as are bound to be in a co-pastorate. The young man too is peculiarly adapted for work with young people. They are naturally drawn to one of their own age. Again, the age and experience of the pastor forces the young man to remember that he is only the associate or assistant pastor. As such, he should show in every way possible his respect and regard for his senior. It is a sad commentary on the plural pastorate that a prominent church in one of the Eastern cities was well-nigh disorganized because of personal differences between the pastor and his associate. Let the associate pastor never listen to any word of depreciation of the pastor, but rather magnify him and his office in every way possible. A compliment given at cost to another may well be regarded with all suspicion! On the other hand, the pastor will do well to magnify the office of his assistant, and so add to his influence and usefulness in the church which he serves.

One difficulty that has been experienced with associate pastorates is the shortness of their duration. When acquainted with the people and in a relation of highest usefulness, the associate is often called to other fields. This doubtless will largely continue. It is only a question of time till most young men will be controlled by a desire for churches of their own. Yet many assistants would probably remain longer, with advantage to the church and themselves, if given opportunity for that thought and systematic sermonizing on which their future usefulness in so large measure depends. Provision must be made for that, one way or another, or pastors will continue to suffer periodic changes. It is trying and difficult for the young man to preach in the pulpit of another, and that too his elder and superior; but preaching is vital to the young minister's future. Occasional preaching will also give the assistant larger influence in the parish, better equip him for present work as well as future. and in every way enhance his usefulness as a minister of

Jesus Christ. The assistant should be encouraged by the pastor to study. Rev. Dr. Huntington of Grace Church, New York, meets with his assistant clergy two evenings each month, when a paper is read by one of the ministers, and all take part in the general discussion.

In addition to having an assistant minister, some churches also have a lay assistant who has charge of benevolences. It is well that such departments be in charge of laymen, — though only officers or members of the church.

Many churches have a woman assistant who attends to parish matters in which the services of a woman are clearly demanded. She also works in the mission, if there is one under the charge of the church, and gathers children into the Sunday-school. In some cases she acts as the pastor's secretary, and is generally useful in looking up and calling on strangers.

Thus we see the Church is coming to avail herself of the strength which is found in numbers, and of the diversity which arises from differing age and sex. Freed from the dominion of priestcraft, the Church should surround those who are over her in the Lord with the warm atmosphere of appreciation and the buoying certainty of constant prayer. It is not for their own but their works' sake, that the Church is bidden to "very highly esteem them in love."[1]

[1] 1 Thessalonians v. 13.

CHAPTER XXXIX.

THE FREE-PEW AND VOLUNTARY-OFFERING SYSTEM.

WHAT is to be said of the relative advantages of the free-pew and the pew-rental systems? While it is true that a consideration of such a subject should be approached from the highest standpoint, that the question of expediency should be eliminated, it is also true that church obligations are hard facts, and we must consider the subject in a practical way.

I, for one, do not feel that the pew-rental system has come about without some claims for its existence, and we can but recognize that it is the system in use in some of our strongest and most aggressive churches. As to the advantages of this system, it is claimed to be business-like, enabling the officers of the church to determine the income of the year, and not only to determine but also to guarantee that income. This system, it is also said, makes it possible for families to occupy the same pew, and thereby deepens the home idea of the church. On the other hand, the free-pew system has been called the unattainable ideal of the dreamer.

We shall be helped in our study by keeping in mind two things: First, by keeping before us just what the free-pew plan is. In the free-pew system, as commonly operative, the people are free to sit anywhere in the church building, or are assigned to pews in order of application, thus avoiding even the appearance of social distinction; and the people are further free to give to the support of the church and to the cause of Christ as in the sight of God they believe it to be their privilege and duty, instead of giving on a *quid pro quo* or commercial basis.

The second thing to be remembered in this discussion is that the pew-rental system is not the supplanted system, but the supplanter. It is not until the middle of the fifteenth century that mention of pew-rents is made. Before that time the entire floor of the church was open to the kneeling or standing worshipper. But as the founders of churches reserved parts of them for the use of their families, soon there was the spectacle of private rooms with windows, screens, fireplaces and fires, where, as has been said, " the godly *élite* could warm their distinguished persons." Thus the idea of choice places in the sanctuary allotted for a money consideration spread and gave rise to the rental of pews.

Keeping these facts in mind, let us ask by what reason the free-pew plan claims place over the pew-rental system?

1. The free-pew system claims for itself all the advantages without any of the disadvantages of the pew-rental system. The former system also claims to be business-like. A fixed income for a year is secured under the free plan by the voluntary offerings pledged at the beginning of the year. It is further claimed that this income is quite as sure as the income from the rental of pews; and experience seems to bear out this statement. It may be that there is some little loss under the free-church plan, but there is also loss under the other system. I believe it safe to say that pew churches meet with just as heavy losses, if not heavier, than churches with the free-pew system;

and if all the truth were known, we should probably find that many pew churches call upon their faithful officers yearly to make up deficiencies due to the fact that the pews were too high to rent or that the subscribers failed to meet their obligations. As over against this, advocates of the free-pew plan hold that they can appeal to the enlightened consciences of the people, that they can trust those consciences, and that the thought of the *voluntary* offering and responsibility for the work prompts the people to faithfulness, and inspires them to give as largely as they are able. The free-pew plan, it is also claimed, meets the demand that families occupy the same sitting, — provision may always be made for this.

But we have implied that the pew-rental system has real disadvantages. What are they? It may be said that the commercial spirit thus entailed overshadows the thought that we are to come into the sanctuary and there make our "free-will offering with a holy worship."[1] Again, the pew-rental system encourages some persons to give less than they should. Certain prices are placed upon pews by the trustees, say, two hundred dollars for one pew, and one hundred dollars for an adjoining pew; one man worth a million dollars, and ten times as much as his adjoining neighbor worth one hundred thousand dollars, pays only twice as much for his pew, yet he pays all that he is asked, and by no manner of logic can we expect him to give more. On the other hand, under the free-pew plan, the weekly offering is emphasized always as a part of worship, and appeal is made to the people to give each as God hath prospered him. Thus it results oftentimes that a few carry the burden of the expenses of free churches; but in the light of these conditions

[1] Psalm cx. 3.

this is seen to be an argument for the free-pew plan rather than against it. A further disadvantage of the pew-rental system is that it alienates certain classes from the house of God, — such as servants, the laboring-classes, and transient people whose business carries them from place to place, that is, railroad men, commercial travellers, and others. In speaking of the pew-system excluding servants and laborers, Bishop Huntington well says that the church is excluding those "whose children in the next generation will be the 'lords and ladies of the land.'" Bishop Huntington further adds: "By excluding them you not only exclude from the Treasury of the Lord the vast sums which might be gathered in rivulets to swell the stream of Christian benevolence, but you exclude the richer and costlier offering of their children and their children's children. And so the policy in the long run becomes as short-sighted as the piety is pharisaical."[1] Now, as to the alienation of working-men from the church, I firmly believe the welcome of the church to the laboring-man has been real and large. Nevertheless it has not been so regarded by him. In speaking of the Church of England Canon Farrar says: "Not three per cent of the working-classes, who represent the great mass of the people, are regular or even occasional communicants."[2] It has been estimated that the condition of affairs is not much better in this country. While it is true that the poor man may unjustly arraign the church, it is also true that there needs to be sounded abroad a welcome in terms that he cannot misunderstand. And this cannot be done, I believe, save we offer him a place in the house of

---

[1] A Sermon before the Massachusetts Free Church Association, 1894.

[2] Quoted by Dr. Strong, The New Era, p. 209.

FREE-PEW AND PEW-RENTAL SYSTEMS.

God without money and without price, and where he will not be labelled, by his sitting under the gallery of the church or other out-of-the-way place, as a poor man or person with moderate income. These disadvantages of the pew system are too patent to need comment; they are never denied by the strongest advocates of the system, nor is it denied that the free-pew plan eliminates these embarrassments. But there are other things to be said of this latter system.

2. The free-pew plan not only claims the advantages without the disadvantages of pew-rentals, but claims certain advantages over that system. I have already suggested how under the free-will-offering plan a man will give a sum more in proportion to his income than he would be willing to pay for a pew, and that with the free-pew system there is no unpleasant discrimination in the seating of people or grading them according to their gifts. Furthermore, the free-pew idea is Scriptural. "My house," says the inspired Word, "shall be called a house of prayer for all people."[1] The crowning glory of the Saviour's mission was, "to the poor the Gospel is preached," and "the common people heard him gladly," while still down the ages rings the command, "Go preach the Gospel to every creature." The Apostles caught the echo of the burning words, and clearly taught the infant Church that they were "one in Jesus Christ." St. James was very definite in his condemnation of class distinctions in the sanctuary; and his Epistle, as one has said, is very uncomfortable reading for the advocates of rented pews.

The whole matter may be summed up in the one thought of self-effacement. We must learn to think of the church, not as ours, but as God's, in trust for us to

[1] Isaiah lvi. 7.

administer for the benefit of his needy children. We shall then desire to see the best seats given to those who need them most. What we need is emphasis placed upon the brotherhood of man in Jesus Christ, and for this the free church stands. It is not enough that the courtesy or charity of a seat be given. There is a stubborn self-respect that resents this. The remedy must go further than a willingness to give them a part of what we pay for; we must keep resolutely down the thought that we pay for anything. We must simply make an offering to God, must maintain his worship because it is the right thing to do, and then, as God's institution, let the church take its place in the world, his gift to men.

I would not make any sweeping denunciation of those who yet employ the pew-rental system. We are the heirs of many mistakes, and this making the Father's house a "place of merchandise" may be one of them. But with a minister consecrated to the great work of saving souls, and with a people impelled by the Christ spirit of love, why would not the free-pew plan be wholly practicable in any church and in any community? Certainly it is in keeping with the thought and feeling of this age and the larger Christian life into which we believe the Church and the peoples of the earth are moving.

I had purposed to give extracts of letters received from pastors showing the success financially and spiritually of the free-pew system in their churches, but space does not permit. In answer to the question which I sent to pastors, "What have been your encouragements and discouragements spiritually and financially?" I received many letters telling of large gains spiritually, of congregations that had doubled and trebled in size, and of contributions that had doubled and trebled in size; others spoke of smaller results, but nearly all were positive in their statements of real encouragements. The discouragements mentioned were such as might be incidental to the pew system, — as, want of spirituality, lack of interest on the part of the people, apparent estrangement of the community from the church; only one pastor expressed the belief that more money could be raised by the rental of pews than by the voluntary-offering system.

It is interesting to state in this connection that about ninety per cent of the Episcopal churches have free sittings; and the Methodist Episcopal Church is fast crowding this noble record. There is a growing tendency on the part of all denominations to return to the simple plan of free pews and voluntary offerings. When the sittings in the Church of England a few years ago were made free, the increased attendance upon the Sabbath services was at once apparent. The records of St. Margaret's Church, London, under Canon Farrar show that with the abolition of pew-rents the congregation grew until it overflowed into Westminster Abbey. Many more illustrations might be given, showing how the free-church plan has been blessed with great increase spiritually and financially. But we do well to recall the words of Bishop Huntington: "We do not expect free churches to be proved to be right because they are successful, but that by and by they will be successful because they are right. God will bless them if he approves them; and if he blesses them they will succeed."[1]

While it is true that the renting of pews is a departure from the methods of the early Church, it is also true that this method of securing revenue has been the estab-

[1] A Sermon before the Massachusetts Free Church Association, 1894.

lished custom of the Church during many years. It thus becomes necessary that the church which would discard the pew system must stand ready to put something satisfactory in its place. The voluntary offering, when carried out in a wise and systematic manner, has proved such a substitute. Some churches have abused the system by making it a sort of tariff levied by the church officers as appeared in their judgment just. This, however, is not the common or the Scriptural practice. Mr. Robert C. Ogden, in his "Pew-Rents and the New Testament: can they be Reconciled?" urges that the church should have no pledges of any kind for the support of its work. It may be that Mr. Ogden is right, but he largely stands alone in this view of the matter. Most churches having the voluntary-offering system, ask their members at the beginning of the financial year to indicate in writing (cards having been provided for this purpose) the amount that they desire to contribute weekly to the support of the work of the church for the ensuing year. The amount of such contribution is left to the individual conscience, enlightened by a clear and definite statement as to the needs of the church. The amount of the pledge is known only to one officer, and may be revoked at any time. A package of envelopes — an envelope for each week in the year — is sent to all pledging a weekly offering. This plan enables the church officers to calculate approximately the income of the year from the envelope system. This is a large gain over the plan suggested by Mr. Ogden; and to say that this plan is not *voluntary* seems to be a narrowing of the meaning of that word. When the aggregate amount pledged is not sufficient to meet the expenses of the year, a special offering is sometimes taken to cover the balance needed, and is usually taken on Easter Sabbath, when it is called an Easter Offering. As an aid to memory in the use of the envelopes, the Faith Presbyterian Church, New York, has a card hanging in the vestibule. This card contains a record by Sundays for an entire year. At the left is the number of every pledge envelope, and every week the amount contributed by the person whom this number represents is filled in. No names appear, but the pledger by a glance at the card is enabled to tell whether or not he is in arrears, and the amount. Also any person interested may estimate how much is being paid in weekly to the treasury of the church. The pastor, Rev. James S. Hoadley, D.D., has found this plan to be of great aid in educating the congregation to regularity in their offerings. Similar plans have been used elsewhere, and are regarded as being of great service. There are churches too which provide envelopes bearing the date for the offerings, for the Boards and benevolences of the church.

Granting that the free-pew and voluntary-offering system is the better system, how can its substitution for the pew-rental system be brought about? The Rev. Howard A. Bridgman, D.D., in his crisp and persuasive article, "A Plea for Free Pews,"[1] makes the following admirable suggestions for bringing about such a change: "Begin at once a campaign of agitation and education. Scatter suitable literature. Bishop Huntington's sermon, 'God's House Open to God's Children;' Dr. Rainsford's pamphlet, 'Let us Anchor our Churches and make them Free;' and Robert C. Ogden's little book, 'Pew-Rents and the New Testament: can they be Reconciled?' all treat the subject in a judicial and admirable spirit. In endeavors to secure the desired result the 'don't's' are

[1] Published in leaflet form, 1 Somerset Street, Boston, Mass.

quite as important as the 'do's.' Don't be impatient or scold. Don't claim everything for the free system, or make the pew system responsible for all the failures of the Church to reach the masses. It is n't. Moreover, it is not a specific for all the diseases or a solvent for all the problems now afflicting the Church. Don't bring things to a head prematurely. Quiet, persistent, patient effort is what tells."[1]

A pastor of a large church in a New England town of some ten thousand inhabitants mailed leaflets and literature on the free-pew question to members of his parish as often as once a month for nearly a whole year. An influential member of the congregation strongly opposed anything that looked like a change from the pew-rental system, but yielded to the quiet invitation of the minister to investigate the matter, with the result that he became a strong advocate of the free-pew plan, although not a Christian man.

One thing should be guarded against: leaving the free-pew system to take care of itself. It demands thought and time, sympathy and support, as does every good work. The plan will serve no better than any other, unless along with it there is the Christ spirit of welcome, and the heart warm and aglow with divine love. Well says Dr. Bridgman: "Better the rental system with a real cordiality pervading the church than the free-pew system where no hands are extended in welcome and no hearts beat in sympathy for the stranger. It is asking too much of even the best system in the world to expect it to flourish in an environment of icebergs."[2]

[1] A Plea for Free Pews, pp. 16, 17.   [2] Ibid. p. 12.

CHURCH PROGRAMMES.

CHAPTER XL.

CHURCH PROGRAMMES, YEAR-BOOKS, BULLETINS, VESTIBULE CARDS, PAPERS, LETTERS, AND ADVERTISING.

1. The Sunday programme in use in so many of our churches is of service in many ways. The programmes of larger churches are usually a four-page leaflet, the first being in the nature of a titlepage; the second giving the programme of worship; the third, notes relative to church matters; and the fourth a calendar of the services of the Sabbath and the meetings of the week. In looking over different programmes, I find it the custom of some churches to give usually one or two notes relative to the work of the church at large. Sometimes helpful quotations are given from writers like Charles Kingsley, Phillips Brooks, and others. This page also gives opportunity for public recognition, in one form or another, of services to the church which may be deserving of mention. Notes relative to the meetings and work of various societies magnify their importance, and show that their work is known and appreciated by the pastor and the church-members. The names of new members received into the church and into the several societies from time to time, appear on this page.

On this page of notes some churches give the record of the parish work for the month, under such subjects as, "Visits Made and Received," "Strangers

Greeted," "Number of Meetings," "Classes Conducted," "Baptisms," "Marriages."

There is opportunity in this bulletin also for the pastor to say many things which he cannot always say from the pulpit; and say them in the hope of having them remembered through the calendars being carried into the homes represented in the church, and having the programmes reach members who from one cause or another are necessarily absent from the church service. Everything that can be said in favor of church papers may be said in favor of church programmes. He certainly has a peculiar church who cannot utilize every line of space in such a Sabbath calendar.

The fourth page of this Sunday programme usually contains the announcements of the meetings for the week, giving the day, the hour, and the place. In a large congregation where the meetings are many, a printed list becomes absolutely necessary, and even in smaller congregations where the notices are few it has been found advantageous. Some village churches instead of four-paged programmes use only a single leaflet, omitting the order of services and indicating only the meetings of the week, and giving notes relative to various departments of church work. In addition to the convenience to the people of a memorandum of the meetings, the programme saves the time and distraction of making announcements from the pulpit. The cost of such a slip is very little.

In addition to the important service of a Sunday programme in keeping the weekly meetings before the people and acquainting them with the work of the church, the calendar makes the best kind of an invitation to the services to send to strangers and non-

CHURCH PROGRAMMES.

church-goers. Many pastors send these calendars every week to those persons whose names have been obtained through the pulpit reception and by other means. Large numbers are also left in hotels and public places. For this mailing-list and public distribution the Marble Collegiate Church of New York City has a special programme, with the announcement leaf bearing a special invitation to strangers and people who are without a church home.

A simpler way of giving such invitation is by pasting the following slip on the regular Sabbath programme: —

The Madison Avenue Presbyterian Church
extends a cordial invitation to transient guests and to all who are without a regular church home in our city, to attend the services indicated in this Bulletin.

The Madison Avenue Presbyterian Church
is located on Madison Avenue and Fifty-third Street, and may be conveniently reached by the Madison Avenue cars.

If you are a Stranger
we ask that you make yourself known to one of the ministers or to one of the ushers, thereby enabling them to give you a special welcome. Ushers will be in attendance to show you to a sitting. All seats are free.

The above is a slight modification of one used by the Westminster Church, Buffalo, N. Y. When the slip is printed, one end is gummed for the purpose of attaching to the calendar.

MODERN METHODS IN CHURCH WORK.

Many churches always have a prominent note which expresses the welcome of the church to strangers. The following appears on every calendar of the Marble Collegiate Reformed Church, New York: —

ITS WELCOME.

Welcome is the shibboleth that will win the people, so long as there is a vacant seat in the sanctuary no person shall be kept waiting in the vestibule. Welcome to lofty and lowly! Welcome to old and young! Welcome to capital and labor! Welcome to the wise and the unwise! Welcome to all to a place in our Father's house!

2. CHURCH YEAR-BOOKS. In comparing a large number of year-books which have been received, there appears a suggestive difference in them. Several manuals give only the names of the officers and committees, the several societies of the church with their officers, and the church roll with the residence of the members. Others include the rules of the officers of the church and their duties, the Articles of Belief, and lists of accessions and deaths during the year. Some contain an historical sketch of the church. The majority of the year-books, however, while incorporating some or all of the above facts, have a yearly pastoral letter and reports from the secretaries of the several societies, stating briefly the object of the society, the work which it has been doing, sometimes indicating mistakes that have been made, and suggesting ways for improvement, and mentioning opportunities and possibilities which may awaken more earnest effort. Such a year-book is of great value in bringing before the church-members the work of the several societies, and showing their inter-relation as an organic whole.

CHURCH BULLETINS.

It is an innocent mistake, but a serious one, to assume that all other church-members are acquainted with the work of the society which is nearest our own heart. Many of them are as much absorbed with the work of their own society as we with ours. Much will be gained, and a common inspiration given, when we learn of the work which *all* are trying to do, and realize that after all we are but parts of one harmonious whole.

The expense of the year-book may be met, if desired, by filling the last pages of the book with advertisements.

3. CHURCH BULLETINS. Bulletins on the outside of the church are more and more coming into use. These have permanent letterings, with name of pastor, and calendar of services for the week. Below this, a space is left for putting in a lettered card, by which the pastor announces weekly the subjects of his sermons. The bulletin also gives opportunity for special notices during the week. It is a simple arrangement, and is an outer indication that the church is alive within. In the case of a church that is open daily for prayer and meditation, a bulletin announcing this fact may be placed on the outside. Many churches are so arranged that it is necessary to call attention to the fact that they are open; and it is comforting and inspiring to the passer to read this invitation, whether he avails himself of the privilege or not.

4. Vestibule and motto cards are also becoming more largely used. The vestibule cards, for the purpose of expressing the welcome of the church to strangers, are in attractive but plain lettering, and are hung in prominent places near the entrances. The following illustrates the general character of these cards: —

MODERN METHODS IN CHURCH WORK.

> "ALL YE ARE BRETHREN."
> "THE RICH AND THE POOR MEET TOGETHER."
> THE SEATS IN THIS CHURCH ARE FREE.
> VOLUNTARY OFFERINGS SUPPORT THE WORK.
> YOU ARE WELCOME TO A CHURCH HOME HERE.

Other churches have similar messages of welcome lettered on the wall; and in their lecture and society rooms have a large number of pretty cards bearing Scripture passages hanging about the rooms.

The motto cards are as helpful in awakening sentiments of worship as the vestibule cards are of service in expressing the welcome of the church.

5. CHURCH PAPERS. The church paper, published monthly, is another means of increasing the interest in the parish, and of extending this interest to larger spheres. There are publishing-houses which provide papers of from ten to fifteen pages, allotting certain pages to a church for its church news and such advertisements as it may secure. The reading matter provided by the publishing company is of general interest and of such nature as might be expected in a church paper. The publishing company largely covers its expenses by advertisements, so that the cost to a church is only a nominal one, which can easily be covered by a few local advertisements. This provides for free distribution of the church paper, which brings the work of the church before the members and the community, and places helpful literature in many homes.

5. LETTER-WRITING. The value of letter-writing, in the work of the parish, cannot be overestimated. It was Goethe who said, "If you would know how others

think and feel, know thyself." One thing we all know is our appreciation of letters; Uncle Sam's messengers are always welcome, and too are subject to the immediate call of the busy pastor. Letters are the most direct and effective means of all advertising. The pastor who does not thus make use of the pen is letting rust one of the mightiest instruments that God has given him. A warm, kindly letter is as a breath of the soul, and goes directly to the soul. However, the busy pastor cannot write many letters; but by the mimeograph he can write a letter in his own hand to every member of the congregation, and too in almost as short a time as it takes to write one letter. A mimeograph which will last for years, and meet the largest needs, costs only from eight to twelve dollars. It is invaluable, and can be used for all sorts of writing where a number of copies are needed, whether ten copies or a thousand, — letters, special notices, invitations, teachers' reports, etc. I speak at length of the use of the mimeograph, as I know from experience how advantageously it may be used, and how indispensable it has become to pastors who use it.

6. ADVERTISING THE SERVICES. Another important work is advertising the Sunday services. There are a good many ways in which this can be done. Of course, nothing is so good as a personal invitation from one of the church-members. Notices of meetings by hand-bills may be distributed in stores, boarding-houses, and public places. Printed, type-written, mimeographed, or — best of all — personally written letters should be mailed to those who are known to be without a church home, to students, and to transient guests at hotels. News-agents who handle large numbers of daily papers can be hired for a small fee to place the invitation circular in all the papers which

they sell and distribute. Still other means may be employed, such as notices in the papers, church bulletins, hand-bills on the street, framed announcements in hotels and barber shops. Care should be taken to have the circulars printed so that they will attract the eye. This advertising should be continuous and persistent. "'The secret of successful advertising for the gospel's sake is the same as that of the successful advertising of the merchant: "Keeping everlastingly at it brings success.'"[1]

The Rev. William H. Fishburn, D.D., pastor of the Second Presbyterian Church of Columbus, O., has large evening audiences and a most successful plan for advertising his services. When he assumed the pastorate, there was practically no evening congregation, but within a few months he had an evening audience of from one thousand to thirteen hundred people. Dr. Fishburn commenced advertising by issuing large numbers of invitation cards to the church services, printing some weeks as many as fifteen thousand cards. These were done up in packages of one hundred, seventy-five, fifty, twenty-five, and ten, held together by rubber bands. They were given to the people for distribution after a sermon on church work delivered at the morning service. Members were to say, as they passed out of the church, whether they wanted one hundred, fifty, twenty-five, or ten, and received what they asked for. The results were immediate. When the pastor delivers a special sermon or series of sermons, cards are in like manner distributed by the male members of the church to the people sought to be reached. This is accomplished by dividing the city up into convenient districts. The plan of advertising includes also getting the evening audience themselves interested in the

[1] The Fishin' Jimmy Club, by Rev. Dr. John Clark Hill, p. 29.

ADVERTISING THE SERVICES.

distribution of cards; appeal is made to them to take packages of invitation cards to distribute during the week. This at once gives the *new-comers* something to do, and stimulates their interest. At times the cards are taken to stores to be wrapped with parcels; they are carried through the markets and dropped into baskets, and are given to the elevator boys at the hotels. The printing of the cards is in plain bold type, the main object being to convey the message.

A question that naturally arises with many churches which would like to undertake such advertising is, "Can we afford it?" Another question might well suggest itself, "Can we afford not to do it?" The common experience is that the increased collections resulting from increased attendance upon the services of the church covers not only the cost of printing and incidental expenses, but also adds considerably to the general fund of the church. It pays "manifold more in this present time, and in the world to come life everlasting."

CHAPTER XLL

CHURCH ARCHITECTURE.

The new methods of church work are having a marked effect on church architecture. Churches built in years past are totally unsuited to the busy life of the modern house of God. Many of them have neither the grace, beauty, or utility of the ancient temple, nor the practical and æsthetic value that modern architecture gives to buildings constructed for other purposes. Like the Chinese Wall, these churches seem to have been built to keep the people out. Nothing more discouraging can be imagined than the attempt to carry on a broad Christian work in cramped and unattractive quarters!

Let us see what kind of a building the new church requires to carry on her work. In this investigation we cannot do better than to take as an example the beautiful new Pilgrim Congregational Church of Cleveland, O. This noble edifice contains forty-three separate apartments. The spacious auditorium, with its gallery, will seat thirteen hundred. All of the space in the auditorium is utilized, as the seating is amphitheatrical in form, the aisles radiating from the pulpit, which is in one corner. This location of the speaker makes the gallery, which occupies the two sides converging to the corner opposite the pulpit, very pleasant, since every occupant of the gallery is brought into a position facing the speaker. The organ and choir, with sittings for one hundred, occupy an addition on the side of the church at the left of the pulpit. The fourth side of the church, at the right of the pulpit, opens by sliding doors into the Sunday-school room, by the use of which the auditorium may be made to accommodate twenty-four hundred people. The Sunday-school is provided with class-rooms, both above and below stairs, including in all twenty rooms for the use of the school. All the doors of the class-rooms may be opened and closed by steam power, which is controlled by levers from the superintendent's desk. The offices of the pastor, his associate, and assistant occupy the remaining rooms on this floor. On the ground-floor of the church, beneath the auditorium and Sunday-school rooms, are the rooms in which the educational and industrial work is carried on. The gymnasium is found here, with dressing-rooms for men and women. Here, too, are the drill-rooms for the Boys' Brigade, capacious dining-room, kitchen and pantry, ladies' parlor, reception-room, and reading-rooms for the various societies of the church.

Other churches devote the church proper to auditorium, choir-rooms, and lecture-room or chantry, having another building — called the parish house — in which to carry on the institutional work of the church. This is the case with Jersey City Tabernacle, which has the People's Palace for housing every activity of the church. In such a building it is more convenient to have swimming-baths and gymnasiums than in the church proper. Many ministers who are in full sympathy with industrial and educational work urge the use of an outside building for that purpose, — not that the church building would be desecrated by loving ministries "in His name," but for reasons of economy. Other ministers urge that institutional work should be conducted only in the parish house, that the church proper may be associated in thought with the one idea of worship. It is evident that the parish house would meet the need of those churches which are circumscribed in the size of their church lot, or where additions or changes of the church edifice would be impracticable. St. Bartholomew's Church, New York, has a well-equipped parish house, containing accommodations for the Rescue Mission, the clubs, classes, and clinics. The house is fully in use, from the restaurant in the basement to the roof garden on the top. This roof garden is a unique idea, which might well be copied by other churches in the cities. It is open on five evenings in the week. Here, on the hot summer nights, there is music, and an opportunity to breathe a better, cooler air than that of the streets or the stifling rooms below. To prevent overcrowding, the roof garden is open to certain classes on certain nights, and on the evening devoted to women and babies there are refreshments. But the roof garden is adapted to other purposes than amusement. Why not make use of it during the sultry months of summer for preaching services and other gospel meetings?

The Fourth Congregational Church of Hartford, Conn., has drawn plans for a new church edifice, which, in addition to a spacious auditorium, lecture-room, and Sunday-school rooms, will house the various departments of institutional work. The plan also seems to solve the problem of support for down-town churches. The building is to be six stories high, and the three upper floors are to be rented for offices and other purposes, which will in large part meet annually the church expenses.

Attention to minor details in planning a church does much to make it pleasant and homelike. The color of the carpet, the style and coloring of the decorations,

CHURCH ARCHITECTURE.

attention to the heating, lighting, and ventilation, — even to the quality of the carpet lining that softens the footfall, — all play their part in making the house of God a restful place to every sense. The Lincoln Park Baptist Church of Cincinnati, O., will soon erect a church having some new features. Among them is an Old Folks' Gallery, with the most comfortable upholstered seats possible. They also plan having a balcony on the front of the church, where a band may be stationed for summer-evening concerts before services. There is such a balcony on the front of Grace Baptist Church, Philadelphia, and music is rendered there at midnight before New Year's and Easter. In the Hollond Memorial Presbyterian Church, Philadelphia, the stairs to the gallery go up from the auditorium instead of from the vestibule, the idea being to make the occupants of the gallery feel themselves to be an integral part of the assembly.

The study of architecture is a fascinating one, and churches and cathedrals have always stood among the highest types of the builder's art. We need not sacrifice the "frozen music." We may still have our groined arches, our flying buttresses, and our graceful spires, our deep pealing organ, and our stained-glass windows. But with these things we should have the beauty of the practical and the adaptation of structure to the varied uses of the church, which has for its high ideal ministering to the whole man on every day of every week.

CHAPTER XLII.

MOBILIZING THE WORK.

The multiplication of societies in a church incident to the demands of different kinds of work may appear to break the church as an organic whole. The individual society sometimes magnifies the importance of its own sphere of action at the expense of other church work, thus interfering with that perfect unity of feeling and of purpose and that fellowship of believers which should characterize the body of Christ. And where there is want of unity and plan in the various organizations of the church, forces often collide or misspend themselves, and the result is discouragement and sometimes the abandonment of worthy endeavors. To counteract this disintegrating tendency, and to fuse and solidify the work and bring the several parts into such articulate and sympathetic relations that one spirit and purpose shall animate all, a representative council or pastor's cabinet is most effective. The meetings are usually held monthly. This council consists of all the church officers by whatever name they may be known, — officers of the Sunday-school and the heads of all the various organizations in the church. All the societies in the church, both old and young, are represented in the cabinet; thus it is easy to prevent overlapping in work, each society is stimulated by hearing of the work of the other societies, young and old are mutually helped, and all appreciate the

MOBILIZING THE WORK.

oneness of the work. Besides the feeling of unity among the church-workers that such cabinet meeting engenders, it is of incalculable assistance to the pastor by placing him in touch with the various societies without the necessity of going to the various heads for information. At the cabinet meetings he has the opportunity of receiving from the representatives of each society and committee all the facts as to the day-by-day life of the organization, and to give, individually and as a whole, words of advice, sympathy, and appreciation. He in return experiences the encouragement of the presence and discussions of head workers gathered around him, and comes into possession of details which it would be impossible otherwise to obtain, and receives suggestions which could in no other way be secured. We would discount that college president who did not avail himself of the helpful discussions of his college faculty. Can the pastor any the less afford to let pass the helpful suggestions of his workers? True, he has the church officers as advisers, but church officers do not by any manner of means know all the practical workings, the encouragements and difficulties, of the several societies. Such meetings will be of help to the officers as well as to the minister. The ideal church is the unified church, in which the pastor is as one who sits in the midst of a complicated system of machinery all working in perfect harmony, — able to see at a glance just how everything is going, and able to direct and control the energy of every part. Such a church through the subordination of all individual preferences to the one great object of advancing the kingdom of God upon earth, must indeed be a great power. There is one practical suggestion in this connection that ought to be made: the pastor should be an *ex-*

officio member of every nominating committee of every society. Without being dictatorial, he can help to the wisest choice of officers, as no one so well as he knows the influence and qualifications of members for such important trusts.

Incidental to the discussion in the chapter on " Women's Work " are other suggestions for mobilizing church work.

There is yet a broader way of looking at this question of mobilizing the work, — that of mobilizing not merely the work of the several societies of a church, but the work of the several churches of a community. Union effort of churches in certain directions in no way limits or interferes with the regular work of the individual church; rather it enlarges its work and increases its opportunities for doing good. The broader conception of the mission of the Church, that her duty is to work for the salvation of society as well as the individual, at once brings the churches into sympathetic relation and into appreciation of the need of co-operation. Only in union effort can the churches be thorough in their work in the community, or hope to effect a social redemption. The demands are so great that if the churches stand alone the work will remain undone. There is need of the power of concerted action that comes through organization. There may be other societies in the town which aim to raise the tone of citizenship, work for civic improvements, promote the interests of labor, arouse the public conscience, and influence legislation in the interests of temperance, education, equity, and morals, but the churches have a duty in this matter which cannot be delegated to another. This great work has been placed on the children of God, and we should bring the tremendous influence of the churches into all that affects the interests of society, civic interests as well as religious, and work together for the public weal.

The plan suggested for church co-operation by the Evangelical Alliance [1] is a very simple and comprehensive one; namely, a Board of Managers or Executive Committee, consisting of the pastor and two members from each church. A Standing Committee is then appointed on each line of work which the Executive Committee decide to undertake, the names being selected from the lists of individual members of the local church alliance. Of course, every community will have its own problems and needs, but for general lines of work the Evangelical Alliance suggests, among others, the following: Committee on (1) Social Conditions; (2) Evangelization; (3) Relief; (4) Temperance; (5) Sunday Observance; (6) Law and Order; (7) Municipal Reform; (8) Civic Improvements; (9) Labor; (10) Education and Recreation.

The object of such church co-operation is not to compete with other societies in the community working to the same end, but is to co-operate with them. "Thus the Alliance Standing Committee on Temperance appoints a sub-committee to confer with whatever temperance organizations there may be in the town, and ask how the churches can best co-operate with them to serve the cause of temperance. The Alliance Standing Committee on Labor appoints a sub-committee to confer with labor organizations and arrange for such co-operation as will best enable the churches to serve the interests of labor, etc." [2]

[1] Rev. Josiah Strong, D. D., General Secretary, United Charities Building, Fourth Avenue and 22d Street, New York.
[2] Evangelical Alliance, Leaflet No. 6, p. 7.

Since the Church has no right to delegate to another this work for society, the churches should not hesitate to form an alliance, although there may be existing organizations in the town for similar purposes. The Church Alliance will then be able, usually, not only to co-operate in, but also to co-ordinate, the work of the several societies.

The Evangelical Alliance, which was formed in England in 1844 and in the United States in 1867, and which has done such a large and praiseworthy work, is always ready to co-operate in the organization of a local alliance of churches by sending helpful literature, and in other ways as it may be able.

I do not believe it possible to over-emphasize the urgent need of church co-operation. Union effort will open many avenues of service before unknown, place the churches in possession of invaluable facts for their work, prevent needless overlapping, and the greater crime of new churches being built when not needed, or where they would only deplete other churches and force all to suffer a struggling existence. Greater inspiration would come to all the churches because of this larger view of their mission in their co-operation for the great end of social regeneration. And we *must* work for the regeneration of society. The sooner we give ourselves to the task, the sooner will God's Kingdom come. It would be praiseworthy to save what people we could from a sinking ship, but it were better to save both ship and people. With church co-operation denominational differences could still continue; but with the churches working together to extend the Kingdom, with eyes fixed alone on Jesus Christ, and hearts filled with the Holy Spirit, our churches would make a resistless march, without one wavering line, till soon the world, with all its business, all its learning, all its art, all its kingdoms, would be gathered up into the one unified and perfected Kingdom of our God.

CHAPTER XLIII.

RESULTS OF THE NEW METHODS.

Every good tree bringeth forth good fruit, but a corrupt tree bringeth forth evil fruit. A good tree cannot bring forth evil fruit, neither can a corrupt tree bring forth good fruit. . . . Therefore, by their fruits ye shall know them. — ST. MATTHEW.

AMONG the first questions asked regarding churches which are carrying on institutional work are: How have the new methods succeeded? What have been the spiritual results? Is the work a success financially? These questions may be said to go to the heart of the matter; they at once determine the kind of tree, whether it be good or evil, and the leaders in the new movement willingly give answer.

But in noticing the results of the new methods in churches we must bear in mind two things: First, that the *new methods* in many of these churches *have succeeded where the old methods failed*, or that the new methods have met with much *larger results than the old methods*. Second, in measuring the new methods we must measure them as we would measure a projectile, — not only by the work accomplished, but also by the resistant force which they have had to overcome. It is comparatively easy to build up a large and strong church where the conditions are favorable, — an increasing population of a church-going and an accessible people. But when, by birth and training, environment, inaccessibility, and other conditions, people are alienated

RESULTS OF THE NEW METHODS.

and separated from the Church, her task in winning them is far more difficult.

Now, as to some of the results of the new methods, what are they?

The Central Presbyterian Church, Rochester, N. Y., Rev. Henry H. Stebbins, D.D., pastor, has grown under the Open Church system, since Dr. Stebbins assumed the pastorate in March, 1888, from a membership of 885 to 1,688, and the membership of the Sunday-school has grown from 800 to over 2,500.

In the Westminster Church, Buffalo, N. Y., Rev. Samuel Van Vranken Holmes, pastor, the gain in attendance at the services of the church under the Open and Free system, has been one hundred per cent, and the financial gain has been fully fifty per cent.

Rev. G. R. Robbins, pastor of Lincoln Park Institutional Baptist Church of Cincinnati, O., reports that though that church is poorly located and unattractive in outward appearance, God has blessed them wonderfully. During the seven years of institutional work the membership has increased from 240 to 707.

Rev. John C. Emory, pastor of the Waverly Congregational Church, Jersey City, N. J., in answer to the question, "What have been the gains, financially and spiritually, of the new methods?" writes: "Five times as many converted and uniting with the church. Collections double." In Mr. Emory's address before the Open Church League, New York, 1894, he said, in speaking of his church: "The income was formerly each year $700 to $800 behind. It is now ahead, and a $25,000 mortgage is being paid off."[1]

Berkeley Temple, Boston, Rev. Charles A. Dickinson, D.D., pastor, has grown in seven years from a membership of about 300 to over 1,100. About half the

[1] Report of League Conference, p. 11.

additions have been on confession. The congregations, which formerly numbered about 250, now fill the house. They frequently have 1,500 at an evening service. From 8,000 to 12,000 pass through their doors in the aggregate during each week. This church is now the largest church of its denomination in New England.

Rev. S. Sherberne Matthews, pastor of the Hanover Street Congregational Church, Milwaukee, says: "Institutional methods have been in use here for some three years, during which time I think the membership has nearly doubled."

Rev. Warren G. Partridge, pastor of the Ninth Street Baptist Church, Cincinnati, O., reports an addition of 854 members during four years, and says, "We usually have conversions every week of the whole year."

The membership of the Calvary Methodist Episcopal Church, New York, Rev. A. B. Kendig, D.D., pastor, increased from 1,200 to 1,500 during two years of the new methods.

Dr. John L. Scudder, pastor of the Congregational Tabernacle, Jersey City, N. J., says: "Without these methods we should have died long ago, but with them we have steadily grown in numbers and power."

The Pilgrim Congregational Church of Cleveland, O., has been employing the new methods during the five years of the pastorate of the Rev. Charles S. Mills, D.D. During that time they have built a beautiful new church, and undertaken many kinds of Christian work. Their morning congregations have increased from 250 to over 600, and the evening from 100 to 1,200. Attendance on the prayer meetings has proportionately increased. This church is a family church as well as a people's church; and its benevolent work is only supplementary to strong aggressive methods of evangelization and Christian nurture, with the result

RESULTS OF THE NEW METHODS.

of doubling its church-membership, and increasing the Sunday-school from 680 to 1,250.

St. George's Episcopal Church, New York, Rev. W. S. Rainsford, D.D., rector, inaugurated some forms of institutional work in 1882. At that time the church-membership had dwindled down to not more than seventy-five communicants. The neighborhood was becoming more and more a tenement-house district, and the outlook for the church was very unpromising. To-day, under the new methods, there are about 4,000 communicants. Of these, Dr. Rainsford says, "four-fifths live in boarding-houses and tenement houses. More than half are genuine working-people whose daily bread depends upon the work of their hands." In St. George's Sabbath-school there are 3,000 children, and more might be gathered if there were sufficient accommodations.

Grace Baptist Church, Philadelphia, Rev. Russell H. Conwell, D.D., pastor, inaugurated institutional work in 1887. Since then they have built the beautiful new Temple, have founded the Temple College and the Samaritan Hospital, besides carrying on all the other work of the church. The total amount expended has been more than $300,000. This amount has not been given in large donations. It has been the result of self-denial on the part of the members, many of whom are of the working-class. It has meant walking instead of riding, doing without luxuries and even things that almost seemed necessities. It has meant the enlistment of childish interest so that the children's contributions swelled the fund. Along with this, hand in hand, was the increase in church-membership and all good works. There were 899 church-members in 1887; now there are about 2,600.

The Armour Mission, Chicago, has also been blessed

with large increase. The prominent religious feature of this institution is the Sunday-school. When the beautiful Armour Mission building was completed and swung wide its door of welcome on the Sabbath of December 5, 1886, the Mission Sunday-school of Plymouth Church, two blocks away, was invited to make the spacious Armour Building its home. This invitation was accepted, the new mission Sunday-school opening with a membership of 500. The enrolment of this Sunday-school at the present time is over 2,200.

The Madison Avenue Presbyterian Church, New York, Rev. Charles L. Thompson, D.D., pastor, has had four years of Open Church work. In his last anniversary sermon Dr. Thompson said: "During the four years we have been engaged in this work we have contributed for benevolent purposes a total of $20,851, and for our own work $74,787, making a grand total for all purposes of $95,638. . . . All but perhaps $8,000 of the total has been given by our own people, and on a purely voluntary principle. . . .

"During the past four years we have received 302 new members: 152 by examination and 150 by letter from other churches. . . . The noblest thing by far that has been achieved in these four years of struggle has been the development of a rare spirit of Christian service."

"The Outlook" for June 30, 1894, in an article "Spirituality and the Institutional Church," by the Rev. William Cross Merrill, presents some interesting statistics as to the work of the Berkeley Temple, Boston, and other churches employing similar methods. It is as follows: "The Berkeley Street Church furnishes the history of a long and arduous struggle for survival in a rapidly changing environment. Meanwhile it enjoyed pastoral leadership of exceptional

RESULTS OF THE NEW METHODS.

ability, and yet, some eight years ago, it became the deliberate conviction of the ablest judges that the field must be abandoned. To some church about to surrender its field of labor, it may be of interest to compare the last six years of the Berkeley Street Church with the first six years of its institutional work as Berkeley Temple. The table gives the year, membership, additions by conversion, percentage of gain by conversion, and gain over all losses by letter and conversion: —

BERKELEY STREET CHURCH, 1882-1887.

Year.	Members.	Received on Confession.	Percentage of Gain on Confession.	Percentage of Net Gain by Letter and Confession.
1882	604	16	2.65	2.45
1883	598	2	.33	(1.00) loss
1884	595	15	2.52	1.51
1885	597	7	1.17	.33
1886	597	17	2.88	.83
1887	605	12	1.98	.50
Totals.	...	..	11.53	4.62

BERKELEY TEMPLE, 1888-1893.

Year.	Members.	Received on Confession.	Percentage of Gain on Confession.	Percentage of Net Gain by Letter and Confession.
1888	590	26	4.41	14.40
1889	597	31	5.19	12.56
1890	711	66	9.28	13.22
1891	812	63	7.76	12.32
1892	894	52	5.82	9.39
1893	957	51	5.39	6.45
Totals.	...	..	37.85	68.34
1894	1020	62	6.07	6.17
1895	1063	39	3.66	4.04 [1]

[1] The statistics for the years 1894 and 1895 I have added to those given by the "Outlook," for the purpose of showing what has been the continued increase in the membership of Berkeley Temple.

MODERN METHODS IN CHURCH WORK.

"This is a comparison of a church with itself under old and new methods of activity. As Berkeley Temple, working under the Divine injunction, ' Go ye into the highways and hedges, and compel them to come in, that my house may be full,' its accessions on confessions are more than three-fold, and its total net gain is almost fifteen-fold. . . . Berkeley Temple has had unusual difficulties to encounter, and yet the test is most favorable to the modern methods of work. Let us take four other institutional churches, widely separated, under more favorable conditions, figuring, as before, the percentage of gain by confession on the basis of membership less absentees. We take the years 1887–1892, and the churches Pilgrim, Worcester; Fourth, Hartford; Tabernacle, Jersey City; Plymouth, Milwaukee, and the combined Congregational churches of the United States, of course not deducting the absentees from the latter. Should that seem just, however, a little less than one per cent would be added (about .93).

	Pilgrim, Worcester.	Fourth, Hartford.	Tabernacle, Jersey City.	Plymouth, Milwaukee.	United States, combined.
1887	18.54	20.83	16.81	14.79	8.99
1888	7.86	4.87	9.23	10.94	5.47
1889	3.83	10.75	9.19	5.73	5.95
1890	5.15	11.56	22.01	5.57	5.44
1891	12.38	9.34	3.84	8.44	5.83
1892	3.75	9.47	5.71	1.05	5.82
Totals.	51.51	66.82	66.79	46.52	37.50
Annual Average.	8.58	11.14	11.13	7.75	6.25

"Had all the Congregational churches of the United States attained the same average of gain on confession during these six years, with the institutional churches,

RESULTS OF THE NEW METHODS.

it would have increased their total by a **hundred thousand converts.**"

I add to the above table given by the "Outlook" statistics for the years 1894 and 1895, which show that these churches have continued to realize about the same relative increase on confession as during the previous years of the new methods.

	Pilgrim, Worcester.	Fourth, Hartford.	Tabernacle, Jersey City.	Plymouth, Milwaukee.	United States, combined.
1893	5.66	5.62	6.24	17.10	5.59
1894	6.16	9.25	8.84	——[1]	6.09
1895	4.36	9	2.52	3.05	5.34

It is to be said that some of the churches carrying on this larger work are unable from the contributions of their own membership to meet the heavy expenses involved. We could hardly expect it to be otherwise with those churches situated in down-town districts and whose constituency is largely of the laboring-class. But the large spiritual results attendant upon institutional work, together with the leavening and uplifting influence that comes with the personal touch of these churches upon the community, commends the movement to those congregations which have the means to place such work among needy people.

It must not be inferred from this remark, however, that many churches, and in fact the majority of those churches which are trying to "heal" and to "teach" as well as to "preach," are not meeting their expenses from the gifts of their people. Many such churches have proven not only that the consecration of their people is equal to all the demands of this great work,

[1] No report in the Congregational Year Book.

but also that the gifts of their people to missions, benevolences, and Church Boards was showing an annual increase. The promise, in more ways than one, has been fulfilled unto these churches: "Give, and it shall be given unto you; good measure, pressed down, and shaken together, and running over, shall men give into your bosom. For with the same measure that ye mete withal it shall be measured to you again."[1]

[1] Luke vi. 38.

CHAPTER XLIV.

THE INSPIRATION OF THE NEW MOVEMENT AND THE REALIZATION OF THE KINGDOM.

THERE is no mistaking the fact that our churches are tremulous with the mighty spirit of a new life. We have seen that the Church, under the stimulus of the new movement, is yet "holding fast to that which is good," but that along with this there is "life more abundantly." Co-existent with the larger conception of the humanitarian and civic mission of the Church, it has been ordained that there should be a deepening of the spiritual life of the members of the Church of Christ. Never throughout the whole Christian era has there been such eager seeking for the life of privilege, or so wide-spread and deepening appreciation of the gift and office of the Holy Spirit. The tendency, therefore, is not that the material will overshadow the spiritual in the life of the Church, but that the sphere of the sacred will be extended to all secular life, and all things held in holy trust for God, "whose we are and whom we serve."[1] The new movement comes, then, with this double gift (the larger conception of the mission of the Church, and a larger reliance on the presence and work of the Holy Spirit), and comes into the closing century with such force and with such promise in the sweep of its power, and

[1] Acts xxvii. 23.

under the impulse of so mighty an inspiration, as only the Infinite can supply.

The new movement, too, finds inspiration in the *time* of its coming. We are familiar with the threefold preparation for the coming of the Messiah. The intellectual preparation by the Greeks, or the use of the Greek language as the common vehicle of thought; the political preparation by the Romans through their almost universal empire; the religious preparation by the Jews, or the preservation of the monotheistic idea. Similarly it may be said that there has been a threefold preparation for the new religious life and work in our churches.

1. The first preparation is the religious preparation, or the deepening of the spiritual life and the conception of the larger mission of the Church to which we have referred.

2. The intellectual preparation. The great doctrines of the Church were fought out in the early centuries of the Christian era. The fires of polemical discussions wrapped their flames about the very life of the Church; that it stood such stress is unanswerable argument for its divine origin. Sometimes the fires of controversy have been fanned anew, and have shot their flames into succeeding centuries; in notable instances the Church has risen out of these trials greater in power, and adorned with a purer, sweeter, and a nobler life, — but at other times the Church has suffered irreparably! We have appreciated, even in some of these latter days, what Gibbon wrote of the early Church, "that the Christians, in the course of their intense dissensions, have inflicted far greater severities on each other than they had experienced from the zeal of infidels." [1]

[1] Milman's Gibbon's Rome, vol. ii. p. 84.

INSPIRATION OF THE NEW MOVEMENT.

But there has come a hopeful change. The Church is weary of controversy; weary of dry doctrinal discussions, this quibbling over the "nice sharp qualities of the law;" talking about things of which, as Rev. Dr. Parkhurst has said, "We none of us know much, and most of us know nothing, and none of us need know anything."[1] That the great body of believers to-day are weary and impatient with the controversialists is indicative of intellectual and spiritual growth. If it be argued that "the schools" still seem powerful, it may be answered that things are not always what they seem. It has been said of the heathen temples in Rome that they were never so magnificent, seemingly so powerful, as when Jesus Christ came; yet when he came, great Pan was dead. The controversialists and the schools have built some great temples for the thought and faith of the Church that yet stand; but the polemic, so far as having voice or sway over the life and heart of the Church, is dead. The Church, too, is weary of formalism, which has forced silent assent to Ouida's charge, that Christianity has become a shibboleth, a husk, a robe, with no heart beating within it.[2] The Church, therefore, is longing to-day, as never before, for truth and life in all simplicity, in the helpfulness, hopefulness, and power found in the Son of Man.

Another thing that marks the intellectual preparation for the new movement is the return to Christ that characterizes the nobler scholarly thought of our time, and is noticeably the impulse of New Testament critics, and of what is called the new school of ecclesiastical historians. "Those who are interested in a new theological habitation for faith," says Rev.

[1] Orthodoxy versus Heresy, or the Indwelling Christ, p. 17.
[2] North American Review, February, 1891, p. 211.

Dr. George A. Gordon, "who seek emancipation from the bondage of mediæval opinion, who want the modern world of life in all its richness and compass to be mastered by adequate, ultimate conceptions of God and man, are on a deep return to Christ. The longing for the true word of Jesus, the desire to reach the creative mind underlying Christendom, the hunger for help in the task of interpreting the world and its life, is the great motive in the characteristic criticism, historical research, and theological construction as at present carried on by Christian scholars. The ultimate problems of reason are so difficult, the final questions of faith are so urgent and perplexing, that along a score of different lines Christian thinkers are returning to their Master. It is felt more and more that there can be no substitutes in creeds, in church authority, in patristic tradition, in apostolic interpretation, for him, and that without him there can be no solution of our human problem."[1] Thus the theological demand is for the simple teachings of Jesus, stripped of the metaphysics that has clouded them, that they may stand forth in the singleness of their divine majesty.

Another thing that marks the intellectual preparation is the demand for a return to Christ's ways of working. We have seen that the Church, in departing from those ways, in following Christ only in part, has not fulfilled its mission; as a result, institutions have sprung up outside the Church for doing the work which it should have done; and though addressing herself mainly to the spiritual mission, the results, as we have seen, have been pitifully small. This being so, and with the Church now perceiving more clearly the meaning of the teachings and life of Jesus

[1] The Christ of To-day, p. 248.

Christ, it is not strange that the cry of the Church, from child to scholar, is for the spirit of the Master and for a return to the "Christianity of Christ."

3. The political preparation. Never was the world so ready for the gospel of Jesus as now. Anarchism in Spain, socialism in Germany, nihilism in Russia, Turkish atrocities in Armenia, revolutionary uprisings in nations, and social disturbances in our own country, all tell one and the same story. These various conditions and expressions of unrest are like the flushed face and the quickened pulse of a man stricken with fever. They are symptoms of a disease, and it is a disease that is at the bottom of all our social ills, and the cause of all the world's sufferings. The trouble is a spiritual one. It is because a certain moral leprosy has taken away the nobler sentiments of love, self-sacrifice, and kindness, that nations are disturbed, and the social systems of the world are threatened with grave and imminent danger. Take our own country, for example. We have heard the cry of suffering, and in an appalling manner have felt the dangers of social unrest and class distinction. Some have dared to say that more money was our need, but time has shown that the need of our country is not money. We are the wealthiest nation in the world. Neither is our need legislation. We have been legislated to death; men are afraid of legislation. But how about liberty? Is not that the cure-all of our ills? "The curse of our time," says the anarchist, "is law." Let us then remove all law, start life anew, make an equal distribution of the nation's wealth. How long will it remain equalized? The improvident man would feast to-day and be bankrupt to-morrow, the indolent would lie by until his fund was exhausted, while the careful

manager would gradually add to his wealth; in a few hours the conditions of life would be as uneven as they are now. Said Dr. Johnson, —

> "How small of all that human hearts endure,
> That part which kings or laws can cause or cure." [1]

When Dr. Johnson uttered these words, over a hundred years ago, the people were complaining, as now, that liberty — fewer laws — was their great need, and Dr. Johnson was denounced for fifty years for speaking as he did. It was claimed that he spread a gloom over life and prevented progress from being made; but time has shown the wisdom of his words. Many reforms contended for at that time have been carried through. True, we have advanced somewhat, yet there is just as much suffering, and in many cases as keen a sense of social wrongs, as one hundred years ago. Mob rule in place of law and order will but aggravate instead of ameliorate our suffering. The questions of liberty, law, and a medium of exchange have a grave bearing on the welfare of our people and country, but we cannot by legislation make men just, honest, or kind. As a nation we may legislate until the end of time, have the soundest monetary system in the world, but only as the Golden Rule is operative in our individual and civic life will our ills find permanent relief. The heart of faith and love is the solution of all of our difficulties. As Burns says, —

> "It's no in titles nor in rank,
> It's no in wealth like Lon'on bank,
> To purchase peace and rest;
> It's no in making muckle *mair:*
> It's no in books, it's no in lear,
> To make us truly blest:

[1] Lines added to Goldsmith's "Traveller."

INSPIRATION OF THE NEW MOVEMENT.

> If happiness hae not her seat
> And centre in the breast,
> We may be wise, or rich, or great,
> But never can be blest:
> Nae treasures nor pleasures
> Could make us happy lang:
> The heart aye's the part aye
> That makes us right or wrang."[1]

Men the world over have looked to legislation, to a mechanical readjustment of the social system, have looked to "things" for relief from suffering and for the realization of hopes. But all these various means have failed, and now humanity lies bleeding at the feet of her own broken idols. The world, as never before, is realizing that only as men's hearts are right can we have a government that is just, only as men's hearts are noble will they refrain from that which is ignoble; is realizing that the present suffering of the world will be permanently relieved only as men get back to faith in God! The world is passing through a great moral crisis, and is hungering and yearning for life as found in Jesus Christ. With the political world, therefore, waiting for the comfort and help of Christ's gospel, with the deepening of the spiritual life of the Church, and the apprehension of its larger mission, and with Christian thinkers demanding a return to the spirit of our Master, — with all this we see that the times are ripe for a great onward movement of God's people; it is the hour of opportunity for the Church! But there is yet a greater stimulus which should be mentioned in this connection.

It is in the person and work of Jesus Christ that the creative, formative, and comprehensive spirit of

[1] Epistle to Davie, a Brother Poet.

the new movement in church and Christian life is found. Saul, the persecutor of the Church, only needed to be brought face to face with Jesus Christ to receive that impulse and inspiration which made him a tireless apostle. Those active in the new movement have been stirred by a vision no less real than Paul's. They have seen the gracious, compassionate Christ who wept over Jerusalem, weeping over the cities of our own land. They have heard the same Jesus who went about healing the sick, ministering to the poor, caring for the impotent, ignorant, and sinful, saying, "As my Father hath sent me, even so send I you,"[1] and they have heard the Christ who gave himself a sacrifice for others, say, "Love one another, as I have loved you."[2] The vision is of the Christ whom we cannot disassociate from the miseries and needs of men; and the Church to-day, which seeks to alleviate human suffering and endeavors to meet men's miseries and needs, has gone to the bottom of the whole question of reaching the masses. The new movement is trying to represent, or re-present Jesus Christ, both in his putting away disease and demons, sufferings and limitations, and in his positive work of putting a new life within; in humanitarian, beneficent, and philanthropic as well as spiritual work, therefore, the supporters of the new movement find inspiration in doing the will of Him that sent them.

The new movement finds another inspiration in the greatness of the work that yet awaits the Church. The world is white unto the harvest. Out of the fifteen hundred million of the earth's population, but five hundred million are even nominal Christians; in our own country but twenty-one million of our popu-

[1] John xx. 21. [2] John xv. 12.

INSPIRATION OF THE NEW MOVEMENT.

lation (counting Protestants and Catholics, who include children) are Christian people.

There is further inspiration in that the greatness of the opportunity and the magnitude of the work quicken the feeling of insufficiency, and press the worker "back upon the Infinite inspirations." This is working as Jesus worked, who was constantly giving of his life freely, and was as constantly replenishing his life through unbroken communion with the Father. The larger the Saviour's work, the more did he give himself to meditation and prayer. It is significant that it was at the close of days of hardest toil, when weary, exhausted by the work of the day in caring for the sick, the needy, the ignorant, the sinful, that Jesus went apart to pray, to renew his strength through communion with the Father. The greater and nobler our work, the more do we realize our need of divine help. There is a beautiful picture of the Rock of Ages, which pictures a young woman standing on a rock in the midst of the sea, with the waves beating perilously about her feet. With one arm she is clinging to the cross, and with the other arm is lifting up a sister who had fallen into the sea; the arm about the cross is clasped the stronger, as with the other she seeks the harder to save. An inspiration in lifting people up out of disease, ignorance, hindrances, and sin is that it brings the worker more closely to the very heart of the Father, and to a life inseparable from the Lord Jesus Christ.

Again, the new movement finds inspiration in a continuous spirit of revival. I do not mean to imply by this that in the mind of the Open Church advocates the day of the evangelist is past. They welcome the aid of the evangelist, but do not wait for him. It is believed that the Holy Spirit is the gift to the Church, and will work through the people personally, and that God will add to the Church daily such as should be saved.

There is yet another inspiration, that of making good the divine claim of Jesus Christ. He came with the gift of redemptive love, and claimed the world and all things therein, — all men, and all of the man, as the Father's; by going unto the bosom of the Eternal, and there pleading his own atoning work, he has not abrogated one iota of that claim, any more than amid the hosannas of angels he has lost one whit of his suffering, compassionate sympathy. It was life in its entirety that was ever before the eye of Jesus, that was ever the burden of his heart! It is life in its entirety, the demands of the social, physical, and spiritual needs of the world, that summons the Church to-day, and is inspiring and inciting to untiring efforts and greatest sacrifice. A new life thrills the Church; and men fearless as the apostles at Pentecost are holding that the gospel must be supreme in the control of all life; that there must be social and national as well as individual regeneration; that legislation, law, business, commerce, agriculture, labor, art, science, philosophy, schools, institutions, universities, individuals, society, governments, — all must be made subservient to the great end of establishing God's Kingdom. Never was there such unity of thought and effort on the part of any body of Christian workers, never have men so truly comprehended the meaning of the life of Jesus Christ, or so largely recognized the comprehensive claim of his gospel, or so accorded him his true place of supremacy in the individual, the home, the clan, the community, and the nation. Each new day is coming to us with a new consecration of money and of men, and the new movement looks to nothing less than the realization of the Kingdom of God. But a mighty work has yet to be done. God has honored this generation by placing before them an opportunity sublime, awful, and grand, as was never before given to man. I believe the Church universal will rise to the occasion; and that in the fulness and beauty of divine power the Church, through toil and sacrifice with Jesus Christ, through efforts untiring, through energy of renewed courage born of faith in a great cause, through powers strung by the demands of a noble and life-giving work, through over-welling sympathy for the sufferings and sins and miseries of the toiling millions, through faith in God, and by the power of the Holy Spirit, and constrained in all things by the ruling, reigning Christ, — the Church will, I believe, take her place, white-robed, empowered, crowned, God's faithful agency, triumphing over all opposition, bringing in the day of that Kingdom whose gates are praise and whose walls are salvation; when "every star shall point to the Morning Star, and every rock to the Rock of Ages;" when the earth shall be filled with His glory, "and they shall not teach every man his neighbor, and every man his brother, saying, Know the Lord: for all shall know me, from the least to the greatest."[1] The Kingdom shall be realized.

[1] Hebrews viii. 11.

INDEX.

Abbott, Rev. Lyman, D.D., 12.
Aid Societies, 202-204, 208-209.
Alling, Mr. Joseph T., 167, 168, 172.
Andrews, Bishop, 36.
Argyle, Duke of, 9.
Armour Institute, 196, 261.
Armour Mission, 196, 339.
Armstrong, Rev. E. P., 241.
Assistant pastor, 304-305.
Associate pastor, 304-305.
Athletics, apparatus for, 181.
Atkinson, Edward, 267.
Austin, Ill., Presbyterian Church, 27, 77, 89, 94.
Auxiliary League, Salvation Army, 142.

Bacon, Lord, 184.
Bailey, Rev. Melville K., 158, 298.
Band of Hope, 234, 278.
Banner for Sunday-schools, 237.
Baptist Tabernacle, Boston, 136.
Baptist Young People's Union, 119, 120.
Battalion Club, 253.
Bedford, Bishop of, 134.
Beecher, Rev. Henry Ward, 92.
Belden Ave. Presbyterian Church, Chicago, 87.
Beneficiary Associations, 296-298.
Benefit Association, Christian Industrial, 161.
Berea College, 205.
Berkeley Temple, Boston, 72, 94, 191, 195, 337, 340-342.

Bethany College, 196.
Bethany Presbyterian Church, Philadelphia, 25, 56, 103, 106, 170, 196, 295, 297, 304.
Bicycle Club, 183.
Birthday boxes, 232.
Book fund, 114.
Bowling-alley, 160.
Boys' parlor, 212.
Brick Church, Rochester, N. Y., 34, 235, 236, 238, 278.
Bridgeman, Rev. Howard A., 315, 316.
Bridgeport, Conn., Congregational Church, 123.
Broome Street Tabernacle, New York, 99, 135.
Brotherhood of Andrew and Philip, 163, 166-167, 175.
Brotherhood of St. Andrew, 136, 163-166, 175, 294.
Buffalo Plan, 145.
Burlington, Iowa, Congregational Church, 84.
Burns, Robert, 350-351.
Bryan, Rev. W. S. Plumer, D.D., 229.

Cadman, Rev. S. P., 125.
Cadwell, Rev. Newton W., 149.
Calling report, 219.
Calvary Episcopal Church, New York, 281, 293.
Calvary Methodist Church, New York, 13, 338.

357

INDEX.

Campbell, Rev. Frederick, 135.
Card, after-meeting, 109 ; Alling class, 169-171; boys' club, 252 ; chapel, 141; church record, 23; communicant's, 24, 25 ; enlistment, 53 ; pew, 60-62 ; prayer meeting, 123 ; record of church-members, 23 ; reporting unconverted friends, 41 ; silent evangelism, 55 ; Sunday-school, 236 ; Sunday-school evangelization, 56; ushers', 64 ; vestibule, 322.
Card Catalogue, 23-24.
Carpentering classes, 262-263.
Carter, Rev. William, 83.
Central Christian Church, Kansas City, Kan., 294.
Central Church, Rochester, N. Y., 34, 102, 167, 172, 240, 337.
Central Congregational Church, Jamaica Plain, Boston, 65.
Central Metropolitan Methodist Church, New York, 117, 125.
Certificates, church-members, 53 ; Sunday-school, 237.
Chalmers, Dr. Thomas, 9, 35.
Chamberlain, Rev. James A., D.D., 84.
Chapman, Rev. J. Wilbur, D.D., 56, 297.
Chatham Literary Union, 188.
Chautauqua Reading Circle, 187.
Chester, Rev. Carlos Tracy, 235.
Chicago Mail, 18.
Christ Church, London, 112, 159, 207.
Christian Culture Course, 120.
Christian Endeavor Society, 119-121, 150, 151, 288.
Christian Evidence Society, 134.
Christian Industrial League, 160.
Christian Men's Union, 278, 279.
Christian Treasury, 284.
Christianity, of Christ, 3; growth of, 2 ; influence of, 2 ; true view of, 39.
Church, children in, 226-227 ; co-operation of, 332-334; the duty of, to heal the sick, 286-287; duty of, to help to an education, 194-195 ; duty of, to strangers, 58-59, 67; effect on, of young people's work, 118-119; estrangement from, of working-men, 111; failure of, in personal work, 43, 49; forward movement of, 345; great work awaiting, 352; in temperance legislation, 281-282; in the country, 153; men in, 76 ; mission of, 5, 332; music of, 71, 74-75; open doors of, 19-20; unification of work in, 331; up-town movement of,10; value of property of, in London, in Chicago, 18, 19.
Church of the Ascension, New York, 237, 276.
Church of the Covenant, Washington, D. C., 156.
Church of the Unity, Los Angeles, Cal., 203.
Clarendon Street Church, Boston, 73.
Clark, Rev. Francis E., D.D., 121.
Clothing Bureau, 214.
Club-room for young men, 175.
Coal Club, 295.
Cobb, Rev. Henry Evertson, D.D., 229.
Coffee-houses, 280.
Collegiate Reformed Church, New York, 229.
Commons, Prof. John R., 266, 280.
Congregational and Presbyterian Church, Storm Lake, Ia., 240.
"Congregationalist," 6.
Conquest Meetings, 120.
Conwell, Rev. Russell H., D.D., 5, 52, 185, 297, 339.
Cooke, George Willis, 8.
Crawford, Rev. William, 74.
Cumming, Rev. Dr., 40.

DAGER, Dr., 188.
Day, Rev. James Roscoe, D.D., 13.
Deaconesses, 27, 288-290.
DeCosta, Rev. B. F., D.D., 248.

INDEX.

Delaware Ave. Baptist Church, Buffalo, N. Y., 187.
Dickinson, Rev. Charles A., D.D., 72, 94, 191, 195, 337.
Dike, Rev. Samuel W., D.D., 148.
Dodge, Mr. William E., 177.
Drinking-fountain, 280–281.
Drummond, Prof. Henry, 177, 257, 258, 259, 260.
Duncan, Mr. W. A., Ph.D., 239.

Easter offering, 314–315.
Ely, Prof. Richard T., 39, 292.
Emerson, 223.
Emmanuel Chapel Industrial School, New York, 271.
Emory, Rev. John C., 337.
Employment Associations, 205, 293–295.
English, Dr. V. P., 244.
Epworth League, 119–120.
Evangelical Alliance, 333–335.
Evening Home for Girls, 208.
Evenings at Home, 224.

Faith Presbyterian Church, New York, 315.
Farrar, Canon, 310, 313.
Faville, Rev. John, D.D., 89–90.
Fifth Ave. Presbyterian Church, New York, 160.
First Baptist Church, Rockland, Mass., 51.
First Congregational Church, Appleton, Wis., 77, 89, 202.
First Congregational Church, Aurora, Ill., 88.
First Congregational Church, Detroit, Mich., 200.
First Congregational Church, Elgin, Ill., 85.
First Congregational Church, Jersey City, 73.
First Congregational Church, Lee Center, Ill., 88.
First Congregational Church, Michigan, Ind., 231.

First Congregational Church, Muskegon, Mich., 87.
First Congregational Church, Owatonna, Minn., 85.
First Presbyterian Church, Danville, Ill., 87.
First Presbyterian Church, Los Angeles, Cal., 97.
First Presbyterian Church, Sterling, Ill., 84.
Fishburn, Rev. William H., D.D., 324.
Fisher, Dr. C. Irving, 242, 244.
Five Points Mission, New York, 98, 99.
Flower and Fruit Missions, 287.
Flower Festival Boarding-House, Los Angeles, Cal., 294.
Food and Fuel Club, 211.
Fourth Congregational Church, Hartford, Conn., 135, 328, 342, 343.
Fresh Air Fund, 209–210, 215.
Frost, Mrs. William G., 205.
Frost, Rev. William G., Ph.D., 205.
Frost, T. Gold, 182.

Gibbon, 346.
Gladden, Rev. Washington, D.D., 124.
Goethe, 322.
Goff, Rev. Edward F., 88.
"Golden Rule," 120.
Good Templars, 278.
Good-will Home, 294.
Gordon, Rev. A. J., D.D., 73.
Gordon, Rev. George A., D.D., 348.
Gordon, Rev. W. C., 231.
Gospel push-cart, 136.
Gospel tent-meetings, 137.
Gospel wagon, 136–137.
Gough, John B., 98.
Grace Baptist Temple, Philadelphia, 69, 72, 185, 188, 196, 253, 288, 297, 329, 339.
Grace Chapel and Clergy House, New York, 158, 206, 298, 304.
Grace Episcopal Church, New York, 66, 74, 158, 182, 206, 288, 293, 306.

359

INDEX.

Gradgrind Club, 187, 188.
Grant, Rev. Percy S., 276.
Greenstone Presbyterian Church, Pullman, Ill., 35, 157.
Greer, Rev. David H., D.D., 299.
Growing Legion, 231.
Gymnasiums, 178, 181.

HADDEN, Rev. Archibald, 87.
Hadley, Col. Henry H., 282.
Hall, Dr., 245.
Hall, Rev. John, D.D., 160.
Hall, Rev. Newman, D.D., 134.
Hamlin, Rev. Teunis S., D.D., 156.
Hammond, Rev. E. P., 134.
Handbook for Sewing-schools, 271.
Hanover Street Congregational Church, Milwaukee, 338.
Hanson Street Baptist Church, Brooklyn, 35.
Happy Sunday Afternoon, 213.
Harlem Reformed Church, New York, 116.
Harper's Magazine, 179.
Harry Wadsworth Club, 253.
Harvest Home Praise Service, 228-229.
Hastings, Rev. Thomas S., D.D., 125.
Havergal, Frances Ridley, 75, 107.
Hawthorne, Julian, 179.
Helping Hand, 204, 205, 206.
Hill, Rev. John Clark, D.D., 27, 89, 94.
Hill, Roland, 133.
Hoadley, Rev. James S., D.D., 315.
Hollond Memorial Presbyterian Church, Philadelphia, 33, 69, 297, 329.
Holmes, Rev. Samuel Van Vranken, 154, 155, 337.
Home Department of the Sunday-school, 150-151, 238, 240.
Hopkins, Dr. Mark, 147.
Horr, Rev. Elijah, D.D., 125.
House-to-house canvass, value of, 30-33; blank for, 31; directions to visitors, 32; in the country, 152.

House-to-house visitation, 33-37.
Hoyt, Rev. Charles S., 86.
Huff, Mr. J. E., 229.
Hull, H. S., 172.
Huntington, Bishop, 310, 313, 315.
Huntington, Miss Emily, 264, 269.
Huntington, Rev. Dr., 306.

IMMANUEL Presbyterian Church, Los Angeles, Cal., 200.
"Independent," 110.
Institutional Church, 4, 6, 16-18.
Invitations to strangers, 63, 319-320.

JACOB TOME Institute, 261.
Jefferson Park Presbyterian Church, Chicago, 54, 135.
Jersey City Tabernacle, 26, 182, 279, 327, 342, 343.
Johnson, Dr., 350.
Jones, Rev. G. James, 86.
Judson, Dr. Edward, 175, 226.
Judson Memorial Baptist Church, New York, 294.

KENDIG, Rev. A. B., D.D., 338.
King, Prof. Henry C., 40, 50.
Kittridge, Rev. Abbott E., D.D., 124.
Knights of King Arthur, 253.
Knights of Temperance, 253.
Knox, John, 133.

LADIES' Parish Society, 202, 203.
Lay assistants, 306.
Laymen in chapels, 143.
Legal Bureau, 295.
Lend-a-hand Club, 253.
Letters, mimeographed, 140-141, 323; to attendants at chapels, 140; to attendants at prayer meetings, 123-124; to strangers, 63.
Lincoln Park Baptist Church, Cincinnati, 231, 329, 337.
Littlefield, Rev. Milton S., 175.
Livingstone, David, 194.
Loyal Temperance Legion, 234, 278

INDEX.

MacAllister, Rev. J., 240.
MacAuley, Jerry, 282.
Madison Ave. Presbyterian Church, New York, 23, 62, 73, 191, 192, 217, 222, 319, 340.
Madison Ave. Reformed Church, New York, 124.
Marble Collegiate Church, New York, 60, 205, 319–320.
Markley, Rev. J. Munroe, 88.
Mason, Rev. W. A., D.D., 100.
Matthews, Rev. S. Sherburne, 338.
Maywood, Ill., Presbyterian Church, 86.
McAll Mission, 139, 144.
McBee, Hon. Silas, 16.
McNeil, Rev. John, D.D., 134.
McPherson, Rev. John, D.D., 85.
Meeker, Rev. J. M., D.D., 123.
Men's League, 80.
Men's Social Club, 158.
Merrill, Rev. William Cross, 340.
Messemer, Miss Marian, 301.
Meyer, Rev. F. B., B.A., 112, 113, 159, 160, 207.
Miller, Rev. J. R., D.D., 70, 297.
Miller, Rev. Rufus W., D.D., 166.
Mills, Rev. B. Fay, 106, 109.
Mills, Rev. Charles S., 91, 338.
Mission bands, 232–234.
Missionary banks and jugs, 232.
Missionary concerts, 127.
Missionary societies, 200–202, 209–210, 215.
Mizpah Chapel, New York, 175.
Monthly Sabbath service for children, 230.
Moody, Dwight L., 41, 101, 133, 140.
Mothers' Christian Endeavor Society, 206.
Mothers' Meetings, 277.
Music in the prayer meeting, 126.

Name Book, 219, 221.
New Movement, brings young men into the church, 162; discussion of name for, 15–21; continuous spirit of revival of, 353, 354; inspiration of, 346–355; looks to the realization of the kingdom, 355; preparation for, 346–350; represents Christ, 352; results of, 336–344; succeeds when other methods fail, 336.
Ninth Street Baptist Church, Cincinnati, 144, 338.

Oak Park, Ill., Presbyterian Church, 86.
Oberlin, O., prayer circles, 131–132.
Ogden, Mr. Robert C., 314, 315.
Open Church, 5, 8, 18–21, 353.
Oswald, Dr. Felix L., 180, 181.
Oswego, N. Y., Congregational Church, 61.
Ouida, 347.
"Outlook," 340, 343.

Paden, Rev. W. M., D.D., 33.
Parish houses, 138, 327–328.
Park Congregational Church, Grand Rapids, Mich., 202.
Parkhurst, Rev. Charles H., D.D., 347.
Parsons, Rev. Willis E., 87.
Partridge, Rev. W. G., 144, 338.
Pass-book for chapels, 142.
Pastor's woman assistant, 202, 289, 306.
Patterson, Rev. J. M., 122.
People's Mission, New York, 295.
People's Palace, Jersey City, 327.
People's Tabernacle, Denver, Col., 182.
Periodical Club, 186–187.
Piedmont Congregational Church, Worcester, Mass., 125.
Pike, Rev. G. R., 35.
Pilgrim Congregational Church, Cleveland, O., 326, 338.
Pilgrim Congregational Church, Worcester, Mass., 342, 343.
Platteville, Wis., Congregational Church, 86.

INDEX.

Plymouth Church, Milwaukee, Wis., 342, 343.
Pulpit paintings, 99-100.

QUESTION-BOX Meetings, 125.

RAINSFORD, Rev. W. S., D.D., 71, 315, 339.
Ravenna,O.,CongregationalChurch, 197.
Report of Church Committee on strangers, 66.
Rescue Missions, 282-284, 328.
Reynard, Rev. J. H., 85.
Riis, Jacob, 179.
Robbins, Rev. G. R., 337.
Robertson, Rev. F. W., 14.
Rodstock, Lord, 134.
Roll of Honor, 237.
Roof garden, 328.
Ruggles Street Baptist Church, Boston, 24, 41.
Russell, Rev. Frank, D.D., 123.
Russell, Rev. J. L., D.D., 97.

SAMARITAN Hospital, 288.
Sanitation Bureau, 295.
Schauffler, Rev. A. F., D.D., 10, 235.
Schloppe, Rev. W. G., 197, 198, 199.
Schott, Miss Mary, 212.
Scott, Rev. R. D., 87.
Scotter, Mr. E., 262.
Scudder, Rev. H. M., D.D., 124.
Scudder, Rev. John L., D.D., 279, 338.
Second Presbyterian Church, Columbus, O., 324.
Seldon, Rev. Joseph H., 85.
Shawmut Church, Boston, 224.
Shelter of the Silver Cross, 215.
Sidewalk Committee, 66.
Silver Cross Club, 212.
Silver Cross Society, 248.
Simpson Memorial Methodist Tabernacle, Los Angeles, Cal., 275.
Sixty-third St. Mission, New York, 160.

Sloyd System, 261, 263.
Smith, Rev. E. L., 87.
Smith, William A., 255.
Sparta,Wis.,CongregationalChurch, 74.
Sprague Memorial Presbyterian Church, Tacoma, Wash., 85.
Spurgeon, Rev. Charles H., 133.
St. Bartholomew's Episcopal Church, New York, 160, 287, 293, 294, 295, 328.
St. Bartholomew's Mission, New York, 160, 282, 328.
St. George's Chapel, Liverpool, Eng., 116.
St. George's Episcopal Church, New York, 73, 136, 186, 253, 295, 304, 339.
St. Luke's Association, 288.
St. Margaret's Church, London, Eng., 313.
St. Mary's Church, Whitechapel, London, Eng., 134.
St. Paul's Methodist Church, Cincinnati, O., 123.
Statistics, as to evening congregations, 85-90; churches reporting no converts, 47-49; expenses of missions, 144; growth of Christianity, 2; growth of cities, 138; growth of churches under new methods, 337-340; Home Department Sunday-school, 239; loss from waste and bad cooking, 267; people who have never heard the Gospel, 101; rural church-going, 148; St. Bartholomew's Loan Association, 299; work of Brotherhood of St. Andrew, 164, 166; young men in the penitentiaries, 261; Young People's Societies, 119. (See "Table" for further statistics.)
Stead, Mr. W. T., 18.
Stebbins, Rev. Henry H., D.D, 102, 337.
Stephenson, George, 194.
Stewart, Rev. Mr., 134.

362

INDEX.

Strong, Rev. Josiah, D.D., 7, 17, 49, 82, 139, 144.
Sunday evening lectures by laymen, 97.
Sunday-school teachers' tea, 240.
"Sunday-School Times," 235, 241.
Swimming-baths, 182.

TABLE, showing average number of additions per church, and average cost of convert in four denominations for five years, 44–45; showing average number of church-members to a convert, 46–47; showing church communicants in colleges, 162–163; showing comparison of five Congregational Churches with Congregational Church at large, 342–343; showing growth of Alling Class, 167; showing growth of Berkeley Temple, Boston, 341; showing work of Bible Class in Tremont Temple, Boston, 116.
Tenement House Committee, King's Daughters and Sons, 291.
Ten Times One Club, 253.
Thanksgiving donation, 228–229.
Thompson, Rev. Charles L., D.D., 5, 340.
Three Rivers, Mich., Presbyterian Church, 85.
Training-class for Mission Workers, 282–283.
Tremont Temple, Boston, 116.
Tyndall, Rev. C. H., 99.
Tyng, Rev. Stephen H., D.D., 226.

VISITATION block or district plan of, 27; by committee of Pleasant Sunday afternoon, 115; by committee of Mary and Martha League, 219–220; by deaconesses, 3; by laymen, 31; by "sub-pastors," 26.

WADSWORTH, Rev. Arthur Leonard, 51.
Walla Walla, Wash., Congregational Church, 88.
Wanamaker, Mr. John, 170.
Water Street Mission, New York, 282
Waverly Congregational Church, Jersey City, N. J., 337.
Welcome to strangers by church officers, 60.
Wells, Amos R., 121.
Wesley Chapel, Columbus, Ohio, 228.
West Presbyterian Church, New York, 125.
Westfield, N. J., Presbyterian Church, 149.
Westminster Presbyterian Church, Buffalo, 154, 319, 337.
Westminster Presbyterian Church, Detroit, Mich., 122.
Westminster Presbyterian Church, San Francisco, Cal., 255.
White, Rev. Frank Newhall, 84.
White Cross Society, 247.
Wight, Rev. C. A., 86.
Wilder, Prof. B. G., 243.
Willard, Frances, 280.
Woffendale, Rev. Mr., 134.
Woman's Christian Temperance Union, 234, 278, 279, 280.
Woman's Employment Association, 205.
Woman's Friendship Club, 206.
Woodyard, 283–284, 293.
Worker's Handbook, 52–53.

YOUNG CRUSADERS, 253.
Young Men's Christian Association, 178–179.
Young Men's Institute, 157, 158.
Young Woman's Christian Temperance Union, 210.

363

www.ingramcontent.com/pod-product-compliance
Lightning Source LLC
Chambersburg PA
CBHW032022220426
43664CB00006B/336